INSIDE POLITICS;

THE NATIONAL CONVENTIONS, 1960

America's Politics Series: No. 2

Inside Politics:

The National Conventions, 1960

edited by

Paul Tillett

Published for The Eagleton Institute of Politics at
Rutgers—The State University

By Oceana Publications, Inc.
Dobbs Ferry, New York
1962

Library of Congress Catalog Card Number: 62-15974

TABLE OF CONTENTS

AMERICA'S POLITICS SERIES

Published for the Eagleton Institute of Politics
Rutgers—The State University
New Jersey
PAUL TILLETT, *General Editor*

Volume 1. RELIGION AND POLITICS, Peter H. Odegard

In a year when the religion of a Catholic presidential candidate was a burning issue, this book unhesitatingly reaffirmed
the principle that bigotry has no proper role in American
politics. A book of current interest, this also reflects many
years of research and reflection by Dr. Odegard. RELIGION
AND POLITICS is a culmination of his political experience,
and his career-long interest in the religious influence on the
American political scene. Dr. Odegard, former President of
Reed College, is Professor of Political Science at the University of California at Berkeley. He is presently on leave of
absence, and is conducting a two-semester course on "The
Structure and Functions of the American Government" for
the National Broadcasting Company's "Continental Class-
room." 219 pp, Index. $5.00

Volume 2. INSIDE POLITICS: The National Conventions, 1960
Paul Tillett

Here is a probing of the happenings at the 1960 national
conventions held in Los Angeles and Chicago, with an intel-
ligent interpretation of the significance of each party's
decisions and nominations. Professor Tillett is general editor
of the America's Politics Series, and Assistant Director of
the Eagleton Institute of Politics. 288 pp., Index. $6.00

Part I:

Introduction

Preface

Under the auspices of the Eagleton Institute of Politics of Rutgers, The State University, and the National Center for Education in Politics, twenty-four instructors and assistant professors of political science were selected, in a nationwide competition, to attend the 1960 Democratic and Republican National Conventions. Fourteen of the Fellows were Democrats; ten were Republican.

Democratic Convention Fellows:
Lucius J. Barker, University of Wisconsin (Milwaukee)
Daniel M. Berman, Washington College
George F. Brasington, Emory University
Fred G. Burke, Syracuse University
Malcolm E. Jewell, University of Kentucky
Eugene C. Lee, University of California (Berkeley)
Karl O'Lessker, Wabash College
James A. Robinson, Northwestern University
Robert L. Sawyer, Central Michigan University
Bert E. Swanson, Hunter College
Richard W. Taylor, Coe College
Aaron Wildavsky, Oberlin College
J. D. Williams, University of Utah
Sidney Wise, Franklin and Marshall College
Republican Convention Fellows:
George S. Blair, Claremont Graduate School
David R. Derge, Indiana University
Houston I. Flournoy, Pomona College
Robert J. Huckshorn, University of Idaho
Charles O. Jones, Wellesley College
John H. Kessel, University of Washington
Karl A. Lamb, University of Michigan

Donald W. Marshall, Western Illinois University
Thomas Payne, Montana State University
Harley J. Stucky, Bethany College

The first responsibility of each of these political scientists was to use his opportunity to gain new insights into the national convention process which might later be applied in his teaching and in his own research program. Some gained access to the organizations of candidates for the presidential nomination and were allowed to observe operations at close range. Others worked with committees of their respective conventions.

A large majority of the Fellows were attached to state delegations. Many were accepted to such an extent that they moved with and within their delegations almost as if they had been delegates or alternates.

Although each Fellow was asked to write an article based on his experiences, no attempt was made to impose an overall research design. This volume, therefore, is not *the* product of the of the Eagleton-National Center for Education in Politics Fellowship Program at the 1960 convention. It is, rather, a by-product. In spite of the limited research objectives, however, it is our judgment that political scientists, their students, and others interested in American politics will find much that is useful in these articles.

Representing a variety of approaches to the 1960 national conventions, the chapters of this book develop important information on many aspects of the convention process, some of which have previously received little or no attention from political scientists. Beyond that, taken together, the chapters do provide a fairly complete story of what did happen in 1960 at the Democratic Convention in Los Angeles and the Republican Convention in Chicago.

In Part I, the director of the Fellowship Program at the Democratic Convention, Professor Austin Ranney of the University of Illinois, and the director at the Republican Convention, Professor Ivan Hinderaker of the University of California, Los Angeles, summarize the Democratic and Republican 1960 preconvention campaigns and developments at the conventions.

Part II, Nominaton Campaign Organizations, shows the very great extent to which both conventions were dominated by the front-running candidates for the presidential nomination—Kennedy at Los Angeles and Nixon at Chicago. And more important, the concern is with *how* this was done.

Part III, Kennedy and Nixon Leadership on Party Platform, develops the conflicts between national platform requirements for the presidential nominees and the pressures from party wings, sections, or states for planks more suited to the political needs of their more limited constituencies. While at the Democratic Convention the most dramatic story was Kennedy's organization and how it went about winning the nomination; at the Republican Convention, it was Nixon's leadership in the formulation of the Republican platform.

Part IV, State Delegations: Leaders and Followers, focuses on the relationships between state delegation leaders and the delegates, and on the behavior of individual delegates. In some states, the leaders are firmly in control and in others leadership is badly split. Some of the rank and file delegates accept the minor roles assigned to them and the reactions of others range from hurt to throwing their weight around on such matters as allocation of convention tickets. In each delegation, the business of *state* politics goes on without interruption at the national convention.

Part V, State Delegations: Organization and Candidate Communications, represents a miscellaneous category. It includes one chapter addressed to the question of how a delegation organizes itself to perform its several convention functions, and another to the question of what kind of presidential and vice presidential candidate communications reach the delegation, and in what form.

Except for Part I, the chapters are developed from a worm's eye view of the conventions—through the eyes of individual delegates, or from the vantage point of a state delegation, convention subcommittee or committee, or a presidential candidate organization. Though these chapters may seem made up too much out of the particular, they are based on enduring patterns of American political behavior. Much more work of this type remains to be done before those who are working from the bird's eye view will understand fully the convention process.

Not all of the project reports of the Fellows warranted inclusion as chapters in this book. Two topics which appeared to have excellent promise before the conventions were wiped out by the fast flow of political events, and in two other cases problems of

access arose to prevent the kind of observation which would have
led to meaningful results.

The 1960 national conventions project was made possible by a
Ford Foundation grant to the National Center for Education in
Politics and the Eagleton Institute of Politics. To the Ford
Foundation we are deeply grateful, and we wish also to thank
the University of Southern California which provided facilities
for the Democratic pre-convention seminar and Beloit College
which provided similar facilities for the Republican group. We
should like also to acknowledge the contribution of Rhoten A.
Smith, Director of the National Center for Education in Politics
when this project was conceived and executed.

Bernard Hennessy, Director
National Center for Education in Politics
Donald G. Herzberg, Executive Director
Eagleton Institute of Politics

2. The 1960 Democratic Convention:
Los Angeles and Before

By

AUSTIN RANNEY

University of Illinois

The 1960 Democratic Convention adopted the most liberal
platform in the party's history, and nominated to run on it
Senators John F. Kennedy of Massachusetts and Lyndon B.
Johnson of Texas. To understand how the Convention arrived
at these decisions, the essential points to note are these:

The Convention's choice of Kennedy registered and formal-
ized a decision already made in the course of perhaps the longest
preconvention campaign in American history.

The essential story of this campaign was Kennedy's long climb
from being one of many possibilities in 1957 to nomination on
the first ballot at Los Angeles in 1960.

The main themes in this story were: the critical role played
by Kennedy's sweep of the presidential primaries; the outstand-
ing competence and success of his organization of "young pros";
and the combination of these and other factors to overcome his

handicaps of youth, opposition from many farm and labor leaders, and, above all, his Roman Catholicism.

This striking success story may be highlighted as follows.

The Preconvention Campaign

The 1956 Convention. The 1960 preconvention campaign began about a month after the 1956 Democratic Convention when John Kennedy and his advisors decided to make an all-out try for the party's presidential nomination four years hence. They were encouraged to undertake this ambitious quest mainly by the surprising strength he had just shown in his near-miss of the vice-presidential nomination in the dramatic struggle with Estes Kefauver. This was by far the most exciting episode at either party's convention in that rather dull political year. As a result, Kennedy, who had gone to the convention as the nice young junior Senator from Massachusetts, emerged as an attractive, sportsmanlike, powerful vote-getter of national stature. Recognizing his new status, he decided almost immediately to try for the top spot in 1960.

1956 to 1960. By early 1957 the consensus among the "inside dopesters" was that there were at least nine serious possibilities for the 1960 nomination: Averell Harriman, Hubert Humphrey, Lyndon Johnson, Estes Kefauver, John Kennedy, Robert Meyner, Adlai Stevenson, Stuart Symington, and Mennen Williams. The Gallup polls showed Kefauver and Kennedy well out ahead of all the others among Democratic voters, and Kennedy running better than any other Democrat, including Kefauver, in the "trial heats" against Richard Nixon. A Chicago *Daily News* poll of the delegates to the 1956 Convention showed Kennedy having more votes than the next three hopefuls combined, although well short of a majority.

The 1958 congressional and state elections produced considerable reshuffling of the prospects. Harriman and Williams were eliminated from presidential contention by poor showings at the polls. Kennedy swamped his hapless Republican opponent in Massachusetts by a record-smashing 74 per cent of the vote. And the election of a number of other prominent Catholic Democrats, such as "Pat" Brown, Eugene McCarthy, Michael Di Salle, and David Lawrence, set some commentators to saying that Catholicism might have become more of an advantage than a handicap to a candidate in many parts of the nation.

By 1959 the analysts generally sized up the situation thus: the only remaining serious possibilities were believed to be Humphrey, Johnson, Kennedy, Stevenson, and Symington. Of these Kennedy was clearly the front runner, but his chances of winning were thought to be slim. He was in front too early; he was young and could afford to wait; most labor and farm leaders were cool toward him; and most party leaders were still not prepared to saddle the party with a Catholic candidate unless they had to. So each of the five "possibilities" was expected to come to the Convention with enough strength to produce the greatest deadlock in years. After a number of ballots (National Chairman Paul Butler was predicting at least five) the party's old pro's were expected to pick the most acceptable compromise, and this was believed most likely to be either Stevenson or Symington. The "smart money," indeed, was predicting a Stevenson-Kennedy ticket.

Kennedy's Strategy. The Kennedy organization agreed that their man would have no chance for the top spot in a deadlocked convention. They therefore had no choice but to try all-out for a first- or second-ballot victory. Starting from their base of solid New England strength they planned to enter Kennedy in just about every presidential primary and to do their utmost to sweep them all. If they succeeded, they would not only win a lot of votes; they would also get Kennedy national attention and win him a national "image" enjoyed by none of the other hopefuls except Stevenson; and, above all, they would convince the party's leaders that Kennedy was the Democrat's best vote-getter, the man who could beat Nixon. Kefauver's failures using similar strategy in 1952 and 1956 proved this is a hard road to travel, but no other offered Kennedy any chance at all.

Kennedy's Organization. This strategy was designed and executed by a group of young men who have come to be regarded as one of the great presidential campaign organizations of history, ranking with and perhaps surpassing such redoubtable predecessors as the Farley-Roosevelt and Brownell-Dewey operations. The organization was headed by Senator Kennedy, who served skillfully as his own campaign manager. His principal lieutenants were brothers Robert and Edward Kennedy, brothers-in-law Stephen Smith and Sargant Shriver, and non-relatives Theodore Sorensen, Lawrence O'Brien, Kenneth O'Donnell, Pierre Salinger, Robert Wallace, and pollster Louis Harris. Operating from a nine-room headquarters in the Esso Building in Washington, the organization compiled a card index of information about upwards of 29,000 influential Democrats and established "field" organizations in every state in which there was the remotest possibility of Kennedy votes. Well financed, well organized, and boundlessly energetic, the "young pros" raced into the critical period from January to July, 1960, determined to bring off the coup most of the "old pros" thought impossible.

1960. The climactic period from January 1, to July 10, 1960, featured the following main episodes.

1. Ohio. As Professor Wildavsky's paper relates, Governor Di Salle of Ohio wanted to run as a favorite son in the presidential primary so as to hold his party together and maximize its bargaining power at the Convention. But Kennedy needed Ohio's votes, and he informed Di Salle that he would contest the primary unless Di Salle pledged his support at the Convention. A private poll convinced Di Salle that Kennedy would sweep the state—with disastrous consequences for Di Salle's local position. Accordingly, in early January Di Salle announced that he would run in the primary as a favorite son but would deliver the entire delegation's vote to Kennedy on the Convention's first ballot. This was the first major break in the campaign, and it got Kennedy's drive off to a winging start.

2. Wisconsin. The only other presidential hopeful who felt he needed some primary victories was Hubert Humphrey. Operating with very limited funds, Humphrey selected Wisconsin for his first effort. Widely known by the state's Democrats as "Wisconsin's third senator" for his years of effort in the state's behalf, Humphrey felt he could count on their support. But a Harris poll taken in late 1959 showed Kennedy could beat Humphrey, and the organization felt that beating a midwesterner in his own back yard might make believers out of a lot of the skeptics. So Kennedy entered the Wisconsin primary, and from late January to early April both senators shuttled back and forth between Washington and Wisconsin campaigning hard. The Kennedy organization added to its swiftly growing reputation for thoroughness and efficiency by sending at least one Kennedy brother, sister, or in-law at least once into every Wisconsin town with a population of over 300! In the face of such

formidable opposition, Humphrey ruefully remarked to reporters, "I feel like an independent merchant bucking a chain-store operation!"

The primary drew a record vote, and Kennedy won 56 per cent and 20½ delegate votes to Humphrey's 10½. While this was a Kennedy victory, it was no knockout. Some observers, indeed, said that the Catholic bloc vote for Kennedy in Milwaukee and other heavily Catholic areas plus his failure to do better in the heavily Protestant rural areas might well have made it more of a defeat than a victory.

3. West Virginia. The great break-through came in the West Virginia primary a month later. Despite an early private poll showing Kennedy in the lead and despite Kennedy's far greater financial and organizational resources, most analysts felt Humphrey had most of the advantages. The state has few Catholics and many fundamentalist Protestants, and its depressed economic condition was made to order for a strong liberal like Humphrey. Both candidates put in a month of intensive and sometimes bitter campaigning, and by election day in early May, Humphrey was widely expected to win. In a smashing upset, however, Kennedy polled 60 per cent of the vote and carried 48 of the state's 55 counties. Humphrey formally withdrew from the race, and many party leaders for the first time came to believe that a Catholic—at least this particular Catholic—could win a lot of Protestant votes. It was now clear that Kennedy was going to be very hard to stop.

4. The Preconvention Snowball. After West Virginia Kennedy went from one success to another. He challenged favorite son Wayne Morse in Oregon, and won an astonishing 73 per cent of the vote. He won uncontested primaries in Indiana, Nebraska, and Maryland. In early June Governor Williams swung the Michigan delegation to Kennedy. By late June the Kennedy organization publicly claimed firm commitments for at least 710 first-ballot votes (761 were needed to win), and few doubted their claim. From January to June, then, Kennedy had moved from having a slight lead over a large field to almost holding the nomination in his hand.

5. The Belated "Stop Kennedy" Movement. In late June, the camps of the remaining active candidates, Johnson and Symington, launched a belated and desperate drive to keep Kennedy from winning on the first ballot. Johnson formally announced

his candidacy and maneuvered a recess of Congress until after the Convention—an implied reminder that Speaker Rayburn and he would still be running Congress in August and might remember who supported whom at Los Angeles when congressional favors were again being passed out and withheld. Former President Harry Truman, a Symington supporter, held a press conference to publicly advise Kennedy to withdraw in favor of some other man who would have the experience and maturity needed by a good candidate and president. This Kennedy refused to do, and shortly thereafter Truman announced that he would not attend the Convention because, as he said, it was "rigged" to force Kennedy upon the party when the party did not really want him.

By Convention Eve, the dopesters agreed that, "barring a miracle," Kennedy would be nominated on the first ballot. But, some said, miracles *do* sometimes happen at national conventions —remember Willkie in 1940? The question was, would a comparable miracle happen at Los Angeles in 1960? If so—if Kennedy could somehow be prevented from winning on the first two ballots—then his strength would rapidly crumble, and someone else, probably Stevenson and possibly Symington, would win after all.

The Convention

The Presidential Nomination. By the end of the Convention's first day, the chances for a miracle looked even dimmer than before. True, Kennedy had received his only noteworthy setback when the California delegation, despite Governor Brown's endorsement of Kennedy, gave him only 33½ votes out of 71 (see Professor Lee's paper). But much of the sting was removed when Chicago's Mayor Daley delivered 59½ of Illinois's 69 votes to Kennedy (see Professor Robinson's paper). The Pennsylvania delegation, at Governor Lawrence's urging, gave Kennedy 64 of its 81 votes (see Professor Wise's paper). If all held firm, Kennedy now had more than enough first-ballot votes to win.

The opposition, however, was still not ready to surrender. Johnson took advantage of a routine Kennedy request for an invitation to appear before the Texas delegation to challenge him to a face-to-face debate. Kennedy appeared to have little to gain and much to lose by accepting, but, after some hesitation, he agreed to come. The debate itself was anticlimactic: before the

Texans (interlarded with an agreed 20 members from the Massachusetts delegation) Johnson and Kennedy spent most of their time complimenting each other. Aside from a few implied but not explicit attacks by Johnson on Kennedy's Senate voting record, no forensic fireworks were set off, and Kennedy emerged unscathed.

The last effort of the stop-Kennedy movement came on nomination night when Minnesota Senator Eugene McCarthy's * impassioned speech nominating Adlai Stevenson touched off a 25-minute demonstration that sent the obviously pro-Stevenson galleries wild. Some television viewers may have wondered whether a Willkie-like miracle might not after all be in the making, but observers on the spot noted that most of the snake-dancing demonstraters came from outside the hall and that most of the delegates sat unmoved until the noise finally died down.

The first ballot ended all dreams (and nightmares) of a miracle, and capped with victory the four-year effort of Senator Kennedy and his redoubtable organization. The results:

Kennedy	806
Johnson	409
Symington	86
Stevenson	79½
Meyner	43
Humphrey	40½
Others	57

If further proof were needed of the "young pros'" calibre, it was provided by the fact revealed in Professor Burke's paper that the Kennedy organization's final estimate of his expected vote turned out to be exactly one-half vote short of his actual vote! No campaign organization has ever had better intelligence information or analysis, and few have fought so difficult a fight so successfully.

The Vice-Presidential Nomination. As it became more and more evident that Kennedy would be the Convention's presi-

---

*The Minnesota delegation set a new record in the 1960 Convention. Nominating speeches for two different candidates were made by Minnesota delegates (McCarthy for Stevenson and Governor Orville Freeman for Kennedy), and on the first ballot the delegation cast its entire vote for yet a third candidate, Senator Humphrey!

dential choice, there was increasing speculation about whom he would choose as his running mate. The names most frequently heard in this regard before the Convention were Humphrey and Symington, Governors Freeman, Docking, Loveless, and Nelson, and Senators Jackson and Engle. Johnson's name was also mentioned, but it was generally agreed that Kennedy would not name him and Johnson would not accept if he did.

The rumors continued to fly at the Convention, but they increasingly centered on Freeman, Jackson, and Symington. Immediately after Kennedy's nomination, most observers felt Symington had the inside track although each of the other two was believed to have a chance.

A stream of visitors passed through Kennedy's hotel room giving him their views: among others, David McDonald, Walter Reuther, and Arthur Goldberg from labor; and Robert Wagner, David Lawrence, Richard Daley, and Sam Rayburn from the party's "old pros." When the consultations were completed, Kennedy caught almost everyone by surprise with his announcement that he had asked Johnson to accept the vice-presidential nomination and Johnson had accepted.

A number of liberals were greatly disappointed and even bitter at this "betrayal," especially the Michigan delegation (see Professor Sawyer's paper). The following day some voted a resounding "No!" on the voice vote to nominate Johnson by acclamation. Most, however, were willing to go along with Kennedy's choice, and in any case they regarded the platform as so great a victory for liberal principles that Johnson's selection did not unduly disturb them.

The Platform. Like almost every other aspect of the Convention, the platform bore a strong Kennedy stamp. Chester Bowles, who had already declared his support for Kennedy, was named as the Chairman of the Platform Committee. He, in turn, appointed a 20-man drafting panel containing many strong liberals and only four southerners. The liberal majority produced a platform, appropriately entitled "The Rights of Man," which was by far the most liberal ever adopted by either major party. Yet its adoption produced nothing resembling the 1948 southern revolt. Why? For one thing, the failure of the 1948 Dixiecrat bolt convinced most southern leaders that this form of protest is futile. For another, Johnson was the first serious southern candidate for the presidential nomination in a very long time, and they did not want to embarrass him. Perhaps most significant was the fact that moderates outnumbered fire-breathing segregationists among the southern leaders far more in 1960 than in 1948. In any case, southern delegates were largely silent during the platform committee's hearings, and were content to propose for home consumption a ten-state minority report which they knew would be defeated on the floor (see the papers by Professor Taylor and Professor Brasington).

THE SUMMING UP

There are at least two schools of thought about how a party should pick its presidential candidate. The Harry Truman school holds that primaries are "eyewash" and that at the Convention the party's most mature, experienced, and respected leaders should by secret negotiation pick the right man, with due consideration for every faction's interests and feelings. The John Kennedy school believes that the nomination should go to the man who establishes the best claim to it by proving his vote-getting ability in the primaries as well as by his ability to negotiate effectively in the smoke-filled rooms.

In 1957 it appeared that the plethora of strong candidates would in all likelihood force the 1960 Convention to follow Truman's prescription, but this was not to be. The Kennedy organization's nearly flawless execution of the only strategy that could bring them victory made the Convention a decision-registering, not a decision-making body.

There will be other conventions, other candidates, and other years; but the "young pros'" success in overcoming all handicaps and making the "old pros" play the new game in all probability will mean that the presidential nominating process will henceforth be more like that of 1960 than like most of those before 1960.

3. *The 1960 Republican Convention: Chicago and Before*

BY

IVAN HINDERAKER

University of California, Los Angeles

❋   ❋   ❋

From 1940 through 1952, Republican National Conventions were the scene of major public battles between the so-called liberal and conservative wings of the party. Willkie, Dewey, and Eisenhower were the men around whom the "liberals" rallied. Robert A. Taft was the leader of the "conservatives." By any standards of judging the intensity of intra-party division, the split on each occasion was both bitter and deep.

With President Eisenhower in complete control, the keynote of the 1956 Convention was harmony. Though Eisenhower had not lived up to the expectations of many "Eisenhower Republicans," they had no place else to go. Eisenhower had been enough of a "Taft Republican" to preclude opposition from that group. And beyond that, everybody liked Ike.

The temporary peace of 1956 did not mean, however, that the divisions within the Republican party had been resolved. For Richard M. Nixon, working from his position as Vice President and as almost *de facto* head of the Republican party, it was important to keep intra-party conflict as subdued as possible. Chances for Governor Nelson Rockefeller of New York, as the potential leader of the "liberal" wing, and U.S. Senator Barry Goldwater of Arizona, of the "conservative" wing, rested on a resumption of open intra-party warfare.

The story of the 1960 Republican National Convention was mainly the story of Nixon. He had the presidential nomination in hand well before the Convention. And without driving off the "conservatives," he provided the leadership which produced a party platform and a vice presidential nominee which fell well within the specifications of the "liberal" wing of the party.

THE PRECONVENTION CAMPAIGN

The Presidency via the Vice Presidency. Traditionally, the office of Vice President of the United States, in the event the President did not die during his term, has been a political dead end street. Yet in 1960, for Nixon the vice presidency served as a stepping stone for advancement. Several factors operated to produce this result:

1. The opportunities, either delegated or as a result of President Eisenhower's serious illnesses, which enabled Nixon to demonstrate his abilities in a way that no Vice President had been able to do before.

2. The necessity, in this era of "cold war," of a kind of training and experience in foreign affairs and national security matters which Vice President Nixon was able to acquire through such activities as service on the National Security Council, as a roving ambassador on assignments abroad, and through the process of being kept informed by the President.

3. A publicity buildup over an eight-year period in which the Vice President was often in the national news spotlight.

4. And perhaps most important for the immediate purpose of securing the presidential nomination, the fact that Nixon had stepped actively into a party leadership role—a function for which President Eisenhower had little taste and one in which he generally took little interest.

By 1960, then, Nixon appeared to be as well or better qualified, by virtue of ability and experience, as any other potential Republican presidential candidate. He had had the benefit of more publicity over a longer period than any potential candidate. State party leaders throughout the United States were deeply indebted to Nixon, and with few exceptions those state leaders were committed to his candidacy.

As Vice President, still another factor was working in Nixon's favor. Because of his position, he was free to avoid commitments on issues which might have made it possible for either Rockefeller or Goldwater to amass large followings by the time of the national convention. "Conservative" Republicans could and did, though not with complete confidence, regard Nixon as one of their own; "liberals," on the other hand, could also feel that he would be their kind of candidate and President.

By 1960, only major Nixon mistakes or an adverse recommendation from President Eisenhower could have denied the Republican nomination to the Vice President, and perhaps even Eisenhower would not then have been able to change the course of a "preconvention" campaign which had, in fact, begun in 1953.

1956 to 1960. At the 1956 Republican Convention in San Francisco, Harold Stassen had led a movement to "dump" Nixon from the Republican ticket and replace him with Christian A. Herter of Massachusetts. Stassen was routed, and Herter joined in nominating Nixon.

Three events occurred in the elections of 1958 which had a bearing on the 1960 Republican Convention and preconvention campaign. One was the removal of William F. Knowland as a potential rival, with "conservative" wing support, to Nixon's presidential candidacy. Republican Senate Floor Leader Knowland, feeling that the office of Governor of California would be a better springboard to the presidency than the U. S. Senate, suffered a disastrous defeat which removed him, with finality, from contention.

The second and third events took place in Arizona and New York. While Republicans were suffering reverses all over the country, Goldwater was re-elected to his Senate seat and Rockefeller upset incumbent Averell Harriman for the office of Governor of New York.

Goldwater stepped up his speaking campaign, and by the summer of 1960 he had become the acknowledged leader in the "conservative" wing of the Republican party. With most of the support which he would need for a presidential nomination already commited to Nixon, however, the route from Arizona to the White House was blocked until such time as the Vice President would remove himself or could be pushed out of the way. For Goldwater, the time was not right. He did not become an active candidate for the Republican presidential nomination.

Nor did the time appear right for Rockefeller. For the first half of 1959, he was kept busy in New York by the Legislature. After adjournment, he did give the appearance of being an active presidential candidate, speaking in other states and criticizing quite sharply the posture of he Eisenhower Administration in several areas of national policy. By Gallup Poll standards, at least, Rockefeller did not make much headway. Among Gallup's sample of Republican voters in December, Nixon was the choice by 66 percent and Rockefeller 19 percent.

On December 26, Rockefeller announced that he would not be a candidate for President. Those who would control the nomination, he had found, were already committed to Nixon.

With this development, the Vice President now appeared to have a clear field. President Eisenhower, however, had not yet given his endorsement, insisting at his January 14, 1959 press conference that there were "half a dozen, or ten, or maybe a dozen fine, virile men in the Republican party that I would gladly support."

Nixon's Startegy. Vice President Nixon "officially" became a candidate for the presidential nomination on January 8, 1960 when he allowed his name to be entered in several presidential primaries. In the Democratic party, Senator Kennedy had chosen to follow the presidential primary route, but there was a great difference between the Kennedy and Nixon situations. For the former, the presidential primaries would make or break his chances for the nomination. For the latter, without open opposition and therefore without much risk, the primaries offered an opportunity to prove vote-getting ability as a presidential candidate, to acquire some first ballot convention votes, to insure that no rival would be able to use the primaries to build up strength, and to keep his name before the public at a time when the Democratic primaries would make it difficult to compete for front page newspaper space.

Until President Eisenhower's endorsement was in hand, Nixon had to avoid speeches or actions which might endanger the prospect of receiving that endorsement. It was necessary, likewise, to avoid giving cause to either the Goldwater or Rockefeller forces to go into active opposition early enough to amass a substantial counterforce or forces by national convention time. Also, a holding operation made it possible to postpone some strategic decisions which would be important in the general election campaign until after the Democrats had acted in Los Angeles, particularly the decision on how much emphasis should be placed on an attempt to win the South. As surely as Kennedy's situation dictated that he should early take the initiative and do it vigorously, Nixon's situation for most of the pre-convention period of 1960 demanded that he hold back and play a "waiting game."

1960: The Presidential Primaries. As expected, the Republican presidential primaries provided little excitement. No other Republicans were entered and, whether Nixon's name was on the ballot or not, the write-ins for Rockefeller represented only a tiny fraction of the total Nixon vote.

Inevitably, reporters looked for news in comparisons between Nixon and 1956 Eisenhower strength or between Nixon and Kennedy vote-winning ability. In Pennsylvania on April 26, Nixon received almost as many votes as had Eisenhower four years before. In Indiana on May 3, with both Nixon and Kennedy on their respective party primary ballots. Nixon led by a substantial margin. In Nebraska on May 10, though Kennedy was on the ballot and Nixon was not, Nixon's write-in votes came close to the Kennedy total and, Nebraska Republicans claimed, if many ballots had not been disqualified because of improper marking, the Republican candidate would have been in the overall lead.

In Nixon's home state of California on June 7, he received 43 percent of the total of Republican and Democratic votes while the Democratic "favorite son" candidate, Governor Edmund (Pat) Brown got 39 percent. From this, Nixon forces could claim that prospects were good in November. Democrats, however, could point to the fact that Brown and his Democratic opponent had together drawn 57 percent of the total Republican and Democratic vote.

For Nixon, the whole series of Republican presidential primaries turned out well. Though the results for him were not spectacular, the total effect was on the plus side.

Much more important for the Vice President than the Republican presidential preference primaries, in the events of 1960 leading up to the Republican National Convention, were his relationships with President Eisenhower and Governor Rockefeller, and developments which affected the political prestige of the Eisenhower Administration.

1960: Nixon and Eisenhower. The greatest political blessing which the Eisenhower Administration could have bestowed upon the Vice President would have been two-fold: (1) an early and unmistakably enthusiastic endorsement of his candidacy for the Republican nomination for President; and (2) new heights of peace and prosperity during the last year of the Administration. Neither the endorsement nor the record met those specifications.

It was not until March 16—over two months after Nixon officially became a candidate—that the President publicly came out in his behalf. The form of the endorsement, whether so intended by the President or not, tended to raise doubts about the enthusiasm behind it.

Events in the spring of 1960 were less than ideal for Republican development of a campaign based on the "peace and prosperity" themes. The economy had slanted down into a recession phase. On the "peace" front, matters were even worse, with apparent confusion within the Administration on the handling of the U-2 incident and the collapse, on May 16, of the Paris summit conference. Though the political consequences of these events would surely be felt in the fall, they also had implications for the Republican pre-convention campaign—Rockefeller began to look once again like a candidate for the Republican nomination for President.

1960: Nixon and Rockefeller. Rockefeller had withdrawn as a candidate for the Republican nomination the preceding December. But beginning on May 14 he took a series of steps which made it appear that his hat was again in the ring.

On that date his office made public the fact that he had declined a prominent role in the Republican National Convention and, to quiet talk about a possible second place for him on the Republican ticket, he indicated he might not attend the convention. The following day, Nixon asked that the New York Governor's wishes be respected since he clearly did not want to be considered for the vice presidency. On May 25, Rockefeller decided he might attend the convention, and at the same time said he would accept a draft for the presidential nomination.

After breakfast with President Eisenhower in the White House on June 8, Rockefeller flew back to New York City and issued a strongly worded challenge to Nixon to make known his program and policies *before* the Republican Convention. We cannot, said Rockefeller, proceed "to march to meet the future with a banner aloft whose only emblem is a question mark." The nature of this challenge was such that it required an immediate reply, and that was forthcoming the next day. He had, said Nixon, explained his positions "more precisely and in more detail" than had the New York Governor in his statement, and Rockefeller was offered an opportunity to publicly question him. This was declined by

Rockefeller, but with the barb that the public was entitled to "no less than a clear and candid statement."

Such was the nature of relations between Nixon and Rockefeller during the pre-convention period. Nixon, for reasons which have already been noted, was engaged in a holding operation.

Rockefeller, who had little or no chance of a presidential nomination for himself, was trying to pressure Nixon into a definite commitment of support for such Rockefeller positions as: (1) the need for a stronger defense posture; (2) a national economic growth rate of five to six percent; (3) an aged health insurance program under the Social Security System; (4) a strong position on civil rights. At least the first three involved direct criticism of the Eisenhower Administration. Implicit in Rockefeller's challenge was the possibility of some kind of opposition in the Republican Convention, or in New York after the Convention, which might have the effect of damaging the possibilities for a Nixon victory in the fall.

Finally, on July 22, after the Democratic Convention and on the weekend before the Republican Convention, Nixon made his move for an accommodation with Rockefeller. In a session which began early in the evening and lasted into the early morning hours of July 23, in the latter's Fifth Avenue apartment in New York City, the two men concluded a fourteen-point compromise agreement on what should go into the platform of the Republican party.

Goldwater, understandably, was angry. He called the Nixon-Rockefeller "Treaty of Fifth Avenue" a "Republican Munich." A large number of the delegates felt the same way. Nixon was accused of everything from a "double cross" to "selling out to Rockefeller."

Through the joint statement with the New York Governor, Nixon won a very necessary type of support while, at the same time, he was able to move out of the Eisenhower Administration and onto his own in a dramatic fashion. For the Goldwater forces, Nixon's movement was much too far and in the wrong direction. Though it was too late for them to make a serious attempt to win the presidential nomination, there was an opportunity to fight on the platform. This the "conservatives" did.

THE CONVENTION

The Platform. The extent of the pressures within the Republican Convention for a "conservative" platform is suggested in several of the chapters of this volume. Montana delegates came to Chicago with a state platform that differed sharply in most of its important planks from the Republican national platform which was adopted—in international affairs, foreign aid, taxation of cooperatives, development of water resources, federal aid for education, and immigration. (See Professor Payne's paper). At a pre-convention meeting in July, the Indiana delegation went on record for a conservative platform which would not attempt to out-promise the Democrats, and one which would preserve the integrity of the states against federal encroachment. (See Professor Derge's paper). Of the 14 members of the Idaho delegation, three favored Goldwater for President and five of the eleven for Nixon expressed themselves as ideologically oriented toward Senator Goldwater. (See Professor Huckshorn's paper).

What Nixon thought to be the facts of political life in 1960, however, led him to design an appeal aimed first at trying to win the voters of the large and doubtful states with their big blocs of electoral votes. That meant planks attractive to urban communities, to minority groups concentrated significantly in major cities, and to those who felt strongly that the United States has a significant stake in world affairs.

Yet, because each state delegation had two representatives on the Platform Committee regardless of the state's population or contribution to party strength, those large and doubtful states were very much under-represented. Because a state delegation's two representatives on the Platform Committee must be able to afford an extra week in the convention city, there is a tendency to get a membership more conservative than the cross section of convention delegates. Compounding Nixon's problem was the fact that to a large extent membership on the subcommittees was the result of an indication of the individual's personal preference.

The operation of these factors was most clearly evident in the fight over the party's position on civil rights. The Civil Rights Subcommittee adopted a "southern" plank. The full Platform Committee did likewise. Only heroic efforts on the part of Nixon and his convention organization made possible a reconsideration, by a narrow margin, of that position. Rockefeller, with this assurance, announced that his name would not be placed in nomination for President. (See Professor Lamb's paper).

In its entirety, the final platform draft was a Nixon document. Where other recent Republican national platforms had heavy injections of negativism, a positive tone ran throughout the 1960 version. In unmistakable language, the Republican party sought to show to those who still doubted that it too was firmly committed to solving the new problems of a new age, and to providing national and world leadership. Northern "liberals" were well satisfied. "Conservatives," though not entirely happy, were willing to go along in the name of party unity.

The Ticket. Only two names were placed in nomination for the office of President—Nixon and Goldwater. The latter withdrew immediately after the demonstration in his behalf had been completed. The official vote was 1,321 for Nixon and 10 (from Louisiana) for Goldwater. Arizona's motion for a unanimous ballot was then adopted.

With Rockefeller standing firm against becoming the vice presidential nominee, those still in the running at Convention time were Republican National Chairman Thruston B. Morton of Kentucky, Secretary of the Treasury Robert B. Anderson of Texas, Congressman Walter Judd of Minnesota whose keynote address elevated him into the ranks of the available, and U. S. Ambassador to the United Nations Henry Cabot Lodge. Morton and Anderson were ruled out after the Democrats nominated Johnson who was expected to exert a strong influence in the South. Judd ruled himself out. The nomination, in large part an attempt to focus attention on Republican capacity to provide sound leadership in national security and foreign affairs, went unanimously to Lodge. (See Professor Kessel's paper for an analysis of Nixon's organization and the manner in which it functioned on selection of the vice presidential nominee, and in influencing decisions on the platform).

Conclusion

What little doubt may have existed about Nixon's nomination for President vanished in December, 1959 when Rockefeller formally withdrew from the contest. Accordingly, Nixon's primary concern at the Chicago convention was to get a platform and a vice presidential nominee that would unite the Goldwater and Rockefeller wings of the party behind his drive for victory in November. Thus he did not need an elaborate organization for the "care and nurture" of delegates as did Kennedy.

Most of the decisions which still had to be made at Convention time he made himself, and he also assumed much of the burden of getting those decisions accepted by the delegates. When the Republican Platform Committee was moving off toward a position too far to the right of the Vice President, he took personal charge of reshaping the platform into a document designed for winning the general election. It was Nixon who selected Lodge as the vice presidential nominee in spite of very real opposition to Lodge in many quarters. In short, through his personal leadership Richard M. Nixon dominated the Republican National Convention of 1960.

Part II:

Nomination Campaign Organizations

4. *Senator Kennedy's Convention Organization*

FRED BURKE

Syracuse University

One aspect of the national party conventions that has received relatively little consideration is that of the presidential candidate's organization. The purpose of this paper is to examine the convention organization of Senator John Kennedy, the successful aspirant for the Democratic nomination. No attempt is made to assess its relative importance, or to determine to what extent the senator's nomination can be attributed to this much discussed organization.

It is possible only to separate analytically the Kennedy Los Angeles organization and its functions from the months of previous work and organized activity that culminated in the nomination. It is probably true that the Kennedy organization at Los Angeles was more efficient and effective than was that of any other candidate. However, it is obvious that the best of convention organizations, in the absence of months of earlier work, would be insufficient for the task of winning the nomination. Thus, to view the convention organization separately is liable to tend to exaggerate the significance of what transpired at Los Angeles, as contrasted to that which came before. The staff members of the Kennedy organization, themselves, are less inclined to attribute the nomination to the convention process and the convention organization than they are to the months of hard work in West Virginia, Wisconsin, and elsewhere, which preceded the convention. In other words, the nomination was won, not because Kennedy was organized in Los Angeles, but rather because he arrived at Los Angeles in possession of sufficient delegate votes to win the nomination on the first ballot. This is an important distinction, for it determined the primary strategic role of the organization in Los Angeles. The major task of the candidate's organization at the convention site was that of maintaining the strength which he had when he arrived. This contrasts with the task faced by the organizations of the other would-be nominees, which was to secure at the convention site a majority of the delegates votes for their respective candidates. As the goal sought by the various candidate organizations differed, it is also quite likely that the nature of the organizations themselves varied. Thus, the Los Angeles operation of the Kennedy organization, seen primarily as a defensive mechanism, was in essence a communication system and can be most usefully studied from this angle.

Communication Structure

In the tradition made famous by Jim Farley, the Kennedy organization, billeted for at least a year before the convention in the Esso Building in Washington, had long been preparing a political personality file of immense proportions. Kennedy supporters in every state had been instructed to compile lists and background information on all important Democrats, including, of course, likely delegates to the national convention. The task at Los Angeles, in one sense, was considerably easier because the groundwork had been laid.

The greater part of the convention organization was located in the Biltmore Hotel. For the purposes of our analysis we might conceive of each separate room or unit in the Biltmore as a radio receiver, whose frequency was controlled by a predetermined crystal set to receive only those transmissions for which it was cut. In this manner the input to any single aspect of the communication system was regulated so as to keep the system from becoming cluttered by transmissions from organizationally irrelevant sources. Pushing the analogy a bit further, we might say that that receiver with the widest wave band was the so-called music room located on the mezzanine of the Biltmore Hotel. It was here that huge, gaily colored signs, and even more striking Kennedy girls, welcomed the delegates with music, food and much hoop-la. Behind a partition, strategically located to give the impression of exclusiveness, the curious delegate could see a number of desks, and if he had studied the pictures of the Kennedy organization's key personnel which had appeared in *Newsweek* and nearly every important daily paper, he would have recognized political veteran Hy Raskin, talking possibly to Governor Williams of Michigan, or he might have glanced at the scholarly Dr. Robert Wallace, discussing Kennedy's views on water power with a delegate from Utah. Here the senator and other members of his family made scheduled appearances, and here campaign literature and souvenirs were distributed to all comers. The more important delegates, newspaper reporters, important Democrats, and hotel employees knew, however, that the music room was but the surface of the communications system. Its substance was to be found hidden in as many as twenty hotel rooms or suites on the second, third and eighth floors of the Biltmore. Even the private quarters of the twelve to fifteen most important individuals in the permanent Kennedy organization were also parts of the communication system.

Organizational Problems

Newspaper columnists and spokesmen have called the Kennedy apparatus a ruthless, and efficient machine. The image drawn by the mass media was one of a very careful and methodically constructed organization, wherein each individual was recruited to play a well-defined role and was systematically responsible in a hierarchical fashion to the senator himself. The constant emphasis by the mass media upon the efficiency, ruthlessness and method of the Kennedy organization is less a tribute to the senator's organization than it is a commentary upon the generally disorganized and inefficient nature of most political organizations. Far more striking than the well-oiled Kennedy machine was the relative absence of comparable organization and efficiency on behalf of the other candidates.

The Kennedy organization at Los Angeles was not designed on a drafting board and then implemented according to plan. Rather, it grew pragmatically to its convention proportions from the original small group of men that surrounded the senator at the time of his decision in 1956 to try for the presidential nomination. Rather than being a cold and infallible mechanism, this organization, like most others, possessed its human frailties. As it expanded in response to the senator's progress toward the nomination, it was not spared the usual pains of rapid organizational growth.

A political organization differs from most others in two interesting and important ways. Inevitably, a large number of the participants in a political organization are volunteers, whose compensation is in some form other than economic. To the extent that this is true, economic sanctions are not available to ensure conformity to organizational norms. If for some reason it becomes necessary to coerce the volunteers, coercion must take the form of depriving these individuals of the satisfactions they seek to derive from their service. This, of course, is extremely difficult, as the motives for involvement are often personal and psychological; consequently deviation tends to be relatively high. The absence of well-structured sanctions, alone, may account for the lack of rigor in political organizations.

Second, it is very difficult for a candidate organization to rid itself of dead weight or to discard undesirable members. Thus, functional assignments to an individual tend to become permanent and are not easily altered because a candidate cannot afford the adverse publicity and threat to organizational morale which would result from an internal struggle culminating in the discharge or in the downgrading of an important member of the organization. The victim might also defect to the enemy. Dysfunctional organizational elements of this type were evident in the Kennedy organization, as they probably are in any large-scale political undertaking. The Kennedy organization operated relatively efficiently, it would seem, not because of its size and complexity, but often in spite of it.

Delegation Liaison

As a defensive system, the Kennedy organization required an almost hourly measurement of its standing with the many state delegations at the convention so as to detect defections early enough to apply effective counter-action. This required the almost constant presence of at least one organization representative or communicant with each state delegation. Strikingly, as a matter of fact, the Kennedy organization reached this height of organizational readiness in Los Angeles. There seemed to be several patterns to the recruitment and the types of persons selected to fill the liaison roles. While in some instances this person was a delegate, it was not uncommon for a governor or a senator who was not a delegate to fill this role. The Kennedy representative with some delegations was not even a resident of that state, and in several instances his association with the state and its delegates originated during the primary and preconvention campaign. In this fashion some permanent and semi-permanent members of the Kennedy organization, such as Byron "Whizzer" White, Robert Kennedy, Ted Kennedy, Claude Desautela and others, were associated with specified state delegations. This arrangement, whereby the liaison man was an organizational regular and not a resident of the state to which he was assigned, was most common in those states where the party was divided, or in the home states of other presidential or vice presidential candidates. The reasons, of course, are obvious. Wherever the selection of a liaison or representative from the state itself would have jeopardized relationships with another faction, it better served the organization to select its liaison man from the outside. If the person responsible for liaison with a given delegation was neither an important political personage nor a delegate from that state, it was more than likely that he was a member of the permanent and paid staff of the Kennedy organization. With few exceptions, these liaison men were selected in advance of the convention and had been instructed to make careful studies of their respective delegations prior to their arrival in California. The organization assisted them with their homework by supplying information which had already been collected and analyzed by the Washington staff.

Input and Output

The delegation liaison men who were not already in Los Angeles with the permanent organization arrived considerably in advance of their respective delegations. In Los Angeles each liaison man was supplied with a kit containing instructions and a set of delegate cards. These cards, duplicates of which were kept at the Biltmore, had been brought from the Esso Building headquarters in Washington. The card files provided the liaison men with all the data that the organization possessed on each delegate and delegation. The amount of information on these cards varied considerably, but in addition to such face-data as name and residence, most cards included some information on the delegate's religion, occupation, political party position, or local office, and sometimes even on his personal ambitions. Particular note was also made of the delegate's relationship to Senator Kennedy, to members of the Kennedy family, or to important political figures very close to the senator. The delegate cards also recorded pertinent correspondence between the senator's office and the delegate. Of course, the card also included the delegate's anticipated vote in the convention. The liaison men were instructed to add data to their cards where possible.

Each liaison man was required to attend a morning staff meeting, at which time he deposited with a secretary a written report of the previous day's activities, including new information obtained on any delegate or delegation. Individual liaison reports were gathered and sent to what some referred to as the "secret room." Here four highly trained and very responsible young ladies, each charged with responsibility for approximately one fourth of the states, extracted the data and transferred it to the corresponding state briefing files. It was from these files that Robert Kennedy, and other key men in the organization, prepared, on numerous occasions throughout each day, an estimate of Kennedy's delegate strength. The scheme was carried to the lengths of maintaining and checking, at least daily, a preference card on every delegate to the convention. The periodic daily tallies of delegate strength were derived from a calculation based upon these individual cards. Access to the "secret room" was restricted, and even the liaison man's knowledge of this data center was limited to a telephone number.

The liaison men were instructed to keep the "secret room" constantly informed of their whereabouts. This was done because, in addition to the regularly appointed liaison men, an undetermined number of official and semi-official members of the Kennedy organization, including important political figures, were constantly circulating and absorbing information which they fed into the system. Upon occasion it was necessary to instruct a liaison man to verify reports concerning his delegation or individual delegates, to request that he act immediately to block a threatened defection or to spike an unfavorable rumor.

A special frequency or channel was reserved for communication between liaison men and headquarters. The system worked something like this. Assume that a liaison man, talking to a personal friend, discovered that a key New York delegate was under considerable pressure to support Adlai Stevenson openly. He would call the "secret room" and pass on his discovery to the young lady in charge of the northeastern delegations. She, adjusting action to the significance of the information, might take it upon herself to inform the liaison man assigned to the New York delegation, or relay the information to some one higher in the organization. Let us assume that she has decided to inform the liaison man with the New York Delegation. To tell him, she must now locate him, no easy task in the confusion of a convention. However, each liaison man was required to report his location and anticipated movements at regular intervals. Once located and informed that an important person in the New York delegation was under pressure to support Stevenson, the liaison man for New York immediately would seek to verify this information by questioning delegates, including influential Kennedy supporters in the New York delegation, who perhaps would assist him, or who might advise him how to proceed. In any case, the liaison man would attempt, on his own initiative, and with the assistance of Kennedy supporters in the New York delegation, to offset the pressures being applied by the Stevenson organization. If the rumor proved well-founded and if, despite his best efforts, the delegate continued inclined to announce publicly for Stevenson, the liaison man would phone the intelligence headquarters and report his inability to cope with the situation. In the case of a serious defection, someone high in the organization—a member of the Kennedy family, or an eminent political figure—would be dispatched to the Ambassador Hotel to persuade the wavering delegate of the advantages to be gained by staying with Senator Kennedy. If necessary, and if the delegate or delegation were sufficiently critical, the senator himself might be advised to phone the ambivalent delegate or ask him to visit the senator at the Biltmore.*

Within the central organization, four highly placed individuals were charged with the responsibility for maintaining, and if possible, increasing delegate support in a region assigned to each. The data constantly being processed by the communications network enabled each regional coordinator to maintain a running file on every delegate in his region. For example, the person responsible for the midwestern block of delegations was aware that within the Iowa delegation there were three or four Stevenson delegates, who could conceivably be brought around to support Senator Kennedy. He also knew which Stevenson supporters in

---

*Some New England delegates were heard to grumble that their loyalty to Senator Kennedy was being taken for granted, and that their position was not unlike that of a loyal ally of the United States. They maintained that if they wanted attention from Senator Kennedy or his organization, it was necessary to flirt first with the Johnson, Stevenson or Symington camps.

the Iowa delegation were beyond persuasion, and upon whom little time should be wasted.

The so-called soft delegates were under constant pressure, not only from the Kennedy organization, which more likely than not was attempting to keep them in line, but from representatives of other candidate organizations who were seeking to pry them loose from the Kennedy majority.

Key Communicators

There were approximately forty to fifty key persons at Los Angeles associated with the senator's cause in one way or another and for one reason or another. Although there was some overlapping, it might be useful to categorize this upper echelon as follows:

1. *Permanent Policy Staff.* Unlike the organizations of other presidential candidates, the Kennedy organization did not possess a staff czar—at the convention, as in the campaign, the senator made his own major decisions. Nevertheless, Robert Kennedy assumed a relatively broad range of responsibilities for campaign tactics and strategy. Other members of the permanent staff who held responsible functions in Los Angeles were the senator's long-time assistant, Ted Sorensen, his brother-in-law, Steve Smith, who assumed primary responsibility for the compilation and organization of the delegation files, Lawrence O'Brien, Robert Wallace, Pierre Salinger, Dave Hackett, Byron White, Edward Kennedy, and Mike Feldman.

2. *Politicos.* A number of leading political personalities cooperated with the Los Angeles organization, providing advice, lending prestige, and frequently reinforcing wavering Kennedy delegates. Some, such as Governor Ribicoff of Connecticut, were intimately involved in the day by day operation of the organization; others, such as Governor DiSalle of Ohio, were available upon request. Governor Williams of Michigan and Chester Bowles of Connecticut also had significant roles.

3. *Issue Specialists and Egghead Generalists.* The upper echelon of the organization also included a number of scholars and experts whose major concern was with specific issues or with particular interests groups. This category included nationally known scholars, such as Arthur Schlesinger, Jr., and John Galbraith of Harvard; a labor specialist, Ralph Dungan; and Frank Reeves, national committeeman from the District of Columbia

who maintained liaison with Negro delegates. The interest group specialists were not assigned specific delegations, but provided liaison with delegates and delegations associated with these interests. They and the scholars were available to critical delegations or individuals.

If glamour was required, rather than an exposition of the issues, a member of the Kennedy family—a sister or sister-in-law, or possibly even the candidate's mother—would take over the assignment.

Locator System

Over 80 telephone lines had been run into the Biltmore Hotel for the exclusive use of the Kennedy organization which alone among the Democratic aspirants operated a central telephone switchboard. The switchboard operators were in special communication with two women, referred to as "locators." It was the function of the "locator" to know at all times where every important member of the organization could be reached.* Before a staff member left his post in the Biltmore or elsewhere, he was required to phone the "locator" and report his intended movements, where he could be reached, and when he expected to return to his post. The switchboard and "locator" were coordinated in the following manner: to reach a member of the staff, one first dialed the Kennedy organization central number (Madison 6-3592) and asked for his party. If the person sought did not answer his extension or was not at his post, the switchboard operator referred the call to the "locator." The locator, upon checking her file, would inform the caller where his party was located, how he could be reached, and when he was expected to return. Like all human institutions, the locator system was fallible and did not always perform according to design or expectation. Nevertheless, by the standards prevailing among the short-lived convention organization, the locator system permitted unusually rapid communication.

Communication in the Sports Arena

This somewhat elaborate, and at times cumbersome, convention organization existed to further Senator Kennedy's bid for

---

*The "locator" should not be confused with the "secret room," for communication with the "secret room" was limited to the liaison men and to the organization's upper echelon.

the Democratic nomination. The ultimate test of the effectiveness of the communication system awaited the casting of ballots on the night of July 14. The senator's press agents had reported to the public, as early as July 11, that their candidate already possessed sufficient delegate strength to win the nomination on the first ballot. This was disputed by some media correspondents, who attributed this claim to campaign tactics rather than to objective assessment. However, it is now evident that the senator did in fact arrive in Los Angeles with sufficient strength to win on the first ballot. The major task of the organization, therefore, was that of making certain that the votes committed to the senator were forthcoming when the roll of delegations was called.

Kennedy Floor Telephones

Possibly the elaborate communications network within the sports arena itself best illustrates the thoroughness and imagination of the Kennedy convention organization. Six telephone stations were strategically located beneath the seats of the chairmen of ideally placed friendly delegations. Telephones were located in the Illinois, Massachusetts, Michigan, Wyoming, New York and Rhode Island delegations. Each of these phone stations was designed to serve a distinct area. For example, the station located in the Illinois delegation served not only Illinois, but Wisconsin, New Mexico, Minnesota, Ohio, New Hampshire, Arizona, Louisiana, Vermont and Utah as well.

The liaison men, nearly all of whom had managed in one way or another to obtain access to the floor, hovered about their respective delegations like mother hens, clucking reassurances while casting a wary eye for outside threats. Little was left to chance. The interdependent elements of the Kennedy communications system performed reasonably well, in part because they had been subjected to thorough pretesting during the early stages of the convention. The telephone system not only provided communication on the convention floor, where physical movement was often all but impossible, but more important, the six telephones were connected to the Kennedy headquarters located in the model house at the rear of the sports arena. At this control point sat Hy Raskin and other members of the permanent organization, who, by scanning a number of television sets, were often able to spot the activity of opposition candidate organizations, or incipient defections, more quickly than could the

Kennedy people on the floor of the arena. The telephone system provided the television scanners with an opportunity to immediately relay their intelligence to the appropriate telephone location on the floor. In the event that the telephone system was sabotaged or failed to function, an equal number of walkie-talkie sets were available, had been tested and could have been pressed into service.

Man and Machine

The effectiveness of this communications system on the floor of the arena was apparent to most television watchers, who were generally impressed by the fact that soon after or immediately upon a visit to a delegation by the supporters of another candidate, there would follow a visit by a member of the Kennedy organization. Robert and Ted Kennedy, as well as the candidate's sister, Patricia Lawford, were very much in evidence as they circulated from delegation to delegation. This circulation was not so haphazard as it might have appeared. The seemingly friendly visits of a Kennedy staffer or member of the family generally followed receipt of information to the effect that such a visit would be useful. Let us assume that the Illinois liaison man learned indirectly that delegate X had been overheard threatening to defect. Immediately he relayed the tip by phone to the control center in the model house at the rear of the arena. The delegate's card was pulled from the file, while the phone system was employed to transmit word of the threatened defection and relevant information about the delegate to Robert Kennedy, standing by at the Massachusetts delegation phone station. After first checking with the Illinois liaison man, Robert Kennedy would approach delegate X as if he recognized him, address him by name, remind him of earlier associations with the senator, and talk him back into line.

Floor Demonstration

The Kennedy floor demonstration was not so much designed to communicate with delegates as it was directed toward the TV viewer and the morning headlines. Organization of the demonstration is worthy of some description, for it posed a difficult problem of coordination and rapid communication in a situation conducive to neither. The delegation liaison men, the issue men, and all other members of the organization who normally attended the morning staff meetings, were given elaborate instructions concerning the preparation and strategic location of demonstration materials, the proper time at which these materials were to be brought into the arena, and alternate procedures to be used in the event of unforeseen complications. Every one was provided with a detailed diagram of the sports arena, showing the exits and entries that were to be used for this purpose.

Evaluation

Possibly the best testimony to the effectiveness of the communication system lies in a comparison of the estimate of delegation support prepared by the Kennedy organization with the actual votes cast for Senator Kennedy on Wednesday night. By nine o'clock Wednesday morning, 60 or more weary Kennedy workers crowded together for the last convention staff meeting. Present, as on past mornings, were the state delegation liaison men, the special issues and general purpose eggheads, and most of the senator's permanent staff members. The meeting was shouted to order by Robert Kennedy, perched percariously on the edge of a coffee table. After the usual locker room exhortations and warnings of overconfidence, the senator's brother, for the last time, called upon the liaison men, state by state, to report their assessment of Kennedy's strength. This was not a group of politicians telling each other what each wanted to hear. Robert Kennedy compared critically each state assessment of the senator's strength with his own tally sheet. Not once did he attempt to elicit a higher estimate from a liaison man. But on a number of occasions he questioned the report as being too high. For example, the liaison man from the Illinois delegation reported that he was sure of 64 votes. Robert Kennedy responded by carefully studying his data, based in part upon earlier reports of this same liaison man, but also upon additional intelligence which had been fed into the system throughout the previous day and night. Wasting little time on pleasantries, he informed the gentleman from Illinois that he was inaccurate, and that on the first ballot Senator Kennedy would receive only 62, and not 64 votes from the Illinois delegation. Robert Kennedy then questioned the Illinois liaison man about two delegates and the tenacity of their support for Senator Symington, indicating the scope and quality of the information fed into the system, and its uses. With few exceptions, the delegate liaison report tallied fairly closely with the information already possessed by Robert Kennedy. The staff meetings early in the week, however, showed considerable discrepancy between the often inflated figures reported by the liaison men and the conservative estimates of Robert Kennedy. A quick computation and recording of the tally taken on Wednesday morning, plus three additional votes which were later secured from California, revealed that the organization expected to receive a total of 780½ votes on the first ballot, with 761 being required to nominate. (See Table I). If the 21 votes cast by the Kansas delegation are excluded, it will be seen that the total vote for Senator Kennedy was in fact 785.* A total of 39 delegations, including Wyoming, cast some or all of their votes for Senator Kennedy.**

The organization's estimates and the votes cast were identical in 19 of these 39 delegations. In six delegations the organization was only one half vote off. In four delegations only one vote separated Wednesday morning's estimate from Wednesday night's balloting. In two delegations the difference was one and one-half votes, and in three delegations, two votes. Significant underestimates were made only in the cases of Alabama, Kentucky, and North Dakota, among which the senator picked up a total of eleven votes that he had not anticipated. The organization overestimated the senator's strength only in Nebraska. (See Table I). On Wednesday morning the Nebraska delegation was thought to be unanimous in its support of Kennedy, but he received only eleven of the state's sixteen votes. North Dakota, which had been counted on for seven votes, nearly made up for this loss by casting all of its eleven votes for Kennedy.

During the balloting, Robert Kennedy kept a close watch on the relationship between the estimated cumulative vote and the actual cumulative vote. According to the calculations of the Kennedy organization, the senator's vote would go over the top either with the 8½ votes which were anticipated from Wyoming, or with

---

*The organization did not anticipate any support from Kansas on the first ballot. It will be recalled that the Kansas delegation was in caucus and did not cast its 21 votes for Kennedy until after he had already received a majority and the roll call had ended.

**The organization anticipated receiving 8½ of Wyoming's 15 votes. It will be recalled that when the Wyoming delegation realized that Kennedy's nomination was inevitable, and that by casting all of its votes for him it could gain the distinction of putting him over the top, it cast all 15 votes for Senator Kennedy.

TABLE I

First Ballot Estimate Morning of July 14 Compared to Votes Cast

	Estimate	Estimate Running Total	Actual Vote Cast	Actual Running Total	Difference
Alabama	0	0	3½	3½	+3½
Alaska	9	9	9	12½	0
Arizona	17	26	17	29½	0
California	33½	59½	33½	63	0
Colorado	12	71½	13½	76½	+1½
Connecticut	21	92½	21	97½	0
Hawaii	2	94½	1½	99	− ½
Idaho	7	101½	6	105	−1
Illinois	62	163½	61½	166½	− ½
Indiana	34	197½	34	200½	0
Iowa	20½	218	21½	222	+1
Kansas	0		(passed)		
Kentucky	0		3½	225½	+3½
Maine	15	233	15	240½	0
Maryland	24	257	24	264½	0
Massachusetts	41	298	41	305½	0
Michigan	42	340	42	348	0
Montana	9½	349½	10	358	+ ½
Nebraska	16	366	11	369	−5
Nevada	7½	373	5½	374½	−2
New Hampshire	11	384	11	385½	0
New Mexico	5	389	4	389½	−1
New York	104	493	104½	494	+ ½
North Carolina	7	500	6	500	−1
North Dakota	7	507	11	511	+4
Ohio	64	570½	64	575	0
Oregon	16½	587½	16½	591½	0
Pennsylvania	68	655½	68	659½	0
Rhode Island	17	672½	17	676	0
South Dakota	6	678½	4	680½	−2
Utah	7½	686	8	688½	+ ½
Vermont	9	695	9	698½	0
Washington	15	710	14½	712	− ½
West Virginia	16½	726½	15	727	−1½
Wisconsin	23	749½	23	750	0
Wyoming	8½	758	15	765	+6½
District of Columbia	9	767	9	774	0
Puerto Rico	7	774	7	781	0
Virgin Islands	4	778	4	785	0
(Kansas)			21	806	0

the nine votes from the District of Columbia. The Wyoming delegation was expected to cast 8½ votes for Senator Kennedy, bringing the total to 758½. By the time the balloting reached Vermont, it was evident to Robert Kennedy that if Wyoming cast fifteen votes for Kennedy, the long campaign would be over. While West

Virginia and Wisconsin were still balloting, young Kennedy moved into the midst of the Wyoming delegation, urging and cajoling the delegates to cast all of their votes for Senator Kennedy, and thereby achieve the distinction of nominating the next president. As the morning headlines were to testify, he was successful. Wyoming's votes gave the senator a total of 765. Had they given him only the anticipated votes, Senator Kennedy would have had at that point 758½ votes, or one half vote more than the organization had estimated at that point.

This discrepancy probably best sums up the effectiveness of the Kennedy convention organization.

5. Political Leadership: The Nixon Version

JOHN H. KESSEL
University of Washington

In the sixties, in addition to knowledge of the issues, in addition to an understanding of world affairs, in addition to the basic ability that any leader must have to gain support for his policies —the American people and the free world need in the American presidency a man who has sound and sober judgment. They need a man who will resist the temptation—and the temptation will sometimes be great—to give the appearance of leadership when, actually, any rash statement or action might set off a chain of circumstances that would be disastrous to the whole world. I would urge that those who are examining this problem of leadership not be fooled by appearances. The American people must look beyond gestures and flamboyant speeches to what is actually accomplished. Accomplishment is the lasting measure of true leadership.[*]

By urging observers to look to the substance of leadership, Richard Nixon invites inspection of what he is able to accomplish himself. The Vice President's behavior at the Republican National Convention provides evidence that his talents are genuine indeed. This is not said simply because Mr. Nixon was nominated for President. Such a claim could be made on behalf of John F. Kennedy. He came to Los Angeles hoping the Democratic Party would accept the credentials of leadership he had gathered in the

---

[*]Richard Nixon, Press Conference, Miami Beach, Florida, January 16, 1960.

primary campaigns. Once Wyoming's votes gave the Massachusetts senator a majority of the votes for the nomination, it could be said that he had achieved his goal. Richard Nixon's position was different. His nomination was expected. Vice President Nixon was an understudy who was inheriting power from an incumbent administration. Moreover, he had been exercising considerable power within the party for some time. Since Nixon came to Chicago in a position of established power rather than as one who was asking the party to grant him power, more could justifiably be expected of him.

In order to show that he could lead the 1,331 delegates, many of whom were preoccupied with home state affairs, Vice President Nixon had to do at least three things. He had to surround himself with a staff which would be responsive to his wishes and which could effectively communicate his desires to the delegates. He had to work for a platform which would reflect Nixon views without disavowing established Eisenhower policies. He had to secure the nomination of the best available man as his running mate. And all of these things had to be done in such a way as to attract the independent voters whose support would be crucial to a minority party candidate.*

The political staff which backstopped the Vice President at Chicago was not formed by the enlargement of an existing group. Rather it was created through the marriage of two staffs. The first group was the Vice President's personal staff which normally had quarters in the Senate Office Building; the second was a campaign organization which had had its quiet beginnings when a primary contest was thought to be likely. The Capitol Hill contingent was headed by Nixon's brilliant young administrative assistant, Robert H. Finch. The campaign group was supervised by former Republican National Chairman Leonard W. Hall.

Finch and Hall have many characteristics in common. Both are unquestionably devoted to advancing Nixon's interests. Both are very hard workers. Hall is uncomfortable if left without any work to do for five minutes. Finch usually puts in at least a fourteen

---

*The accuracy of the description which follows would normally depend on information concerning the actions and motives of Vice President Nixon and other central figures. Many of these data are not available. These speculations are logical inferences from observed behavior, are consistent with the data which are available, and fit the explanatory model being used. It should be quite clear, however, that this article is an author's interpretation and not an authoritative account.

hour working day. But the previous experience of the two men had been quite different. Leonard Hall learned his politics in Nassau County, the legislature at Albany, and the House of Representatives—all strongholds of organization politics. Robert Finch came from Southern California. Since California Republicans had been in the minority in recent decades, and since party structure had been amorphous at best, Golden State practice had been to rely quite heavily on public relations techniques to appeal to independent and Democratic voters. Therefore the two men's assignments varied in emphasis. Hall, who had excellent contacts throughout the country, often acted as an intermediary between the Vice President and the political pros. Finch, whose habits of thought were quite similar to Nixon's, frequently was used as an alter ego for his fellow Californian.

Given these differing backgrounds, and given the normal assumption that a staff person's power lies in his undisputed ability to speak authoritatively for his chief, organization theory would lead us to expect a lively struggle for power. Yet there is no evidence that staff rivalries caused any real difficulties at Chicago. The factors which dampened such potential conflict are therefore of real interest, and an understanding of the ways in which the sharp edges were removed from personal rivalries in turn provides some significant insights into the manner in which Nixon used his staff.

One mitigating factor was the pattern of friendships which defied organizational lines. Many staff members developed real feelings of respect for others who were working on similar projects. This extended all the way from the mimeograph room to Messrs. Finch and Hall themselves. Finch and Hall breakfasted together every morning.* At these breakfasts all major policy decisions were discussed, and any differences of opinion were threshed out. Any questions which Finch or Hall felt should go up to Nixon himself, either because of the importance of the subject matter or because Finch and Hall did not see eye to eye, were automatically so referred.

The assignments given the staff members were normally flexible rather than rigid and precisely defined. No one was apt to have a specific formal scope of authority which was his and his alone. Rather all were expected to help out with "the hot ones" as they

---

*This was a normal practice, not a special arrangement confined to the convention.

came along. The list of chores assigned to Charles K. McWhorter, Nixon's legislative assistant, was typical. "I've been working on three things," McWhorter explained. "I've been contacting delegates, working on the platform wording, and helping arrange the demonstrations. I'm not in charge of any of these activities, but I just pitch in and do whatever I can." Staff arrangements of this sort not only increase adaptability, but the ambiguity has the effect of decreasing the chance that one staff member will be envious of the assignment given to another.

The operation of the Nixon staff also reflected the character of Nixon himself. The Vice President was the single source of authority. (Significantly, members of the Nixon staff referred to him simply as "The Boss.") Nixon's singular position was based in part on his undoubted political acumen, and in part on his personality. While the Vice President had real skill in working with people, the "pane of glass" always seemed to be there to prevent friendly contacts from growing into a warmer rapport. For reserved, serious minded Richard Nixon, politics and the political goals to which he is whole-heartedly dedicated are the most important things in life.

These personality characteristics facilitated the tasks of leadership for Nixon in at least two important ways. Since he was essentially un-involved in personal loyalties and conflicts, he could serve as a neutral arbiter. If there was any difference of opinion between members of his staff, they could take their question to Nixon with absolute confidence that he would decide the matter strictly on the merits of the case. And if staff members were expected to "drop everything" to take care of matters of great urgency that developed from time to time, no one could concentrate on the emergencies more closely than Nixon himself. Given his single mindedness, in a crisis Nixon works calmly, rationally, and incredibly hard.

Achievement of a platform which accurately reflected Nixon's views required not only hard work at the convention, but also a harmonization of his positions with those taken by other leaders in the Republican Party. A simple analysis of the actual and potential centers of power shows that there were at least five groups of persons who were in a position to affect the content of the platform if they chose to do so. These include, aside from the Vice President himself, President Eisenhower, members of the platform committee, Governor Rockefeller, and a grouping of conservatives.*

When the drafting process began some weeks before the convention, three of these parties were represented. The National Committee designated Charles H. Percy, Chairman of the Republican Committee on Program and Progress, who had issued four task force reports under the title *Decisions for a Better America,* as chairman of the platform committee. President Eisenhower's principal spokesman on platform matters was Robert E. Merriam, Deputy Assistant to the President for Interdepartmental Affairs.** Merriam was assisted by Stephen Hess. Assigned to represent the Vice President in these discussions was George L. Grassmuck, a University of Michigan political scientist who had taken a year's leave of absence to work with the Nixon Capitol Hill staff. In typical fashion, position papers were circulated, reviewed, marked up, and passed on to the next interested party. By the time the platform hearings opened in Chicago, Percy Merriam and Grassmuck had a series of draft planks ready, and had secured the approval of President Eisenhower, Vice President Nixon, and other party leaders for these tentative proposals. Charles Percy had been the most active partner in this operation, but Robert Merriam and George Grassmuck had the right to veto any wording which seemed exceptionable to either the President or the Vice President.

While some thought had been given to the content of the platform, no effort had been made to guarantee that the draft proposals would be accepted by picking platform committee members known to favor the proposals. The Vice President had not attempted to influence the selection of the committee members in any way. The only such effort had been a routine exhortation from the national committee asking that the state committees designate responsible, literate, forward-looking delegates who

---

*Some of the conservative delegates were responsive to Senator Goldwater; some were simply prepared to fight the inclusion of particular liberal viewpoints in the platform.

**While Eisenhower was personally concerned with some areas (at Chicago he was to oppose vigorously any implication that the United States' defense posture was less than adequate), his general attitude could be summed up in one statement he made on arrival in Chicago: "Maybe you've forgotten, but there is a political campaign on and us old fellows are supposed to be forgotten."

would reflect credit on the Republican Party. Even though many states attempted to follow these instructions, the selection process permitted less progressive forces to speak with unusual authority. For one thing, the two-from-each-state representational scheme assured disproportionate influence to the less populous states. Moreover, while subcommittee chairmen known to be sympathetic to the draft proposals were picked, the other members of the subcommittees were selected on the basis of *their own* preferences.

The platform committee convened in Chicago on the Monday preceding the convention. For the first few days everything went smoothly. Hearings were held before the full platform committee and before the several subcommittees. Robert Merriam and George Grassmuck were on the scene, but very few committee members were aware of their roles. Grassmuck's instructions were simply to keep an eye on things, and be available in case any questions were raised about the Vice President's views on some topic or other.

But late in the week trouble began to develop. It became apparent that the planks being drafted by certain subcommittees, notably civil rights, might well depart from the tone of the tentative proposals which had been cleared previously. At the same time, members of the platform committee began to see signs that they were not the only ones working on "their" platform. On Thursday night Deputy Attorney General Edward Walsh arrived with a sixteen page brief containing draft civil rights planks and explanatory material. It was understood that these planks had the explicit approval of the Vice President and Attorney General Rogers. And on Friday night Nixon and Nelson Rockefeller held their widely publicized meeting in New York.

Up to this point, three of the five centers of leadership within the party had been involved in the drafting process. The effect of the meeting with Governor Rockefeller was to involve him as well. The decision to go to New York was made by Nixon himself without any consultation with or advance notice to his staff. The Vice President's reasons for making this decision can be discerned by putting together statements made at his press conference on the following day:

> In the preliminary stage of a campaign for the nomination inevitably there arises in the public mind ideas with regard to how the candidates may disagree on issues which are somewhat exaggerated. In Governor Rockefeller's case and mine, however, we

share the same basic conviction on the great issues confronting this nation—domestic economy, and the issue of human rights. That was why I called the Governor on the phone yesterday afternoon. I told him that I had noted the concern he had expressed with regard to the Republican platform, and I told him that I thought that it might be helpful if he and I personally could discuss the platform and see where we agreed, where we disagreed and what particular principles and policies we felt were essential to incorporate in the platform. The Governor indicated he very much would like to follow that procedure. We met at 7:30 last night in New York, and after discussions lasting 3½ to 4 hours, talked to members of the platform committee meeting in Chicago. These telephone conversations lasted for approximately 3 hours, and in these conversations we conveyed those general principles and policies on which we agreed to Mr. Percy, Mr. Mel Laird, Gabriel Hauge, Roswell Perkins, and Dr. George Grassmuck. And the net result of these conversations was the preparation of, and the approval of, the (fourteen point) statement which the Governor issues.

The Nixon-Rockefeller statement did not represent any change or concession in either Nixon's or Rockefeller's views. Despite much published nonsense to the contrary, their opinions had been quite similar all along. The principal effect was to emphasize this agreement. And because of the dramatic circumstances, it did get this point across to many who previously had missed it.

The issuance of the Nixon-Rockefeller statement created a very difficult situation at Chicago. By underscoring the relatively liberal nature of Nixon's views, it put certain conservatives—members of the fifty power center—on notice that the platform might not be entirely to their liking. And quite aside from philosophic considerations, many Republican politicians objected to the preferred treatment being given Rockefeller on the ground that he had been publicly criticizing the Eisenhower administration. Professional politicians were critical of Rockefeller for this. If one didn't like Eisenhower's policies, party folkways called for private expression of dissent, support of the party candidates, and work to modify the objectionable policies when the next administration took office—not public criticism. Open censure of Republican administration would only win votes for the Democrats.

Since the Nixon-Rockefeller statement antagonized some conservatives and some professional politicians, it would have caused enough trouble even if it had been communicated to the platform committee in the most diplomatic manner. But many platform committee members learned about the accord from Saturday morning's newspapers. And they were indignant. Not only were they expected to make their platform conform to someone else's specifications, but they were being given these specifications *after* they had already been working on the platform for a week's time. As one might expect, most of the platform committee were angry about this procedure. Some of them concluded that *they* were going to write the platform now; they were not going to be dictated to by Richard Nixon, Nelson Rockefeller, or anyone else.

No one concerned with the platform got much sleep that week end. There were now two major jobs to do. The platform had to be compared with the working of the Nixon-Rockefeller statement, and members of the platform committee had to be persuaded to accept the type of document desired by Nixon. From Saturday morning until Tuesday evening, Nixon and Rockefeller staff members were working closely with one another to achieve these ends. A group of Nixon staffers which included George Grassmuck, James Shepley, John Hamlin, Rita Hauser, and Charles Lichtenstein* conferred in a Blackstone Hotel suite with a Rockefeller team made up of Roswell Perkins, Emmet Hughes, Bruce Chapman and Joseph Carlino. Working in constant communication with their respective chiefs, these two groups went over the platform drafts to make sure that they accorded with the Nixon-Rockefeller statement. This negotiation was arduous. The principal difficulty was that since the New York meeting had been private, and since the fourteen point statement was so much more synoptic than the platform, it was difficult to be certain what some of the allusions in the brief document meant. But if progress was slow, it was also sure, and by Tuesday morning full agreement had been reached on platform language which both Nixon and Rockefeller could support—language, significantly, which did not vary in substance from the draft proposals approved by Nixon *before* his conversations with Rockefeller.

Reaching agreement with the Rockefeller forces, though, was the less difficult half of the job. At the same time that the research staffs were working out acceptable wording, many other people were undertaking the job of selling this relatively liberal

---

*In view of the amount that has been written about the use of intellectuals by other candidates, it is worth noting that here were three Ph.D.'s in this small group.

platform. At Nixon's headquarters the group most concerned was the delegate contact organization which had been put together by Leonard Hall. Hall, assisted by Under Secretary of the Treasury Fred Scribner, worked through four regional chiefs. The northeast was handled by former national chairman Meade Alcorn of Connecticut. Midwestern delegations were contacted by Ray C. Bliss, Ohio State Chairman and longtime head of the Conference of Midwest and Rocky Mountain State Chairmen. I. Lee Potter, who had been supervising the G.O.P.'s Operation Dixie, continued his work with southern Republicans. Delegations from the Pacific Coast heard from Mort Frayne, long prominent in the politics of Washington. These "regional whips" in turn passed the word through a contact man in each state delegation.

These political veterans were not working alone. They were joined in their task of persuasion by Rockefeller adherents, by close Nixon associates such as Attorney General William Rogers and Senator Hugh Scott, by administration spokesmen such as Robert Merriam, and by the chairmen of the platform subcommittees. But even with this impressive roster of political talent, the pro-Nixon forces were unable to have their way at once on civil rights. At 3:30 a.m. on Monday morning the full platform committee voted to accept a southern-backed, moderate civil rights plank.

This situation confronted Vice President Nixon when he arrived at Chicago. His first order of business was therefore a press conference at which he explicitly associated himself with the civil rights proposals which were being advanced in his name:

The civil rights platform is now under consideration by the platform committee. At the present time the committee has adopted a majority report which is unsatisfactory as far as I am concerned. I believe that it is essential that the Republican convention adopt a strong civil rights platform, an honest one which deals specifically and not in generalities with the problems and goals that we desire to reach in these fields. Now, on this particular plank, I have taken a personal interest. For several days—as a matter of fact, for several weeks, before I left Washington—I studied the various proposals for specific legislative and administration action which had been suggested. I determined which of those proposals I believed were obtainable objectives which would further the cause of civil rights and would not be of a type which would be counter-productive by reason of their extremity. And then, after having done that, I suggested that those particular specific proposals be put into language for consideration by the platform committee. I am not wedded to any specific language. I do support the specific proposals.

He then took personal charge of the drive to get enough votes on the full platform committee to obtain reconsideration of the civil rights plank when the committee reconvened the following morning. While his lieutenants and associates continued to explain Nixon's views to all concerned, the Vice President himself met with delegates who could not be moved by anyone of lesser stature. The closed-door meetings in which Nixon participated lasted until the small hours of Tuesday morning. In these meetings Nixon had two objectives. He wanted to ensure that the civil rights plank represented his views, and he wanted to find language which would be acceptable to all wings of the party. His technique was reminiscent of the one he used in the steel strike negotiations in early 1960. The Vice President simply pointed out the objective situation as he saw it. He told the delegates that the proposals represented his own views on the matter, and that while he would not insist on any inflammatory language, he did want to see these proposals incorporated in the final platform. He much preferred that the changes be made in the platform committee rather than on the floor of the convention. If, however, a floor fight was necessary, he was prepared to lead it, and he could undoubtedly command the votes to win. In short, it was made clear to the conservative delegates that their real choice was whether they were going to have other language imposed on them in a floor fight.

The combination of persuasion from the Vice President and pressure from his emissaries gave the liberals a slight majority by the time the full platform committee reconvened on Tuesday morning. The committee voted to reconsider the civil rights plank and spent much of the day doing so. By late afternoon they had adopted a plank which incorporated the specific proposals mentioned in the Nixon-Rockefeller statement,* but which generally used language calculated to give the least possible offense to the conservatives.

Televiewers who watched the convention proceedings the next evening saw the platform accepted by a voice vote. There was no public evidence of disharmony, nor was there any indication

---

*At this point Nelson Rockefeller immediately announced that he would not permit his name to be placed in nomination for President.

of the leadership job which had been done behind the scenes. But the final platform was tailored to Nixon's guidelines. The southern conservatives were unhappy about the civil rights plank, but appreciated the changes in language which had been made and which would spare them some embarrassment in their attempt to build a Republican Party in the south. Northern liberals were very pleased. They felt that the time of testing had given the party a stronger position in the civil rights field than it had had before.

It is the Vice President's habit to make up his mind by stages. There are occasions when he simply decides something himself,* but in relaxed circumstances he likes to "try out" ideas on close associates first. If he finds the initial response favorable, he will pursue the discussion with all those he feels should be consulted. When all of these conversations have been completed, the decision is firm. This process makes it difficult to say at just what point the decision is made. As Nixon consults more and more people, it is progressively less likely that he will alter his tentative conclusion. At the same time the decision is always subject to modification should some unexpected development occur or some new piece of information come to the Vice President's attention.

This was the manner in which Henry Cabot Lodge was selected as Nixon's running mate. The Vice President had avoided all public discussion of the question with the statement that his decision would not be made until such time as he was the presidential nominee of the Republican Party. This was an accurate statement of his attitude, but it will be noted that there was nothing in this attitude to prevent preliminary discussions from going forward. And if Richard Nixon was not sure about who he wanted as his running mate, he was quite clear about the characteristics he wanted this potential candidate to have.

At no time had the Vice President given serious consideration to the idea of balancing the ticket either geographically or ideologically. Nixon's criteria were, in descending order of importance, ability to serve effectively as Vice President, ideological compatability with Nixon himself, and ability to add political

---

*The times when he does act independently—as when he decided to go to New York City to meet Nelson Rockefeller—are hard on his staff, but it is characteristic of Nixon that he uses his staff as he sees fit. He is never a prisoner of his staff.

strength to the Republican ticket. Nixon had planned for some time to strengthen the vice presidency by asking his running mate, if elected, to assume direction and coordination of the non-military activities connected with the cold war. Since he envisioned working closely with his own vice president, Nixon thought it essential that the nominee agree with his own views on foreign policy, human rights. and economic policy. And while he was more concerned with the nominee's ability to serve than with political considerations, Nixon did want to secure the nomination of someone who would be able to reinforce the image of the Republican Party as a forward-looking group with positive goals.

In the light of Nixon's plans for the vice presidency, it is not surprising that all of those who were seriously discussed had had experience in foreign affairs. Governor Nelson Rockefeller had been an administrative assistant dealing with foreign policy under Presidents Roosevelt and Eisenhower. Henry Cabot Lodge had served on the Senate Foreign Relations Committee for years before his appointment as Ambassador to the United Nations. National chairman Thruston B. Morton had been an assistant secretary of state before his election to the Senate. And Robert B. Anderson had been involved with the National Security Council both as Deputy Secretary of Defense and as Secretary of the Treasury.

Events in the week before the convention worked to the advantage of Ambassador Lodge. Nelson Rockefeller did not want to run for vice president. Rockefeller and Nixon had talked about the vice presidency when Rockefeller was a White House staffer, and had arrived at a general agreement about the limitations and possibilities of the office long before the New York Governor emerged as a possible candidate. Therefore when Rockefeller, at the midnight meeting in New York, reiterated his determination not to accept even a genuine draft for the nomination, Nixon did not hesitate to repeat his public assurances that the governor's wishes would be respected. The nomination of Lyndon B. Johnson by the Democrats made a strategy of appealing to the south seem less desirable to the Republican leaders. This severely handicapped the chances of Kentucky's Thruston B. Morton and Texas' Robert B. Anderson. So when the convention began, it looked very much as though Henry Cabot Lodge would be Nixon's choice.

An event which occurred on Monday night, while most of the Nixon organization was working for the adoption of a strong civil rights plank, came close to changing this. The event was the keynote address delivered by Congressman Walter Judd of Minnesota. This speech made a great impression both on the delegates and on the general public. Spontaneous public support began to build for his nomination, and Walter Judd, a member of the House Foreign Affairs Committee who had spent many years in China as a medical missionary, emerged as a bona fide candidate for vice president.

On the night of his own nomination for President, Richard Nixon called Congressman Judd from the floor of the convention to his suite at the Blackstone Hotel. This event caused no little anguish among the newsmen who had written stories saying that the decision had already been made to nominate Lodge.* The decision had not been made. In fact, Nixon had summoned Judd for a discussion about the possibility of the Minnesotan becoming the vice presidential nominee. Congressman Judd expressed doubts about whether he could reach the heights of his keynote speech again, and about whether he had the physical stamina necessary for a nationwide campaign. Nevertheless, Vice President Nixon added Walter Judd's name to his own list of eligible candidates.

Nixon had need for such a list. He had determined that he would avoid either extreme alternative of making his own choice or of permitting an open convention battle. Instead the Vice President came up with an interesting institutional innovation: a committee of 36 which would "represent the sense of the convention." This group was to meet away from the prying eye of television so that the participants would be free to speak their minds. It was to be small to permit all to participate in the discussion, but large enough to include all of the leadership elements within the Republican Party. Six senators, six congressmen, seven administration members, four governors, nine party politicians, and four elder statesmen were invited to the meet-

---

*The Nixon-Judd conference took place about 10:00 p.m., not too long before the deadline for the morning papers published on the eastern seaboard. Reporters gathered in anxious groups in the halls of the Blackstone. "Gee, I don't know," a typical conversation went, "I talked to Walter (Judd) just yesterday morning and he told me that he thought it would be Lodge."

ing.* The conferees were also selected from the areas of greatest Republican strength. Fourteen came from the northeast, fourteen from the midwest, four from the far west, and four from the upper south. The harmonious proceedings within this group, which was representative of the real power within the party, furnish an instructive contrast to the difficulties on the platform committee where each state and territory, regardless of its size, had equal representation.

This group convened on the second floor of the Blackstone Hotel after the convention had adjourned on Wednesday night. Most of the conferees had taken part in earlier discussions with Vice President Nixon. They knew what his opinions had been, and he knew what their opinions had been. But this was the first chance the Vice President had had to talk with many of the conferees during the convention and, even if nothing had happened to change the participants' thinking, the Vice President wanted a full and open review before the die was cast. Consequently, there was a serious and constructive discussion of the merits and demerits of the principal contenders.

Nixon opened the meeting by stating the qualifications he thought the nominee should have, and then he asked each participant in turn to state his views as to who would be the best nominee. The conversation was largely limited to two men: Henry Cabot Lodge and Thruston Morton. And as the meeting proceeded it became obvious that there was a genuine consensus for the nomination of Lodge. This is not to say that there were no differences of opinion. A number of people opposing the nomination of Lodge did not hesitate to state their views. But these persons did not represent any solid sectional resistance to Lodge. As much as anything else their opposition stemmed from a different conception of the tactical problem facing the Republican Party. They argued that in order to win congressional seats, the ticket ought to be strengthened by someone who was popular in midwestern areas where the party had been suffering heavy losses recently. Most of the participants whose thinking

---

*Attending the meeting were: cabinet members Mitchell, Mueller, Seaton, Summerfield, and Rogers; Senators Bridges, Dirksen, Saltonstall, Cooper, Fong, and Scott; Congressmen Halleck, Byrnes, Ford, Arends, Reese, and Miller; Republican politicos Finch, Scribner, Hall, Alcorn, Morhouse, Percy, Potter, Martin, and Bliss; White House staffers Morrow and Shanley; and elder statesmen (Milton) Eisenhower, Bricker, Darby and Dewey.

proceeded from presidential premises, however, agreed that Lodge was the strongest available candidate.

After each participant had had a chance to express his views, the Vice President asked if they felt a vote would be in order. The response was that this was a decision that the candidate should make for himself. Nixon thereupon reviewed his own feelings about the four potential nominees: Lodge, Morton, Judd, and Anderson. While each of the four was qualified according to Nixon's own criteria, he felt that the United Nations Ambassador would make the best candidate because of his long experience with foreign affairs. His choice, Nixon concluded, would be Henry Cabot Lodge.

The successful fight for a reasonably liberal platform and the selection of Lodge as a running mate were not the only things which occupied the attention of the Nixon organization at Chicago. There were entire staffs whose existence we haven't even mentioned. Herbert Klein and a dozen others were ministering to the needs of the hundreds of media representatives who were reporting the convention story. Up on the ninth floor of the Conrad Hilton Hotel, Peter Flanigan, Clifton White, Eugene Thumbull, and Edward Harding of the Nixon Volunteers were receiving reports of the progress of the "citizens" groups throughout the country. And literally scores of people were concerned with public hoopla and private administrative chores. But if the two episodes we have described barely scratch the surface, the surface we have scratched is sufficiently close to the nerve center of the Nixon operation to give us some good ideas about the effectiveness of Nixon's leadership.

Richard E. Neustadt, in his skillful analysis *Presidential Power*,* makes it clear that there are at least five factors which are essential to successful presidential command. These are assurance of the personal involvement of the President, clarity in the presidential orders, wide publicity for these orders, possession of sufficient authority by the person charged with responsibility for carrying out the order, and a feeling on the part of those to whom the order is directed that it is right and proper for the President to issue such a command. The first three of these items concern the behavior of the leader and his staff; the latter two are more related to the situation in which the leader finds himself.

*New York: John Wiley & Sons, Inc., 1960

In one of the instances we have been describing these conditions were clearly present. Almost all of the delegates were willing to concede Richard Nixon a right to choose his own running mate, and to make this choice in any way he saw fit. Once the Vice President stepped before the microphone and said: "I have reached the conclusion that Henry Cabot Lodge should be the vice presidential nominee," his further comment that "I think the prospects are good that the convention will accept this recommendation," was understatement indeed.

During the early days of the platform struggle the circumstances making for successful leadership were not present. There was uncertainty about what Nixon's views were; there was confusion as to who was speaking for him; and there were members of the platform committee who thought that *they* should write the platform without guidance from Nixon or anyone else. But by Tuesday morning conditions had changed. In fact, the whole episode may be seen as an effort to assure committee members that the Vice President was personally involved, to publicize the nature of his wishes, and to persuade recalcitrant delegates that Richard Nixon should have a controlling voice in platform matters.

What quality of leadership would Richard Nixon have given if elected President? It would seem unwise to write too optimistic a prognosis on the basis of his success at the convention. It is, after all, a *relatively* easy thing to lead your political party when it is in the process of nominating you for President. Once a man is in the White House, he can make his views crystal clear and still fail to get a response from an independently elected Congress or a foreign leader—to say nothing of the difficulties of dealing with the Communist powers. But if a President cannot command obedience from those who look to other sources for their cues, he can sometimes hold in check those who would injure the nation's interests; he can persuade those who are open to reason; and he can give direction to the government by concentrating on the great questions of the day. If his behavior at Chicago is any indication, it is quite likely that Richard Nixon could do these things very well, indeed.

Part III:

Kennedy and Nixon Leadership on Party Platform

6. *Civil Rights and the Republican Platform Nixon Achieves Control*

KARL A. LAMB

University of Michigan

I don't know whether a Convention representing the divergent interests of the country could write a platform, except a most stereotyped statement in favor of the Bill of Rights and the Ten Commandments, without the influence of presidential candidates. Instead of those candidates interfering with the writing of the platform, it seems to me that maybe they furnish the only meeting ground that makes it possible.*

Party platforms are drafted according to long established rules of formal procedure, but a knowledge of that procedure does not explain how the platform committee makes decisions. The assumption underlying the formal process is that the basic source of party philosophy is the opinion of party members at the grass roots. Each state delegation to the national convention places two representatives on the resolutions committee. After investigating the problems involved, these representatives of the local viewpoint take counsel one with another; then, following the democratic procedures of a legislative assembly, they agree upon a definition of party philosophy.

Just as the voting of senators may be more influenced by negotiations in the cloakroom than by debate on the Senate floor, the real decisions of the Committee on Resolutions may be the result of operations quite outside its formal procedures. Party leaders use many tactics to exert an influence upon its decisions. Partisans generally accept the notion that the party's candidate

---

*Alf M. Landon to Harold Johnson, October 14, 1937

should be able to approve the platform. When their own interest seems threatened, however, platform committee members may insist that no outsider should influence the work for which the committee was officially designated. The story of the conflict in the 1960 Republican Platform Committee could be told as a contest between those who insisted upon the use of democratic procedures and those who were willing to accept the judgment of the party's acknowledged leadership. Unhappily for the development of the drama, neither side acted as though they accepted one theory and rejected the other. Each side extolled either the judgment of party leaders or the sanctity of democratic procedure, depending on which appeal seemed, at the moment, most likely to advance its cause.

A platform by itself can hardly insure party victory, but its potential for negative influence on the party's fortunes is very great. Because the American party attempts to build an electoral majority by appealing to every economic group and geographical region, the platform is used as a device to compromise conflicting interests within the party and win the support of all for the national ticket. The danger is that an unchecked battle between hostile party elements will produce stalemate, and the platform will say nothing meaningful on the crucial issues. On the other hand, platform language may handicap the candidate and his campaign. It may be taken from context by his opponent and used against him. In formulating his strategy, the presidential nominee may decide that the appeal to one group of voters is more important than the support of another group, and he will wish to initiate that appeal in the language of the platform. If an entire region feels that its interests are ignored in the platform, a substantial party faction may desert the candidate or refuse to support him with the enthusiasm necessary to achieve victory. The presidential candidate must attempt to attain a balance between these dangers and potentialities.

The following is an account of the methods by which Richard M. Nixon achieved that balance at the Republican National Convention of 1960.

The Background

The Eisenhower era had been essentially a time of consolidation. The Truman policy of the containment of communism had been further refined by the Eisenhower administration. President

Eisenhower had added an extensive program of personal diplomacy. The social welfare legislation enacted by the New Deal and Fair deal was executed, but little attempt was made to expand, through new legislation, government activity in the field. Reposing great confidence in President Eisenhower's ability in the field of foreign relations, the nation gradually forgot the passions and frustrations associated with the period of the Korean War and turned to the enjoyment of an unprecedented material well-being.

As the era drew to a close, this tranquil outlook was threatened. The Republican party could not depend on the slogan of "peace and prosperity" to win in 1960. The success of Russian satellites challenged the invincibility of American defenses; interest groups within the American population including farmers, the elderly, the Negroes, made renewed political demands; and the summit conference, which was to have been the crowning achievement of Mr. Eisenhower's personal diplomacy, collapsed before it could begin.

The policies of the administration and the outlook of American businessmen, who were conspicuously represented within it, were challenged from many quarters. John Kenneth Galbraith, the Harvard economist, challenged the belief that private consumption should be the central goal of the American economic system. Reports of the Rockefeller Brothers Fund and the Gaither Committee indicated weaknesses in the national defense program, while publicists decried the seeming loss of a sense of purpose and national unity. The most powerful and articulate critic of the Eisenhower administration within the Republican party became Governor Nelson A. Rockefeller of New York. He was considered, by early 1960, as a leading contender for the presidential nomination. But he withdrew from the contest months before the convention, convinced that he could not overcome the strong allegiance of the state party leaders to Vice President Nixon.

One week before the Republicans began their official platform deliberations, the Democratic party in Los Angeles adopted its 1960 platform and nominated Senator Kennedy of Massachusetts for President, and Senator Johnson of Texas for Vice President. The Democratic platform did not seem to represent a compromise between various elements within the party. The liberal views of the northern, urban Democrats, personified by Representative Chester Bowles, Chairman of the Resolutions Committee, dominated the document. The civil rights statement of the Democratic platform was taken to the floor of the convention by the southern conservatives. Because the liberal forces were certain of victory in such a contest, apparently they made little effort to accommodate the southern viewpoint in the executive sessions of the platform committee. The strong civil rights position desired by Senator Kennedy was adopted when the convention overruled a bitter protest by the southerners. Senator Johnson's nomination as Vice President was viewed as an attempt to heal the party wounds reopened by the platform strife.

Perhaps the strongest reaction by a segment of the Republican party to the Democratic convention came in the south. Following the Eisenhower victories in southern states in 1952 and 1956, many persons in such states as Texas and Louisiana began working toward the establishment of a Republican organization which would not exist solely to seek the patronage favors of a national Republican administration. They hoped to use the policy attitudes of the national party as a foundation for local Republican victories. These southerners felt that the strong civil rights plank and the opposition to the oil depletion allowance represented a rejection of the political interests of the south by the Democratic party. The nomination of Lyndon Johnson, they claimed, was a transparent exercise in party hypocrisy which would further weaken the appeal of the Democratic ticket in their region.

Northern Republicans did not agree. The nomination of Senator Johnson, they felt, would do much to mollify the southern Democrats, and the Republican party could not expect a renewal of the electoral support given to President Eisenhower by several southern states. This made the battle for the urban areas of the north take on even greater significance. The Nixon forces were assured of the nomination, barring unforseen circumstances. But the nomination could not be converted to victory in November unless Nixon should win the support of many northern city voters. Governor Rockefeller's criticisms of the Eisenhower administration could hardly go unacknowledged; he was a leader of the northern, urban wing of the party, and there was certainly little hope of winning New York's large electoral vote without the Governor's energetic support.

Preparing to Build a Platform

In 1959, then Republican Chairman Meade Alcorn established the Republican Committee on Program and Progress, headed by Charles H. Percy, a young and capable Illinois industrialist. In accepting his new position, Mr. Percy told President Eisenhower that his purpose would be to modernize the public's impression of the party philosophy. He expected that the Democrats would wage their 1960 campaign on Republican attitudes towards domestic issues articulated in the 1930's.

The "Percy committee" was composed of a broad range of Republican intellectual and legislative leadership. Its report, *Decisions for a Better America,* published early in 1960, was well received by the press, which declared that several of its recommendations were the liberal modifications of traditional Republican attitudes. A copy of the report was sent to every delegate to the Republican National Convention of 1960. Mr. Percy was appointed temporary chairman of the resolutions committee in order that the spirit of his committee's report would be reflected in the 1960 Republican platform; his committee had not, of course, enjoyed any legal authority to speak for the entire Republican party. Mr. Gabriel Hauge, who had been one of the principal architects of the Percy committee report, was appointed executive secretary of the platform committee.

Aside from serving as vice chairman of the Republican National Finance Committee, Mr. Percy was a newcomer to the top ranks of the Republican party. His position was one of independent strength. Unlike Chester Bowles, he was not an acknowledged leader of a party faction. Thus Mr. Percy was able both to seek the inclusion of language from the Percy committee report in the platform and to act as a broker between party leaders concerning the platform statements. Soon after his appointment as temporary chairman, Mr. Percy visited President Eisenhower, Governor Rockefeller, and Vice President Nixon. He was able to define for Rockefeller and Nixon their areas of basic disagreement, which were fewer in number than Governor Rockefeller, at least, had assumed.

Mr. Percy supported the Vice President's nomination and felt that the final platform document should be acceptable to Mr. Nixon. But he felt that the Percy committee report furnished guidelines for the construction of the platform, and he felt that the platform committee as a duly constituted organ of the national convention should exercise the final power of decision in those matters assigned to it. Mr. Percy had no intention of trying to use his group as a rubber stamp. In an attempt to establish harmonious relations, Mr. Percy sent letters to each of those designated to serve on the platform committee seeking their opinion as to the length and content of the final document. The answers he received were overwhelmingly in favor of a short document which would be focused on the "national interest" rather than containing a "grocery list" of interest group demands.

The Committee on Resolutions of the Republican National Convention was composed of two delegates from each state, designated for this assignment by the state organization. The first requirement, of course, was that each delegate be able to spend an extra week in the convention city in advance of the opening of the convention. Those convention delegates who had both the time and money to do this would be those who could easily spend an extra week away from their usual occupation. This suggests that the members of the platform committee were likely to be either wealthier than the average delegate, or older, because they were retired. Many were both older and wealthier than the average delegate. Wealth and age are usually considered to be concomitants of a conservative political outlook. Furthermore, the large, industrial states, which were the home of the more liberal Republicans, did not gain the advantage of their large populations, for each state had equal representation on the platform committee. These two consequences of the procedures for selecting the platform committee membership tended to make that body a more conservative group than the membership of the full convention.

Following time honored procedure, the resolutions committee was divided into subcommittees. Each subcommittee would hold public hearings, hear the representatives of groups interested in their policy area, then debate the language of the platform plank in private. Almost without exception, the southern members asked to serve on the subcommittee on civil rights and immigration, which was limited to fifteen members. The south could hardly be denied representation on this subcommittee, but they could not be given exclusive responsibility in the area. Nearly all members received either their first or second choices, however. This meant that they were assigned to the area in which they had the greatest interest and, consequently, the strongest convictions. If those convictions were hostile to the conclusions of the Percy committee, the members of the platform committee were well placed for the purpose of urging their own views in opposition to the leadership.

On Tuesday, July 19th, the resolutions committee held its first public meeting in Chicago's Blackstone Hotel. The day was devoted to speeches by various leaders in science, education, government, and business. Perhaps the most significant addresses were those by Senator Barry Goldwater and Governor Rockefeller. A week before, Governor Rockefeller had released to the press a detailed list of proposals for inclusion in the Republican platform. He was given the opportunity of presenting his case before the full committee on Resolutions. Although his appearance won special attention from the press and attracted many spectators, Rockefeller was received with relative coolness by committee members themselves. Senator Goldwater, representing the Senate Policy Committee, made a forceful presentation of the conservative viewpoint. The warm reception given him by a large segment of the platform committee showed their real sympathy for the ideology he represented.

The Civil Rights Subcommittee

After a long day of speeches under the blazing lights required for television, the resolutions committee members went into executive session and learned their subcommittee assignments. Each subcommittee was a potential battleground, and, with a single exception, conflict between the members of the eight subcommittees delayed the presentation of the subcommittee reports. On each issue, influence and opinion were marshalled among the members of the platform committee and other delegates to the convention. The following account centers upon the civil rights subcommittee, but many of its features were present in the work of the other seven subcommittees.

The composition of the Subcommittee on Civil Rights and Immigration presaged conflict. Thirteen members gathered at its first meeting.

The Chairman was Joseph F. Carlino, Speaker of the New York State Assembly. Mr. Carlino owed his election as speaker at least in part to Governor Rockefeller, and he was clearly a member of the Governor's inner circle. For obvious reasons, Carlino was adamantly in favor of a strong civil rights plank.

There were five southerners on the subcommittee. None were from those states, such as Georgia, Alabama, and Mississippi, which have changed least from the pattern of race relations established by the plantation system. All were responsible and fairly moderate in their views, but it was clear from the beginning that only a political miracle would lead these five members to accept language which was worded strongly enough to please chairman Carlino.

Mrs. Hazel Barger of Virginia was diligent in her interest. In executive sessions of the subcommittee, she delighted in pointing out that southern voters are not only denied registration because of race. Often they are unable to register because they are Republicans.

Mrs. Louis Rogers of North Carolina was perhaps the most articulate of the southern ladies on the subcommittee, and she was deeply committed to the idea that victory for Nixon lay in a moderate civil rights plank and statements on economic policy that would win the support of the south.

Mrs. Janet Showalter of Florida, an elderly lady with great energy, was greatly attracted by the personality and ideas of Senator Goldwater.

Mr. Thomas E. Stagg, Jr., of Louisiana, a leader of the new Republican organization in Shreveport, a lawyer, was a flamboyant representative of the southern viewpoint. Due to press notices in his own locality, he received the major share of telegrams and letters directed to subcommittee members. His knowledge of parliamentary procedure, coupled with his articulateness, made him a leader of the southern viewpoint in the meetings of the full resolutions committee.

Mr. John G. Tower of Wichita Falls, Texas, had resigned as a teacher of political science in order to become the Republican candidate for the Senate seat currently held by Lyndon Johnson. Quiet-mannered and persuasive, Mr. Tower's personality came to dominate the subcommittee, after the leadership of Mr. Carlino had been rejected, and he was elected their floor leader by the southern members of the full platform committee. Thus he became the chief spokesman for the southern viewpoint in negotiations with Mr. Nixon's representatives and later with Mr. Nixon himself.

Three members of the subcommittee were clearly on the side

of a strong civil rights plank and were prepared to support Mr. Carlino in attaining it.

Mrs. Frances Bolton, United States Representative from the State of Ohio, was asked to serve on the civil rights subcommittee so that her twenty years of legislative experience could be used in that sensitive area. Mrs. Bolton accepted the assignment graciously, although she would have preferred to work in the field of foreign relations, her central legislative interest.

Mr. J. Flipper Derricotte of the District of Columbia carried a special burden as the only Negro member of the entire resolutions committee. He is a lawyer, a teacher, and "a politician the rest of the time." During the hearings, he spoke with restraint to elicit further information from the representatives of pressure groups and to challenge some of the claims of southerners concerning the progress of race relations in their areas. His self-introduction, "this is Derricotte of the District," became a trademark of the public hearings. In the executive sessions of the subcommittee and also in the meetings of the full resolutions committee, he attempted with quiet dignity to put the force of his position as a representative of the Negro race behind the strong civil rights proposals.

Mr. Bayard Ewing, National Committeeman from the State of Rhode Island, is a leading attorney in that state, and a former Republican candidate for the United States Senate. Mr. Ewing favored strong civil rights language which would be approved by Mr. Nixon, but he felt that no party faction can be expected to support a decision in which its own viewpoint is denied consideration. When it became apparent that there was an insoluble conflict between Mr. Carlino and the southern representatives of the subcommittee, Mr. Ewing offered his services as the agent of compromise.

Of the remaining six members of the subcommittee, only four were present. They held the potential balance of power. Mrs. John T. Parker of New Mexico, the wife of a physician, had hoped by her presence on the resolutions committee to defeat any proposal that hinted at socialized medicine. She was not personally acquainted with the civil rights problem in urban areas. Consistent with her conviction that the power of the federal government should never be increased at the expense of local authority, she tended to support southern opposition to promises of new federal activity in the field of civil rights.

Mrs. Arthur Ransohoff, although born in New York City, had spent her early married life in Louisiana. She was sympathetic to the outlook of the southern moderates and deeply resented the tactics of chairman Carlino. As a result, her attitudes on civil rights were probably more conservative than those of the Connecticut delegation which she represented.

Mrs. Edna Simpson, United States Representative from the State of Illinois, had been thrust into the maelstrom of practical politics by the death of her husband. She had agreed to accept the nomination for the seat he had held upon the personal urging of Governor Stratton, and she was now finishing her term.

Mrs. John E. Wise of Wisconsin, president of the National Federation of Republican Women, shared the common midwesterner's suspicion of the concentrated political power of New York State. She resented chairman Carlino's tactics as a representative of Governor Rockefeller.

Mr. Edward E. Johnson of Hawaii was absent for the first three days of open hearings because of transportation delays, but he was present at the executive sessions of the subcommittee. Mr. O. Jacob Tallman of Pennsylvania was absent from all meetings of the subcommittee except for the final crucial session. Because he had suffered a recent heart attack, Mr. Tallman had been warned to avoid excitement and late meetings.

The Civil Rights Hearings

The explosiveness of this issue was not fully recognized by the national committee staff. A room seating only 200 spectators was assigned to the subcommittee for its public hearings, which began on Wednesday, July 20th. That first morning, the subcommittee was addressed by such spokesmen as Mr. Roy Wilkins of the National Association for the Advancement of Colored People and Mr. William Taylor of Americans for Democratic Action, with the full attention of the press. As many spectators were forced to stand as were able to sit. In the afternoon, the civil rights hearings were moved to a larger room.

Perhaps the most poignant moment of the subcommittee hearings came when Mr. Marion Barry spoke for the Student's Nonviolent Coordinating Committee to explain the purposes and practices of the lunch counter demonstrations. In general, the members of the subcommittee listened with interest and respect to the presentations of the various witnesses. Copies of their statements were received by subcommittee members and by the reporters. Several members of the subcommittee spoke of this as being an educational experience, but it would be hard to trace the direct positive influence of any single testimony upon the final platform statement on civil rights. Those who drafted the Nixon statements were not members of the subcommittee, and the southerners on the subcommittee had determined their position through long familiarity with the issues involved. Both Wednesday and Thursday were devoted to the hearings, for the policy of the national committee was to refuse no responsible person or group which indicated a desire to testify. The Minorities Sub-division of the Republican National Committee, headed by Mr. Val Washington, has been very active with Negro groups in Chicago. The leaders of several of these groups testified before the subcommittee, displaying a vast range of oratorical skills, and groups of their followers were present to see their positions presented to the official party organ. The subcommittee hearings thus served at least to add to the stature of local Negro Republican leaders.

Subcommittee Executive Sessions

The subcommittee began its executive sessions at 10:00 on Friday morning. The members were supplied with a condensed list of proposals which had been made by the various witnesses and a list of Democratic promises in the areas of civil rights and immigration. Matters concerning immigration were easily disposed of. Mr. Carlino then announced that he wished to discover the general feeling of the subcommittee and present it to the platform drafters. The most important person in drafting the civil rights plank was at this time identified as Mr. Edward Walsh, an assistant to Attorney General Rogers. The list of proposals was gone through methodically and the general feeling of the subcommittee was ascertained informally and noted by its members.

On the question of the "sit-in strikers," it was felt that the principle of peaceful assembly to protest against injustice should be approved, but that this should not be tied to a specific approval of the "sit-in" strikes. The southerners claimed that, while these demonstrations had so far been peacefully conducted, their leadership was likely to be taken over by Communists, with resulting violence which would embarrass the Republican party.

On the question of Rule 22 of the United States Senate (the cloture rule, which makes it difficult to limit filibusters), Mr. Carlino stated that the practice of every state is that a constitutional majority can control the legislative body. Mr. Stagg felt that Rule 22 should not be mentioned by name, and Mr. Ewing suggested that the question of amending Rule 22 should be submitted to Republican senators to determine whether or not the Senate Republican caucus would approve it. Decision by the subcommittee was withheld.

Mr. Carlino stated that Title Three of the Civil Rights Act of 1957 would be included in the recommended draft. This section, which had been defeated in 1957, gave the Attorney General power to initiate suits in school integration cases. Mr. Stagg and Mr. Tower gave their reasons for objecting to this provision and stated that several Republican Senators had voted against it.

There was general feeling that literacy tests had been administered in discriminatory fashion in some states, and that this practice was reprehensible. There was mention of the possible adoption of a uniform standard of education to substitute for literacy tests, but there was no agreement as to what standard would be acceptable.

On the question of a Fair Employment Practices Commission, Mr. Tower reported that these words were second only to "sit-ins" as a stimulus to southern opposition. Mr. Stagg stated that the endorsement of a national F.E.P.C. would kill the Republican party in the South.

The subcommittee was then recessed until 2:30 that afternoon. At this time, Mr. Carlino was most optimistic concerning the outcome of the subcommittee deliberations. He suspected that the southerners would present a minority report which would be weaker than the Nixon proposals, but he was confident that the Nixon statements would become the majority report of the subcommittee, for the discussion just completed had given the southerners a chance to vent some of their emotional force by reacting to the most "extreme" proposals on the list, such as the proposal for a federal F.E.P.C.

When the subcommittee reconvened, Mr. Carlino reported that his meetings with the platform drafters had not yet been completed, and he suggested a meeting at 4:00 p.m. Mr. Carlino then left the meeting, but the subcommittee continued to meet in an informal manner with Mr. John Tower acting as chairman. Working on the basis of the list of proposals considered that morning, Mr. Tower and Mr. Stagg worked to consolidate the feeling of the subcommittee so that it would be in even greater accord with the views of the southern moderates. Mr. Carlino appeared at 4:00 to report that the draft proposal was not yet ready for consideration. The subcommittee was recessed until after dinner.

Mr. Carlino had spent several hours in the suite of rooms occupied by Mr. Percy and Mr. Gabriel Hauge, President Eisenhower's economic adviser, who was the executive secretary of the Committee on Resolutions. This was the communications center for liaison between the leadership of the platform committee, the White House, and Vice President Nixon.

Working in Washington under the direct supervision of Vice President Nixon, Mr. Walsh drafted a position on civil rights. The version he brought to Chicago contained seventeen pages. Mr. Nixon's staff was willing to have this document adopted verbatim as part of the platform. The statement on civil rights would then have represented nearly half of the entire Republican platform, and at least its length would have demonstrated the sincerity of the Republican bid for the Negro vote. It was Mr. Percy's announced goal to produce a short and readable platform, in contrast to the Democratic document, and he refused to accept the lengthy draft. Mr. Carlino supported Mr. Percy's position, and he worked with Mr. Walsh to reduce the original to more manageable dimensions. A seven page version was completed late in the afternoon, but Mr. Carlino could obtain only two copies of the new proposal. Facilities for duplication were burdened with other work.

The Nixon-Rockefeller Agreement

The proceedings of the Committee on Resolutions were jolted from their planned course on Saturday by the news of Vice President Nixon's visit to Governor Rockefeller. As a result of agreement reached at this meeting, Governor Rockefeller delineated those platform statements which would win his support for the party, and Vice President Nixon implicitly accepted responsibility for achieving their inclusion in the party document.

The wording of the statement had been formulated during a telephone conversation between Nixon and Rockefeller, in New York, and Percy and several others in Chicago, which lasted approximately three hours. In many instances, Rockefeller approved the language which was under consideration by the various sub-committees. But the timing and wording of the release by Governor Rockefeller's press secretary left the impression that the terms of the agreement were dictated by the New York Governor and accepted meekly by the Vice President without consulting the platform committee.

Senator Goldwater held a press conference on Saturday afternoon in which he labeled the Nixon-Rockefeller meeting the "Republican Munich," suggested that the Vice President had abandoned previously held sound principles for political expediency, and had deliberately insulted the members of the resolutions committee by presuming to dictate the platform when that committee had spent a week working on its language. Upon reflection, many members of the platform committee came to agree with at least the last statement.

The members of the civil rights subcommittee were forcefully reminded of the reality of the Nixon-Rockefeller agreement when Mr. Carlino, identified as a Rockefeller spokesman, presented the proposed platform statement on civil rights. Mr. Carlino prefaced his reading of the draft by stating that this language represented the views of Mr. Nixon; that he hoped it would be accepted as its report by the subcommittee, and that it was the meaning and purpose of the resolutions committee to supply Mr. Nixon, the party's recognized candidate, with the platform he felt he could run on. Mr. Carlino, of course, did not mention Governor Rockefeller.

Mr. Carlino presented a very strong statement. When the reading had been completed, Mr. Tower stated quietly that this draft consisted of a re-writing of the Democratic platform, and that, if Mr. Carlino had indeed presented the consensus of the subcommittee to the platform drafters, that consensus had received no consideration. After some minutes of heated discussion, Mr. Carlino admitted his bafflement at the reaction of the subcommittee. Certainly they had been in politics long enough and were familiar enough with the operations of national conventions, he stated, to know that the source of the platform statements had to be the party candidate.

Several members of the subcommittee then demanded that the various platform provisions be discussed separately. This job was undertaken, but tempers flared, until Mrs. Bolton pointed out that the main difficulty was that none of the members could properly consider the language, for they did not have copies before them. Mrs. Bolton and her sister Congresswoman, Mrs. Simpson, agreed that they had never before been asked to approve a document which they were not allowed to read. There was a chorus of agreement with this view, and Mr. Carlino directed the subcommittee's executive secretary to find some sort of duplicating machine and produce fifteen copies of the draft proposal while the subcommittee would remain in session.

It was then 11:00 on Saturday night. The offices of the Republican National Committee were closing down. The resolutions committee staff were returning to their lodgings. A duplicating machine was found in the basement of the Conrad Hilton Hotel, but there was nobody left to run it. Finally, at a few minutes past midnight, the executive secretary returned to the subcommittee meeting with fifteen copies of the first four pages of the proposed draft, which represented the recital of the Eisenhower record, and the promise of the copies of the remaining three pages as soon as they could be completed by resolutions committee typists.

The subcommittee had continued general discussion and had ordered in coffee and sandwiches. It was decided to adjourn until such a time on Sunday as the meetings of the full resolutions committee would allow. Mr. Bayard Ewing then suggested that Mr. Tower be allowed to see one of the completed proposed drafts, when the typing was completed, in order to present his case at the next day's meeting. All members had been instructed to return platform drafts to the executive secretary in order to prevent leaks to the press. Mr. Carlino granted the request, knowing that he would have to deal with the southern resistance at some stage in the proceedings.

Shortly after 1:00 a.m., the secretaries had produced the required sixteen copies of the draft proposal; the pages were then separated and each copy stapled and numbered. The executive secretary then took the one copy as requested to the room of Mr. John Tower of Texas. In that room were gathered Mr. Tower, Mr. Stagg of Louisiana, and Mr. Ewing of Rhode Island.

Mr. Ewing had offered his services to the two southern leaders in preparing their report. He told them that he would not vote for their report, no matter what it should finally contain, for he and his state delegation were committed to a support of the Vice President's views. But he wanted to suggest the strongest language they could accept, so that compromise might become possible on the few differences remaining.

Stagg and Tower objected not only to the specific pledges of legislative action but also to the general tone of the language, which they regarded as typical of the attitudes of northerners who assume that the pattern of hatred and violence of the Mississippi delta prevails throughout the south.

When minor changes had been made in the preamble (the opening "view with pride" section), the work began on the substantive proposals for legislation. In every case, the language written followed the line taken by Tower and Stagg in the informal discussions of the subcommittee. One crucial question was that of the "sit-in" strikers. The proposed draft stated:

> . . . the efforts of Negroes to express by peaceful means their resentment against humiliating acts of private persons have our complete sympathy and support, as long as those means are lawful under the Bill of Rights as interpreted by the Supreme Court. The aspirations for equal treatment which our heritage so fully supports is shown by the "sit-ins" who have peacefully attempted to demonstrate their feelings. We applaud the action of the businessmen who have abandoned the practice of refusing to serve food at their lunch counters to their Negro customers, and we appeal to all others to follow their example.

This language seemed to be based on that of the Nixon-Rockefeller agreement. It had in fact been drafted days before by Mr. Walsh and Mr. Percy. Mr. Percy read it over the telephone, and the language was approved by Governor Rockefeller. Because it had been used in the Nixon-Rockefeller statement, this wording took on a new aura of sanctification in the eyes of the aides of both Governor Rockefeller and Mr. Nixon. The language was deeply offensive to Mr. Tower and Mr. Stagg. Perhaps the word "sit-in" was an emotional symbol to the Negro of a movement attempting to attain human dignity. To the white southerner, they objected, it was a label applied to a movement that was illegal, according to many local laws, and probably the precursor to bloodshed.

The reference to the Bill of Rights in the proposed plank, they said, was a declaration on the part of the Republican party that those local laws were void—the party was therefore usurping the function of the Supreme Court. Substitute language was written as follows:

> We reaffirm the constitutional right to peaceable assembly or resort to economic boycott to protest discrimination in private

business establishments where such protest does not contravene applicable laws. [After brief debate, the word "applicable" was substituted for the word "local."] We applaud the action of the businessmen who have abandoned discriminatory practices in retail establishments, and we urge others to follow their example.

At 3:15 a.m. the meeting broke up. The substitutions were ready for presentation to the subcommittee.

When the subcommittee reconvened, the Nixon proposals were laid before it. John Tower indicated his objections and distributed copies of a statement on moderation which formed a chapter of the recently published book edited from Mr. Nixon's speeches, *The Challenge We Face*, which he felt should be included in the preamble. He then presented the proposed language substitutions with brief summaries of the reasons for his objections to the Nixon language. His approach was moderate and reasonable, and most members of the subcommittee marked the proposed changes on their copies of the draft. They did not demand copies of the Tower language.

Mr. Carlino did not feel that these amendments should be voted on by the subcommittee. Instead, he proposed that Mr. Tower should present his case to Professor George Grassmuck, of Nixon's staff, who had, the evening before, been given full authority to speak for Mr. Nixon in all matters concerning the platform. With the promise that this meeting would be arranged, the subcommittee adjourned. The full resolutions committee was now beginning its executive sessions, and the civil rights subcommittee would be able to meet only when the full committee was not in session.

Mr. Ewing was invited by Mr. Tower to join him in the presentation. Along with Mr. Carlino, they went to Mr. Grassmuck's suite. After Mr. Tower's presentation of the case of the southern moderate, Mr. Grassmuck pointed out that it would be necessary for all statements of the platform to meet both the letter and the spirit of the Nixon-Rockefeller agreement. Mr. Tower agreed and submitted that the substitute his people had prepared did just that. Mr. Grassmuck received a copy of the proposed substitute statement, promised to deliver it to the platform drafters for their consideration, and the interview was ended. Mr. Tower and Mr. Ewing then went on to the full committee session.

By this time, the resistance being made to the Nixon civil rights language had become public knowledge. Because of the experience of the Democratic convention, newsmen were eager for a story concerning the handling of the issue by the Republicans. The disagreement within the subcommittee was too strong, and the outcome too uncertain, for Chairman Carlino to deny that trouble was brewing. In addition, the remainder of the state delegations were arriving just as the Nixon-Rockefeller agreement was released. Platform committee members hurried to the caucuses of their state delegations to make reports and to gain instruction. Conflicting opinions were reported among the top leadership—Leonard Hall, Nixon's principal agent among the veteran professional politicians, felt that the word "sit-in" was not essential. Joseph Carlino felt that it was. Meade Alcorn, leader of the Connecticut delegation, hoped to find a compromise. Representative Melvin Laird, vice chairman of the platform committee, felt that Mr. Nixon would not be as insistent upon specific language as his staff members claimed.

When the subcommittee reconvened on Sunday morning, an interlinear draft comparing the Nixon language and the proposed substitutions were placed before them. But the southerners no longer desired to amend the Nixon language in a piecemeal fashion. Instead, they had prepared an entirely new draft which covered the subject in three pages.

Although it was explained that Mr. Nixon hoped the civil rights plank would be the longest in the platform, so that brevity in itself would be no recommendation, the subcommittee accepted the new southern draft as a working paper and began, as a committee, to make revisions in its language. Before this process could long continue, however, it was time for a further meeting of the full platform committee, and the subcommittee recessed. The new southern draft was very sketchy in its substantive provisions (the "we pledge" sections), partly because the southerners wanted to promise little action, partly because their drafting had been done in haste. Mr Bayard Ewing began to write amendments to the southern draft which would put more strength into the substantive proposals, hoping to achieve language which would be acceptable to both sides.

When the subcommittee reconvened that afternoon there had been no new official draft readied for its consideration. Mr. Carlino announced that this was being done. He suggested that Mr. Tower and Mr. Ewing should meet with Professor Grassmuck, Mr. Walsh, and Mr. Roswell Perkins, Governor Rockefeller's representative, so that their views could be presented before the new draft should be completed. The subcommittee recessed at 5:00 p.m. with another meeting planned at 7:00 that evening.

Walsh and Perkins had in fact been preparing a new draft, but their revisions aimed at improving the prose of the original. The proposal prepared by the southerners had been handed to them, but if read, it certainly had no influence. None of the statements which the southerners found objectionable had been modified.

George Grassmuck was aware of the danger that the Nixon-Rockefeller views would be rejected by a majority of the members of the subcommittee. If the draft prepared by the southern moderates were approved by a majority of the subcommittee, it would gain prestige which might carry it through the full platform committee and necessitate a battle on the convention floor in order to carry out the Nixon-Rockefeller agreement. Before that agreement had been made, there was no indication that a floor fight might be necessary to win a representation of Mr. Nixon's views in the platform, and no preparations had been made for it. Regardless of the need for preparation, Mr. Nixon did not want a floor fight. It would represent a public rejection of his leadership by a large segment of the party.

Governor Rockefeller could only benefit from such a battle. If the views of the full convention—on other questions as well as on civil rights—proved to be more liberal than those of the platform committee, and Governor Rockefeller became identified as the leader of the majority cause, he would be in a position of great strength when the call for nominations should be made. In the early meetings of the full platform committee, Mr. Carlino, speaking for the state of New York, reserved the right to present a minority report to the convention on several platform statements, including the agriculture plank. Mr. Carlino was joined by Miss Wilma Sivertsen, the other committee member from New York. This action preserved for Governor Rockefeller the choice of the issue upon which he would launch his offensive. It also antagonized the members of the committee.

When the subcommittee recessed, Mr. Tower, Mr. Stagg, and Mr. Ewing went to the Nixon staff suite to confer with Mr. Walsh and Mr. Perkins. They were presented with the latest official draft of the plank, which again contained the words and phrases which the southerners had found so offensive. Mr. Tower presented the case of the southern moderate; Walsh and Perkins expressed sympathy, but they made no concessions. After nearly an hour of fruitless discussion, Tower, Stagg, and Ewing hurried to dinner before the meeting of their subcommittee.

Walsh and Perkins, as staff workers for Nixon and Rockefeller, were concerned primarily with the creation of language which would be acceptable to both leaders. They had little knowledge of the clash taking place in the subcommittee. In order to save time, they directed that their draft be typed directly onto stencils; it could then be presented to the subcommittee in a mimeographed form, and the same stencils could be used to produce the material for the members of the full committee.

This action, of course, would have removed the last vestige of pretense that the subcommittee was writing the plank itself. Its members would be asked to approve a mimeographed document, frozen into a form which they could not themselves amend. Aware that such an action would redouble the resentment felt by most members of the subcommittee to direction from the top, George Grassmuck overruled the decision of Walsh and Perkins. The plank was typed with many carbon copies. At the top, it was labeled "Proposed Draft."

Meanwhile, Representative Melvin Laird, vice chairman of the platform committee, had been assigned to the civil rights subcommittee by chairman Percy. In an attempt to restore harmony, Laird prepared compromise language on the single issue of the "sit-in" demonstrations which he submitted to the members of the subcommittee. His language eliminated the word "sit-in" but included the words "lunch counter." He obtained the support of a majority of the members of the subcommittee for this language, but the representatives of Nixon and Rockefeller would not, at this time, accept it. It was a minor concession which, if made early enough, might have soothed the feelings of the subcommittee members.

The Subcommittee Decision

The Nixon staff, meanwhile, was contacting the leaders of state delegations from which the civil rights subcommittee members were taken. At times it had seemed that the entire subcommittee was aligned against Mr. Carlino because of their resentment of the political power of Governor Rockefeller, which Carlino represented. If the voting were influenced only by this emotion, Mr. Carlino, Mr. Derricotte, Mr. Ewing and probably

Mrs. Bolton would be the only supporters of the Nixon-Rockefeller draft. It was necessary to convince the members of the subcommittee that this emotion should not decide their final vote. Contacts were made with the people most likely to influence the subcommittee members. This was a further example of the exertion of leadership from outside the formal procedures of the platform committee. But such pressure, coming from the leadership of their state delegations, was not identified as coming directly from the candidates. It came, rather, from the leaders who had arranged membership on the platform committee for the individual delegates—the leaders who could do most to hamper their future careers if those delegates acted in a manner unpalatable to their own state delegations. That such action was effective was demonstrated in the final vote on the issue. Members of the subcommittee who had expressed nothing but hostility for Chairman Carlino's leadership did accept the Nixon-Rockefeller language.

The final meeting of the subcommittee was held shortly after 7:00 Sunday evening. Because the subcommittees had been expected to finish their work before this time, the Republican National Committee had only with difficulty obtained space from the management of the Blackstone Hotel. It was a small room opening off the ballroom floor of the hotel, which had been used as the headquarters of the Coca-Cola hospitality center during the meetings of the full committee in the Crystal Ballroom. It was full of soft drink equipment, and there was barely room for the conference table and chairs hastily gathered together.

As this final meeting was beginning, the fifteenth member of the subcommittee, Mr. Jacob Tallman of Pennsylvania, made his single appearance. Mr. Tallman had long experience in the field of civil rights as a member of the Pennsylvania legislature, but he was greeted with open hostility by the southerners. They assumed that Mr. Tallman had been sent as a messenger by Senator Hugh Scott, leader of the Pennsylvania delegation and a staunch civil rights advocate.

In an atmosphere electric with unspoken conflict, the Nixon draft was read. Soft-drink machines whirred in the background, and a detective was stationed at the door. Reporters kept their accustomed vigil outside. In order to soothe the affronted feelings of the subcommittee members, there had at last been some changes in wording on two crucial points, with the approval of

Mr. Nixon himself. It was hoped that this would reinforce the urgings of the state leaders and win a majority for the Nixon proposals. But there were determined murmurs of "too late" around the table.

Then the southern draft—which had been used as a working paper that morning—was read again. Mr. Ewing introduced six amendments which were designed to strengthen the substantive provisions. Three of them were accepted and three were rejected. Then the question was to choose which would be the majority and which the minority report of the subcommittee. The decision was by roll-call vote. The five southern members of the subcommittee voted against the draft, as had been expected. They were joined by three other members of the subcommittee, persons who were not from the south, who had exhibited no special interest in the issue of civil rights, but who felt that they had been insulted by what they viewed as attempts to dictate the work of the subcommittee from the top. With a division of eight to seven, the Nixon-Rockefeller views became the minority report of the subcommittee. The majority report of the subcommittee was that drafted by Mr. Stagg and Mr. Tower with the liberalizing influence of Mr. Ewing.

Action by the Full Committee

Time was running out. It was Sunday night; the convention would open on Monday; and the platform committee had finished less than half its business. The full committee session began soon after the subcommittee meeting was adjourned.

The southerners were busy. They had met the Wednesday before to plan strategy. John Tower had been elected their floor leader, and each southerner had been assigned other members of the platform committee to whom he should present the southern cause. By Sunday, circumstances made the task of persuasion much easier. Resentment aroused by the Nixon-Rockefeller meeting, reinforced by an enthusiasm on the part of many of its members for Senator Goldwater, combined to create a climate in the platform committee that was unfavorable to any platform language that seemed to be associated with Governor Rockefeller. Southerners claimed that the minority report of the civil rights subcommittee had been dictated by Governor Rockefeller. The majority report, they claimed, resulted from the use of democratic procedure.

Other matters were first to be dealt with by the platform committee. Several of the subcommittees had failed to produce unanimous reports. The full platform committee, therefore, had to choose in each case between the majority and minority reports of its subcommittees; and the minority members of each subcommittee were prepared to argue the case for their own report in most forceful terms.

The mimeograph machine in the platform committee headquarters was busily preparing the copies of the subcommittee reports. The majority and minority reports of the civil rights subcommittee were prepared by midnight. There was no sign at that time that the committee would be prepared to turn very soon to the question of civil rights. The southerners felt that they could only benefit by making the meeting continue and preventing a recess. It was felt that the northerners would be less interested in the matter and more likely to leave the meeting through sheer fatigue. As the night passed into morning, however, few of the committee members seemed inclined to leave.

At about 3:00 a.m. there was a motion to adjourn from the floor. It was rejected by an overwhelming voice vote. The time had come for the introduction of the civil rights plank.

John Tower of Texas presented the majority report of the subcommittee. It was a moderate statement, going further toward admitting the necessity of federal action in this field than most northerners would have believed possible from a southern group. At that point, Tower felt that he had yielded to the northern viewpoint as much as he possibly could. He had accepted increasingly liberal language. But the Nixon forces had made no important concessions. It was time to make a stand.

Chairman Carlino had now realized that, as Governor Rockefeller's representative, he was deeply resented by most of the committee. Mr. Bayard Ewing presented the minority report of the subcommittee; in hopes of preventing two reports from going to the floor of the convention, he reserved the right to file an actual minority report, while he moved the minority report of the subcommittee as a substitute for the majority report.

This placed the minority report of the subcommittee before the full committee for prior action. Amendments were proposed; debate began in earnest. The minority report was identified by its opponents as coming from Rockefeller. Southerners rose to read from the Vice-President's book, *The Challenges We Face,* in order to substantiate the claim that this report did not represent his actual views. A few of the southerners interpreted Nixon's statement that "federal legislation alone is not enough" to mean that he did not favor any legislation at all.

With discussion at a fever pitch, Thomas Stagg of Louisiana moved that the minority report of the subcommittee should be tabled. In accepting his motion, the language on civil rights approved by both the Vice President and the Governor of New York (and also by President Eisenhower, although this fact was not mentioned) was officially rejected by the platform committee.

Melvin Laird, the vice chairman of the committee, now attempted to amend the "southern" or majority report of the subcommittee in order to strengthen it and make it more acceptable to Vice President Nixon. The longer preamble of the minority plank was substituted for the brief opening statements of the majority report, but other strengthening amendments were rejected. Some proposals which had been considered by the subcommittee but found their way into neither the majority nor the minority reports were considered. At 7:00 a.m., the committee voted to adopt what was in substance the majority report of the subcommittee, written largely by the southern members of the subcommittee, as the majority report of the platform committee. The committee recessed. Some of its members went to bed. Members of the New York delegation began to plan the strategy for a floor fight on civil rights.

Chairman Percy was placed in an embarrassing dilemma. The other platform planks had been released to the press as soon as they had been approved by the full committee. This plank had now been officially adopted. But there were methods by which the language on civil rights could be reconsidered, and this would clearly be attempted. This time, the reporters were denied an interview with Mr. Percy.

Early Monday afternoon, as many of the members of the platform committee were waking from their morning rest, Vice President Nixon arrived in Chicago. His first duty was to hold a press conference, and almost the first statement he made was that, while he could not yield on principle, he would not insist that specific language remain in the platform drafts.

Mr. Nixon then held a meeting with his staff, Mr. Percy, and the subcommittee chairmen, to discuss the progress of several matters, including civil rights. The decision was made to make civil rights the test issue on upholding the Nixon-Rockefeller agreement.

Mr. Nixon offered to serve Mr. Percy and the platform committee leadership in any way possible. The suggestion that Mr. Nixon appear before a meeting of the entire platform committee was rejected. In the tense atmosphere of those meetings, the presence of any outsider, even the certain nominee of the convention, would be deeply resented. Instead, Mr. Nixon cancelled other engagements and held a series of meetings with small groups of platform committee members. Some members of the committee were still acting on the assumption that Mr. Nixon's views on several issues were much more conservative than those of the agreement with Governor Rockefeller and that they would do Mr. Nixon a favor by rejecting them. Mr. Nixon explained that instead of being dictated by Governor Rockefeller, the words of the Nixon-Rockefeller agreement had previously been prepared at his direction by his own staff and members of the Administration. They were Mr. Nixon's own views.

The platform committee reconvened at 3:00 on Monday afternoon, with several important issues before it, including the report of the Subcommittee on Human Rights and Needs, which had been wrestling with the problem of medical care for the aged. Individuals and small groups left the meeting for audiences with the Vice President.

The organizational meeting of the national convention had been held, and the first full session would begin that evening. Typesetters needed the platform texts, so that the report of the platform committee could be printed before its presentation to the convention on Wednesday. In spite of the deadline, the committee leadership had no choice but to allow the minority groups of each subcommittee a full opportunity to present their views. Any other method would have antagonized the committee. Only through careful adherence to formal procedures could the Nixon forces retain the slender majority which they had established through the informal procedures of personal contact and individual persuasion.

The committee recessed in time for its members to attend the first evening session of the convention and hear the keynote speech of Representative Walter Judd.

Neither the Nixon staff nor the directorate of the platform committee had time to seek inspiration from the words of Congressman Judd. Preparations were underway to mount an assault on the membership of the platform committee that would bring its product into line with the Nixon-Rockefeller statement, not only on civil rights, but also on other issues. Leonard Hall, former chairman of the Republican National Committee, gathered together a corps of fifteen lieutenants. Each man was assigned to the delegations with whom he would have the greatest influence. An amendment to the plank on civil rights was prepared which reintroduced the substantive pledges of the minority subcommittee report. A few modifications of language were made in order to meet the objections of the southerners. An example of such a change was the substitution of the words "six primary grades" in the place of "a six-year course of education" as a substitute for literacy tests. It had been argued that, if preschool and kindergarten were included, and the child remained in school for six years but did not pass on to the next grade, an education equivalent to the second or third grade level would be considered proof of literacy for voting purposes. Since the preamble of the minority (Nixon) report had been substituted for the preamble of the majority (Southern) report before that was adopted by the full committee, the new amendment would restore the full substance of the Nixon-Rockefeller views, with a few symbolic concessions to the objections of the southerners.

The amendment was prepared and duplicated shortly after midnight. The fifteen emissaries, armed with the document, were sent out to contact the various delegations soon after they returned from the convention.

This was the hard presentation of the "yes or no" proposition. In his talks with key members of the platform committee, the Vice President did not demand pledges of action, for he did not choose to embarrass those members who disagreed with him in a face-to-face meeting. Once Mr. Nixon's views had been made clear, his assistants were in a position to demand whether individuals were for or against Mr. Nixon on the concrete issue.

The platform committee reconvened the next morning. Due to the careful preparations of a few hours before this crucial meeting, the platform committee leadership was able to obtain a two-thirds vote by which the rules were suspended and the plank on national defense was brought up for reconsideration. Because of his involvement in the work of the Rockefeller Brothers Fund, which had produced important studies in this area, this issue was one of the most important to Governor Rockefeller. After long discussion, the plank (which had already been published) was amended to include the language of the Nixon-Rockefeller agreement, which proposed a reexamination of the defense program and increased expenditures, if necessary. This new language was featured in the television presentation of the platform.

It was mid-afternoon before the platform committee was ready to make the final decision on civil rights. Many of the lady members of the committee were eager to leave and dress for the convention session that evening. Chairman Percy arranged for Melvin Laird to take the chair, so that Percy could speak from the floor. He pointed out that none of the southerners were leaving; he called upon the ladies from the north to put principle above beauty and remain for the crucial voting. His appeal was successful.

Because the platform committee had recessed, rather than adjourning, at the end of its all-night session, it was not necessary for the rules to be suspended in order to reconsider the plank on civil rights. It was only necessary for someone who had voted for the majority plank to move its reconsideration, and a majority vote would reopen it for debate. This was a happy consequence for the Nixon forces. The fifteen ambassadors had attained a slim majority for the proposed amendment, but there was no hope of obtaining the support of two-thirds of the membership for it.*

There were three procedural tests of strength which preceded the consideration of substance. The first was a challenge to the ruling of Representative Laird, that a majority vote was sufficient to open the plank for reconsideration. The second was a motion to table the motion for reconsideration. The third was the vote on the motion to reconsider. On all three, the committee of 104 members voted approximately 55 for the Nixon-Rockefeller viewpoint, and 45 against it, with four members absent or abstaining. Senator Hugh Scott of Pennsylvania later commented that a "liberal" vote of 55 to 45 in the platform committee generally became a liberal victory of 75 per cent to 25 per cent on the floor

---

*Before 1936, the Democratic convention required a two-thirds vote to nominate a presidential candidate. This gave the south the power of veto. If a two-thirds vote had been required to reconsider the plank on civil rights, the southerners would have enjoyed briefly a similar veto power in the Republican party.

of the convention, due to the conservative weighting of the platform committee.

If the amendment proposed by the Nixon forces had been considered as a unit, the procedural vote demonstrated that it would have passed. This was prevented, however, when Mr. Stagg of Louisiana proposed a seven-part amendment to the proposed amendment, which would have restored the "southern" language in the substantive part of the plank. This tactical move, was, of course, necessary, if any of the southern language would be preserved.

The tactic was successful. In debating individual statements, the members of the committee no longer felt bound to their commitment to support the amendment as a whole. The southerners were pleased to discover that northerners broke ranks to join with them on certain issues, including the wording of the endorsement of the "sit-in" strikes. There were seven votes. The Nixon-Rockefeller forces unanimously conceded to the objections of the southerners on one point. Of the remaining six issues, the southerners carried three and the "northern" forces carried three. Thus the southerners were able to adopt four substantial amendments to the Nixon-Rockefeller language. Due to the influence of Mr. Ewing and the basic moderation of the southerners, a close reading of the final plank will not reveal the authorship of each section. The final version was so acceptable that Mr. Derricotte, sole Negro member of the platform committee, moved its adoption by that body. The vote was unanimous.

Conclusions

At long last the platform battle was ended. Southern Republicans, capitalizing upon the hostility of the members of the platform committee toward Governor Rockefeller, had been able to weld together a coalition which momentarily rejected the declared wishes of the apparent Republican nominee. The skillful and energetic use of both formal and informal procedures by the Nixon forces had defeated that coalition, restoring the Nixon-Rockefeller views. Platform planks including those on national defense and medical care for the aged, were made acceptable to both leaders. In the civil rights plank, the southerners had won some concessions in language, and John Tower of Texas advised his followers not to contest the plank unless the New York delegation chose to do so. Governor Rockefeller did not elect to do so. Vice President Nixon had joined the Rockefeller forces in the battle to achieve the inclusion of the liberal views held by both men in the party platform. The success of the effort eliminated any legitimate ground for contention between the two leaders.

Thus, in the last few minutes before the Tuesday session of the Republican National Convention, the main contest of that convention was ended. It was a contest that had taken place principally away from the public view. According to the newspaper headlines, it was a contest on the issue of civil rights. But that issue was only a part of the larger contest, which was between opposing factions of the Republican party for ideological representation in the party platform. The final document represented a viewpoint more acceptable to Republicans in the urban states of New England and the mid-Atlantic than to Republicans in rural areas of the midwest and south.

Each side had made use of what seemed to be the best weapons available. Joseph Carlino, powerful speaker of the New York State Assembly, had approached the subcommittee on civil rights on the basis of a disciplined party which must take leadership from the top. The subcommittee and the full platform committee at least rejected the notion that such leadership should come from the state of New York. Charles Percy and Melvin Laird had labored to protect the integrity of the Committee on Resolutions, while at the same time working to bring the thinking of the committee in line with that of the Vice President. Bayard Ewing, the national committeeman from Rhode Island, believed that the platform should conform to the views of the nominee, but he felt that the acquiesence of the opponents of those views could be won only through discussion and at least the appearance of compromise. Both sides had learned a great deal about the rules of the House of Representatives, which governed the proceedings of the platform committee.

The Republican National Convention was free to parade as planned. Charles Percy finished preparing his presentation of platform excerpts minutes before it was telecast. The proceedings were smooth, the aisles were not filled with wandering negotiators, and no note of disharmony rose to meet the public eye. By guiding a reluctant resolutions committee to accept the liberal attitudes of the Nixon-Rockefeller agreement, Richard M. Nixon had earned the right to the accolade of leadership represented by the presidential nomination.

7. Pressure Groups and the Democratic Platform: Kennedy in Control

RICHARD TAYLOR
Coe College

The object of this study is to illustrate some of the techniques of pressure while tracing the process of platform construction at the 1960 Democratic Convention. Interest group activity at conventions has two major objectives: the nomination of a friendly presidential candidate and the inclusion of a favorable plank in the party platform. To achieve these goals a combination of three methods are often used: groups may seek representation in state delegations;* they may lobby before the convention platform committee; and they may launch other types of publicity campaigns through demonstrations or the press to create a favorable image in the minds of the convention decision makers. The most significant fact to remember about pressure group activity is, however, that these political parties need the support of organized groups as much as these groups need party support. Organ-

---

*The reader may be aware of the glib distinction often made between pressure groups and parties—that groups are interested in issues while parties are concerned with controlling the personnel of government. Evidence from past conventions and observations of the 1960 convention and the delegate selection process suggest that some groups are more interested in candidates than in the platform. In county caucuses, congressional district caucuses and the state convention in Iowa, the Teamsters Union sought to secure delegate strength at the national convention. However, this effort to hinder the nomination of Kennedy was largely unsuccessful at the state level. In the 1952 Democratic Convention 121 delegates held major directorships in important United States corporations, while 139 Republican delegates held similar positions. In 1948 10 per cent of the Democratic delegates were union members while 3 per cent of the Republican delegates were union members. Primary energy of union leaders at the 1960 convention was directed toward the securing of a friendly presidential and vice presidential nomination and pressure on behalf of the candidacy of Hubert Humphrey for Vice President. Finally, dirt farmers are not as easily identified as the former categories, but a number of delegates fit this category at each convention and in the 1960 convention they provided a formidable bloc of potential votes for the nomination of Stuart Symington or some midwestern governor for Vice President should a convention fight have been organized.

izations can provide parties with campaign support in the form of money or trained workers; and the groups represented by these organizations can provide voting support. In this context, it should be understood that platform drafting, like the nominating process, is highly political and that the platforms of both parties in 1960 were the results of candidate pressure and lobbying action, as well as the deliberations of platform committees regarding what might be right policy for the United States and what planks might win votes.

Manifestations of pressure may be found at every stage of the platform drafting process. The 1960 Democratic platform had a long history of development prior even to the selection by state delegations of members to the platform committee. Following the unsuccessful 1956 campaign, national chairman Paul Butler appointed prominent Democrats to a newly formed Advisory Council of the Democratic National Committee. It is significant that this Advisory Council produced policy papers which, in spite of the absence among its party members of congressional leaders of the party, prepared the way for the 1960 campaign document *The Rights of Man*. The Advisory Council appointed committees which prepared pamphlets on such topics as "The Need to Elect a Democratic President," "Foreign and Military Policy for Peace and Security," "Domestic Politics for a Growing and Balanced Economy," and "Science and Technology." The Advisory Committee on Agriculture under the chairmanship of Governor Herschel Loveless provided almost verbatim the agricultural plank in spite of the best efforts of Senator Clinton Anderson. It may also be noted that the late Philip B. Perlman, who was deputy chairman of the Advisory Council, became the vice chairman of the platform committee. Representative Chester Bowles, who was appointed chairman of the platform committee in April, had been a member of the Advisory Committee on Foreign Policy.

Following his appointment, Chairman Bowles undertook a series of consultations with party leaders. These consultations were achieved through regional platform hearings, conversations and letters. In a long letter sent to each member of the Democratic National Committee in May, for example, Bowles explained his method and invited their help in producing a platform. The purpose of the regional hearings, which were held in such places as Philadelphia, Detroit, St. Louis, Minneapolis, Denver, Salt Lake City, and Los Angeles, was described as designed to provide all groups, sections, and interests in the Democratic Party and the nation a greater opportunity to express their point of view than had hitherto been possible in the customary week of hearings by the platform committee prior to the national convention. Bowles wanted adequate consultations with interest groups and time to prepare a draft, so that when the platform committee assembled in Los Angeles it could proceed to work on a draft and produce a platform of no more than 3,000 words with the time-consuming hearings of previous years. The hopes for a short platform and for the elimination of lengthy hearings were unfulfilled.

Work on the first draft of the platform commenced several weeks prior to the Los Angeles meeting of the platform committee. The drafting committee, which included among others Professor Abram J. Chayes of the Harvard Law School, and James Sundquist and Thomas Hughes, legislative assistants to Senator Joseph Clark and Representative Bowles, respectively, had before it abstracts of the regional hearings, reports by the committees of the Democratic Advisory Council, and the results of Bowles' own consultations with Democratic leaders. This drafting work was carried on largely in secret, although the committee occasionally received some public advice, such as Senator Kennedy's recommendations that the civil rights plank deal in specific recommendations in place of the pious generalizations which had found their way into the 1952 and 1956 planks.

In contrast to this careful planning and preparation for the draft of a platform to be presented to the platform committee, the arrangements for members of the platform committee to come to Los Angeles were haphazard. The best information that committee members could receive came from members of previous platform committees. For example, Iowa members of this committee received, in a letter from the National Committee, a few of the reports of the advance hearings, an invitation to appear for additional hearings on July 5 in Los Angeles, information that reservations were being held for them in the Biltmore Hotel, and a statement that a check for *per diem* was enclosed. In fact, checks were only received later, and arrangements for accommodations had to be made in Los Angeles after arrival. The first meeting of the committee opened with a short talk, by Vice

Chairman Phil Perlman, explaining the nature of the public hearings that would follow, and members of the committee remained in the dark regarding when they would start working on a platform. In 1956 Chairman McCormack announced at the beginning of the meetings the appointment of a drafting committee. In 1960 there was again a twenty man drafting committee which examined the early draft prior to its presentation to the full platform committee on Saturday, July 9. However, there was no public announcement of this fact until July 8. In the absence of a more explicit statement one can readily understand the growing bewilderment among members of this committee as they endured four days of hearings and listened to more than seventy witnesses present testimony which, when printed or mineographed, weighed over thirteen pounds*

During the hearings on July 7 and 8, particularly, some of the members of the platform committee organized themselves into dinner and luncheon meetings to caucus on behalf of particular causes in which they were interested. For example, midwestern delegates from Michigan, Wisconsin, Illinois, Minnesota, Montana, Iowa, Kansas, Nebraska, and North and South Dakota held meetings to discuss how they could best ensure that the proposals of Governor Loveless with respect to the agriculture plank could be included in the platform. Professor Willard W. Cochrane of the University of Minnesota was present at these meetings to explain the recommendations and to resist some of the extreme demands made by one of the members of this caucus. The strategic problem as viewed by this caucus was to deal with southern agricultural representatives and particularly Senator Clinton Anderson who has opposed the price support program generally favored by the corn and wheat areas of the agricultural sector. Platform committee members from this area showed considerable disenchantment with the soil bank program.

---

*There is little evidence that these hearings influence the platform. Their primary function appears to be "social." Democrats say they are proud and willing to listen to all sides before drawing up their platform. Some individuals testifying complimented the committee on not following the more effective procedure of the Republicans, who follow the practice of dividing their platform committee into subcommittees on different policy areas and holding hearings at these subcommittees. The Republicans' practice makes it possible for testimony to be presented in greater detail and it means that the members of the platform committee do not need to spend so much time at hearings as their Democratic counterparts.

Following the hearings the platform committee met together through Monday ironing out different planks by a process of marking up the draft which was submitted to them by the twenty-man subcommittee. These sessions were entirely secret. Printed drafts were numbered and could not be taken from the room in which the work was proceeding. One member of the committee suggested that the platform committee made over 100 changes in the draft submitted to them, mostly minor in character; however, the changes may have been around 30. While the committee did not achieve unanimity on many questions, only two minority reports were submitted to the final draft which was brought to the convention on July 12.

After the platform committee assembled on July 5 in Los Angeles, the opportunity of pressure groups to influence its work was only minor. Most of the group representatives testifying before this committee recognized this fact. Consequently, most of the testimony did not present specific wording. The testimony dealt largely with general principles relating to such issues as the recognition of The Republic of Ireland, the freedom of physicians from government control, the right to work, the rights of citizenship, the evils or virtues of the protective tariff, and nuclear armament or disarmament. Speeches were generally short, although one sage legislator remarked that "members of the House of Representatives took full advantage of the absence of the five minute rule to expand on the record." Most of the significant suggestions of groups which were put in the platform had a long history in preceding Democratic conventions, and Representative Bowles' drafting group was made aware of them before the platform committee assembled.

Los Angeles was the scene, however, for a number of last ditch efforts to secure favorable planks. For example, on July 9 there was a dignified parade of over 2500 people organized by the Quakers, and the Women's International League for Peace and Freedom to promote the issue of unilateral nuclear disarmament and peace. The parade passed by the hotels in which most of the delegates were housed, starting at MacArthur Park at 10 a.m. and concluding at 3 p.m. in Exposition Park with addresses by General Hugh Hester, Dr. Linus Pauling and Miss Annalee Stewart. Partisans of Governor Orville Faubus held a demonstration on July 10 in favor of the continuation of racial segregation. This demonstration preceded the mass meeting sponsored by the National Association for the Advancement of Colored People which was held in the Shrine Auditorium on Sunday afternoon. The Faubus demonstration was swallowed up by a large, and somewhat spontaneous, Stevenson demonstration which developed in the center of Los Angeles. During the entire convention week there were pickets outside the convention hall advertising various causes; however, they were mostly concerned with the race question. Although these demonstrations offered public expression of opinion, they reflected largely interests that were not seriously considered by the delegates or the platform committee.

An examination of the strategy and operations of a relatively successful pressure campaign should suggest some of the possibilities of group action at the convention stage. The Leadership Conference on Civil Rights efforts will be illustrative. Mr. Roy Wilkins, Executive Secretary of the NAACP and Chairman of the Leadership Conference, circularized a large number of organizations with a proposed "Program for Civil Rights—1960" over a month before the national convention. These groups responded by accepting or suggesting changes in the proposed stand. Finally, 33 national organizations* joined together in the publication of a common civil rights program under the above title. Representatives of about twenty of the participating organizations met on the evening of July 6 to lay down final strategy for presenting the case. Chaired by Mr. Wilkens, this meeting heard short

---

*Constituent groups included: The American Civil Liberties Union, American Jewish Committee, American Jewish Congress, American Veterans Committee, Americans for Democratic Action, Brotherhood of Sleeping Car Porters, Catholic Council on Working Rights, Catholic Interracial Council, Race Relations Department of the Congregational Christian Churches, Congress of Racial Equality, Delta Sigma Theta Sorority, Friends Committee on National Legislation, Improved Benevolent and Protective Order of Elks of the World, Industrial Union Department of the AFL-CIO, International Union of Electrical, Radio and Machine Workers, Japanese American Citizens League, Jewish Labor Committee, National Alliance of Postal Employees, National Association for the Advancement of Colored People, National Bar Association, National Council of Negro Women, Division of Christian Citizenship of the National Council of Protestant Episcopal Churches, National Newspaper Publishers Association, National Sharecroppers Fund, Southern Christian Leadership Conference, Transport Workers Union of America, Union of American Hebrew Congregations, Union of Orthodox Jewish Congregations of America, United Automobile Workers of America, United Steelworkers of America, United Synagogues of America, Women's International League for Peace and Freedom, and the Worker's Defense League.

speeches from Governor Williams and Walter Reuther which emphasized the need for securing specific platform commitments.

The leadership thought that their major problem was to line up midwestern members of the platform committee to support a strong plank; eastern and western delegates as well as the two new states would generally go along with a strong plank.* Accordingly, members of this civil rights caucus were instructed to contact platform committee members with whom they were acquainted to assure them of the group's wishes, and to report back reactions. It was decided that before Mr. Wilkins presented his testimony he would introduce representatives of each of the constituent organizations. This strategy had been developed out of the collaboration among these groups at the 1952 and 1956 conventions. In 1956 there had been a Sunday evening meeting sponsored by the civil rights lobby which was addressed by prominent Democrats who were pledging their support to a civil rights plank. This meeting was replaced in 1960 by a mass meeting sponsored by the NAACP in the Shrine Auditorium to which candidates for nomination for President were invited to speak. The public posture of the civil rights proponents was limited to the Thursday morning platform appearance and the one mass demonstration and no other activities.**

Almost the entire morning of July 7 was devoted to testimony on civil rights by the constituent members of the Leadership Conference on Civil Rights; this testimony was partially counterbalanced by a moderate dissent by Senator Spessard Holland of Florida, a member of the committee. Wilkens led off the testimony by introducing representatives from many of the constituent organizations, some of whom gave short talks on issues with which they were most familiar. Wilkens made two major points.

---

*This concern for the midwest is curious since the leadership for the 1948 floor fight on civil rights came from Minnesota and Wisconsin. In retrospect a developing alliance between midwestern farm states and labor representatives in the platform making process proved to control sufficient votes on the platform committee to have their way on civil rights as well as farm and labor questions. Midwesterners were very influential in these developments. Furthermore, the largest obstacle of a strong civil rights plank in 1956 were platform committee members such as Representatives Dawson of Chicago, Cellar of New York, and McCormack of Massachusetts.

**Picketing on behalf of civil rights was sponsored by groups other than those collaborating with the Leadership Conference on Civil Rights.

First, "generalizations on civil rights which have been the fashion in platforms of past years should give way . . . to specific language." Secondly, the major civil liberties issue was the illegal barriers to full citizenship of the Negro. But Wilkens did not dwell on specifics of platform language, allowing the seven points in the printed brochure to accomplish this objective. His discussion tended to dwell on the importance of the United States coming to terms with the civil rights problem because of its international, moral and political implications.

The seven point "Program for Civil Rights—1960" dealt with voting, education, housing, employment, the establishment of a permanent commission on civil rights, the integrity of American citizenship, and majority rule in the procedures of the Congress. It maintained that while elementary rights of citizenship were denied to Negroes in the south, northern states fell sadly short of allowing the Negro equal economic opportunity in housing and work. It is significant that the final platform incorporated something of each of the suggestions, although it did not use precisely the same terminology. For example, the suggested platform language of the civil rights group on school desegregation stated: "Require every school district affected by the Supreme Court's school desegregation decision to submit a plan for compliance no later than the close of the 1961-62 school term." The final language incorporated in the platform was: "We believe that every school district affected by the Supreme Court's school desegregation decision should submit a plan providing for at least first-step compliance by 1963, the 100th anniversary of the Emancipation Proclamation." With regard to congressional procedures, the final platform language turned out to be more clear and specific than the language recommended by the Leadership Conference which read: "Improve congressional procedures so that the majority will may prevail, at each stage of the legislative process and the Congress thus may be a more effective and responsible instrument of our national purposes." The platform language as adopted by the convention reads:

> In order that the will of the American people may be expressed upon all legislative proposals, we urge that action be taken at the beginning of the 87th Congress to improve congressional procedures so that majority rule prevails and decisions can be made after reasonable debate without being blocked by a minority in either house.
> The rules of the House of Representatives should be amended so

as to make sure that bills reported by legislative committees should reach the floor for consideration without undue delay[*]

Testimony on civil rights was not confined to the morning of July 7. When collaborating groups like the ADA, UAW, FCNL, and AVC presented their testimony, they always gave a boost to the "Program for Civil Rights—1960." Occasionally, as when Joseph Rauh for the ADA or Walter Reuther for the UAW testified, a substantial portion of time was devoted to this question. However, opposition testimony was muted. Senator Holland made the major answer to civil rights proponents on the morning of July 7. He asked that the platform confine itself to generalities as in 1956. He said, "you can put in what you want. You can put in generalities—don't be too specific." On July 8 Governor Hollings of South Carolina also spoke inviting the Democratic Party to adopt the segregationist position. That opposition strategy was to be non-provocative and generally silent can be inferred by the successful efforts of Senators Eastland and Stennis of Mississippi to persuade the less moderate Governor Ross R. Barnett of Mississippi to remain silent and not testify. Proponents of civil rights were only questioned briefly and occasionally by Messrs. Gray and Bloch of Georgia and Senator Ervin of North Carolina. The object was to make as little of this testimony as possible. The candidacy of Lyndon F. Johnson of Texas for nomination as a presidential candidate was the reason for this southern modesty.

Prior to the adoption of the platform, the mass meeting at the Shrine Auditorium was the second major pro-civil rights move. The 6,000 people crowded into the auditorium cheered Senator Humphrey most loudly for his contribution to civil rights. The three major candidates accepted the NAACP invitation to speak, but only Senator Kennedy and Symington appeared. While Kennedy was cooly received, his talk was applauded, as was Symington's. Oscar Chapman spoke on behalf of Lyndon Johnson, possibly because the audience would have been quite unfriendly to Johnson's own appearance. This particular meeting made explicit the interest of the civil rights forces in the presidential and vice presidential nomination.

---

[*]The first paragraph of this proposal repeats verbatim the promise of the 1956 platform with one exception. The 87th Congress replaces the 85th Congress. The second paragraph is entirely new. It may be added that the Leadership Conference on Civil Rights seemed much more exercised about congressional procedures in 1956 than in 1960.

As late as July 10, some of the civil rights leaders like Clarence Mitchell of the NAACP professed pessimism about the civil rights plank. However, when the platform committee published their report these leaders were jubilant. There were only two minority reports to the platform proposed, and the most important of these was by ten states against the civil rights plank.* This minority report was supported by Alabama, Arkansas, Florida, Georgia, Louisiana, Mississippi, North Carolina, South Carolina, Tennessee, and Virginia. It simply asked that the "proposed 'civil rights' plank" be repudiated. That this was no serious parliamentary maneuver can be gleaned from the fact that proposals relating to civil rights were sprinkled through the platform and not confined to one section under this title.

A short summary of the platform proposals regarding this question may help suggest how the rights issue was one major theme of the total Democratic platform, "The Rights of Man." While the protection of individual dignity suggests the purposes of the foreign policy and domestic economic proposals, specific civil rights recommendations include the following:

1. A pledge that Congress shall enact laws necessary and proper to protect the right to vote.
   a. this would include "whatever action is necessary to eliminate literacy tests" and poll taxes as voting requirements.
   b. this would also include home rule for the District of Columbia and support for the proposed 23rd Amendment dealing with the D. C. franchise.
2. The support of the Supreme Court decision regarding desegregation and concrete proposals relating to integration of schools cited before. Further, specific approval of peaceful demonstrations to advance the cause of the Negro was included.
3. A pledge to end discrimination in federal housing programs, including federally assisted housing.
4. The establishment of a Fair Employment Practices Commission.
5. The establishment of a permanent Commission on Civil Rights.

---

*Virginia was permitted to present a minority report dealing with the national debt without the required signatures of eight state delegations on the platform committee.

6. Protection of rights of United States citizens to travel and engage in business abroad without regard to race or religion.

7. Revision of congressional procedures as cited before.

The reader will note that these points follow the outline of the recommendations found in "Program for Civil Rights—1960." Occasionally they even follow the recommended planks verbatim as in the case of the right to travel referred to in point (6). They do come in different order, and the Democratic platform was concerned with other civil rights questions than those proposed by the Leadership Conference on Civil Rights*

The minority report by the ten southern states included the following arguments: first, the main support for the Democratic Party in 1952 and 1956 came from the states signing this minority report. Secondly, these states were being systematically vilified. Third, the federal system and the separation of powers doctrines of the United States Constitution take precedence over the right to vote. Fourth, questions of public education are under the jurisdiction of the states and no state is obliged by the Constitution to have a system of public instruction. Finally, "the states of the south will not be bribed with 'technical and financial assistance' held out as bait" to change their way of life.

Minority reports were handled under a simple procedure. The proponents of the Virginia dissent urging a planned schedule for repayment of the national debt were given five minutes and Chairman Bowles took five minutes to respond to this attack. The proponents of the ten state dissent were given thirty minutes on the convention floor divided into five six-minute speeches. This minority report was answered by five four-minute talks, and Bowles took ten final minutes to conclude. But minority reports were then voted upon and defeated after which the question was put on the whole platform and "The Rights of Man" was accepted. The fact that Senator Lyndon B. Johnson was a serious contender for the presidential nomination precluded a bolt at this time in the same way that this fact had determined the earlier southern strategy of moderation with regard to the civil rights plank.

---

*For example, the Democrats pledged to improve congressional investigating and hearing procedures, and to abolish the "useless disclaimer affidavits such as those for student educational loans."

Action on the platform did not imply an ending of pressure group activity. Labor and agricultural groups were active in the presidential and vice presidential nominating discussions and struggle; as a matter of fact the organization of agricultural delegates from the midwest in the New Democratic Farm Rally was completed on the day following the adoption of the platform under the co-chairmanship of Iowans Leonard Hoffman and Ellsworth Hays. This group listened to speeches by or on behalf of various presidential candidates as a formally organized bloc of agricultural delegates.

After the nomination of Kennedy and Johnson as the 1960 standard bearers, the two candidates again faced representatives of the civil rights lobby. This meeting took place on Friday, July 15, with about 100 Negro delegates and alternates present. Senator Kennedy introduced his running mate to a respectful but cool audience, and Senator Johnson departed from the meeting without subjecting himself to questioning, after pledging his support to the platform and his leader. To the specific questions regarding the course of civil rights legislation in the short session of Congress after the convention, Senator Kennedy answered in generalities. It was apparent that the leaders had many social appointments to keep and were unprepared to give any specific assurances at this stage. Democrats hoped that the statements by Wilkens of the NAACP in New York on the following Monday defending the Democratic platform against Republican challenge would represent the feeling of Negroes. He said that the Democrats "gave us all we asked." He emphasized the fact that a target date of 1963 had been set for the planning of integration of the schools, and that this was more than the Supreme Court had done in its decisions.

The foregoing discussion should suggest that the national convention may be regarded as only an incident or occasional arena in which groups may seek to advance their purposes. Here candidates may be forced to make rash promises; or they may subsequently change their minds. Strong wording may be secured in a platform, but the candidates in any event will be required to interpret, reinterpret and/or implement the promises made. Platform wording may even be traded for votes for nomination, although it is difficult to see how a trade can be explicitly made. A candidate for President may say to one group, "I will support your plank;" and he may say to an opposing group, "I will support your candidate for Vice President." Consequently, significant groups are interested in both the nomination and the platform. They always know that the convention is no legislative hall and that promises made here require additional work in order to be made effective as part of the public policy of the United States. To observe on the scene in Los Angeles, it was apparent that Kennedy's support of specific civil rights promises was as influential in the platform committee as was his choice of Lyndon Johnson as his vice presidential running mate in the Democratic National Convention. However, candidates for nomination were not the direct authors of any platform recommendation in 1960. The influence of candiates on the platform was usually obscure for the Democratic Party.

8. A National versus a State Approach to Platform Making: Montana Republicans Go Along

Thomas Payne

Montana State University

Studies of interest groups commonly single out the influence of these groups upon the platform making process and the resolutions committee as their principal activity with reference to national conventions. Little attention, however, has been given to the impact of interest groups upon state delegations to national conventions. Inasmuch as interest groups do function at all points in the political process where decisions affecting their concerns may be made, it may be presumed that they are not oblivious to the nature, composition, and work of the state delegations. It was with this assumption that this study of interest group pressures upon the Montana delegation to the 1960 Republican National Convention was undertaken.

It may be helpful to identify some of the principal interests in Montana politics as a prelude to a discussion of their role with respect to the Montana delegation. As a state which is still preponderantly rural, Montana's economy depends heavily upon agriculture; the two principal types which flourish in Montana are ranching and wheat farming. Wheat farmers in large numbers support the Farmers Union, one of the bulwarks of the Democratic Party in Montana, while most ranchers are identified with the Montana Stockgrowers Association and constitute an important element of the Republican Party.

Aside from agriculture, mining looms largest in Montana's economy, and one organization, the Anaconda Company, has attained unchallenged leadership in this area. In recent years the oil interest has become increasingly vocal. There are, moreover, the usual professional and small business interests to be considered. Finally, a big mining industry has resulted in the growth of a strong labor movement. The principal union, the International Mine, Mill, and Smelter Workers Union, is unaffiliated. The Democratic Party has built its coalition around the Farmers Union and organized labor, whereas the Republican Party has found its support among the stockmen, oil industry, and business and professional groups. The powerful corporate interests represented by the Anaconda Company and the Montana Power Company, while normally conservative in character, are not identified with either political party.

The great bulk of Montana's citizenry were unacquainted with the personnel in the national convention delegations and did not exert any pressures. To the extent that pressures were brought upon the Montana delegation, they were brought by organized groups. This reflects the well-known truism of politics that organized groups are in a much better position to exert pressure upon any political institution. Unorganized groups and the citizenry generally are not likely to be aware of the critical role played by delegations to national party conventions, and therefore are unlikely to develop access to such delegations. Organized interests thus are able to capitalize upon their better organization and better access to such delegations.

The most important area of group activity with reference to the Montana Republican delegation was manifested in the conflict between the platform adopted by the Republican National Convention in Chicago in July, and the platform adopted by the Republican State Convention in Helena in June, preceding the national convention. To appreciate the role of this conflict, it is useful to recall that the significance of the platform for interest groups is not so much what the platform actually contains, but in the process by which the platform has been adopted. The platform making is essential in shaping the party's coalition in that it provides a point at which the diverse interests clustering loosely about the party may be reconciled.

The platform of a national party convention must accommodate interests of far greater diversity than a state party platform. This was evident in Montana in that the interests represented at the Republican State Convention were relatively homogeneous, representing the not too diverse views of professional, business, ranching, and mining interests. At the national level it was necessary to appeal to urban, minority, and international interests that were not represented at the state convention in Helena.

To appreciate the difficult position in which the members of the Montana delegation were placed, it is appropriate to identify areas of conflict between the state and national platform. The national platform of the Republican Party evidenced far greater concern for international organization and international affairs than did the state platform. For example, the national platform contained a pledge to work for peaceful settlements of international disputes and extend the rule of law in the world. In contrast, Resolution 11 adopted by the state convention placed the state Republican Party on record as opposed to the repeal of the Connally reservation. Further, the national platform and the state platform diverged with respect to foreign aid. Whereas the national platform espoused foreign aid generally, the state platform urged emphatically that foreign aid be granted to friendly countries only, and this "only in repayable loans with interest."

There was a substantial, and to many of the Montana delegates, intolerable divergence between the two platforms with reference to farm cooperatives. While the Republican national platform included a statement in its agriculture plank favorable to cooperatives, the state platform urged that cooperatives be taxed in the same fashion as privately-owned competitive business. The national platform urged development of new water resource projects while the state platform declared its opposition to "construction of either Paradise or Knowles Dam on the Clark Fork and Flathead Rivers."

The Republican national platform commended the Republican administration for sponsoring the National Defense Education Act. By contrast, the Republican state convention expressed its opposition to the re-enactment "of the temporary National Defense Education Act." The national platform expressed its support of federal aid for school construction. By contrast, the state platform expressed its opposition to any kind of federal aid on a general overall basis for the state. "Rather than calling for increased federal handouts which can mean only higher federal taxes, we urge the Congress to allow the states to retain an adequate portion of federal tax revenue in order that we who are willing to support our schools directly may have greater resources for so doing."

The stark contrast between the national Republican platform and the state Republican platform is nowhere better illustrated than in their opposing views on the subject of immigration. The national platform called for a doubling of the number of immigrants entering the United States and urged the amendment of obsolete immigration laws to establish 1960 census data as a base for determining immigration quotas. Contrasted with this position, the Montana platform asserted: "The McCarran-Walter Immigration Act must be preserved and enforced. It is in the interest of American workers that competition from this source be limited."

Montana delegates arriving in Chicago for the national convention became quickly and painfully aware of the conflict between the positions taken by the state convention and those being proposed in the Resolutions Committee. While they did not recognize that the opposing positions reflected the divergent views of differing coalitions of interests, they were nevertheless mindful of the probable unfavorable impact of the national platform upon leading conservative interests in Montana. Montana's members of the Resolutions Committee took pains to issue press releases informing Montanans through Montana newspapers of their efforts to amend the national platform to bring it more closely in harmony with the position of Montana Republicans. These releases were published in leading Montana daily newspapers.

The publicity received in Montana about the fight by Montanans on the Resolutions Committee provoked concern on the part of delegation leaders. They feared that Republican prospects in Montana might be damaged if the impression were given that extremely sharp differences existed between the Montana organization and the party nationally. In order to minimize this danger, Governor Aronson issued a press release which stated in part: "There have, of course, been differences of opinion in connection with the drafting of a national platform acceptable to the majority of the delegates of the various states. This, after all, is the democratic process, and it would be remarkable only if differences of opinion among and within the several states did not exist." The governor further stated in his press release that he was confident that a platform would be adopted "which carries forward the basic Republican principles of government to victory in November, both in the state and the nation."

An examination of communications addressed to members of the Montana delegation revealed that few interest groups availed themselves of the opportunity to communicate to delegates to the national convention and that most communications were routine in character. Indeed, the following list of seven organizations comprises the total number of groups which wrote to all of the delegates. Each of these organizations sent one form letter, suggesting the desultory character of group pressures on the delegation.

> American National Cattlemen's Association
> The Committee of One Million Against the Admission of Communist China to the United Nations
> Committee for the Effective Use of the International Court
> Montana Farm Bureau Federation
> Americans for Constitutional Action
> Montana Committee for Economic Freedom (an organization seeking to abolish the income tax)
> National Coalition to Combat Communism in the United States

Scanning the list above, one is struck by the limited number of Montana organizations which sought to influence the behavior of the Montana delegation. None of the interests in Montana elected to submit personal letters directly to individual members of the delegation. Evidently no dominant Montana interest felt that there was anything in particular to be gained by this kind of communication.

Further analysis of communications received by delegates from Montana to the Republican National Convention discloses that the great bulk of such communications were not concerned at all with policies, but rather with the aspirations of candidates. Typically, for every communication received from an interest group, the delegate would receive from eight to ten communications in behalf of some candidate. This supports the widespread assumption that national conventions are more concerned with personnel in government than with policies in government.

Most communication in behalf of candidates were also routine in character and included many form letters and printed brochures. A limited number of personal, individually prepared letters were received by delegates. An effort was made by supporters of Senator Barry Goldwater to launch a campaign of letter writing to members of the various delegations. Montana delegates were recipients of quantities of form postal cards advocating the nomination of Goldwater for President. A sizable number of telegrams were received by members of the delegation and became a conversational topic in the closing hours of the national convention. It became apparent that members of the delegation were receiving communications in behalf of Senator Goldwater's candidacy from Montanans of whom they had never before heard. Put differently, Goldwater's organization attempted to mobilize support wherever it could, but, by and large, the letter and telegram campaign did not emanate from regular Montana Republicans.

Some members of the Montana delegation themselves were identified with certain interest groups. A survey of the group affiliations of the fourteen delegates reveals that two were ranchers, four were wives of ranchers, four were attorneys, one was the wife of a deceased doctor, one was a chiropractor, one was an employee of the Montana Power Company, one, of course, was Governor Aronson who in private life operates a ranch, is a bank president, and has been engaged in the trucking and oil business. No delegate was identified with any group interest incompatible with the basic Republican coalition in Montana. None of the delegates were members of organized labor nor were any identified with liberal farm organizations such as the Farm Union, although one was a member of the Montana Farm Bureau Federation.

To a considerable extent, therefore, the background and group affiliations of the Montana delegates determined their thinking and approach to their task. While not apparent in any specific action, their group backgrounds were evident in their general outlook and basic political philosophy. Thus, it was not the pressure of outside interests on the delegation that was notable; rather, it was the pressures inside the delegation growing out of affiliations of delegates and built up over many years that affected their behavior at the national convention.

The social lobby plays a lively, if indeterminate, role in the political process. One would therefore expect to see the social lobby employed at the national convention. One alternate delegate, a lobbyist for the Anaconda Company, maintained a suite at the hotel housing the Montana delegation to provide hospitality for Montana Republicans. Free liquor and other refreshments were provided at this suite. Other activities of the social lobby, if any, were not observed, and one should not attribute great importance to this gesture of the Anaconda Company.

Delegates who discussed Anaconda's hospitality to delegates with the writer concluded that the company simply was being nice to persons who had or might later have influence in Montana Affairs. Anaconda's social activities were also useful as a means of identifying and sizing up potential leaders in the Republican Party in Montana. Some Republicans had the impression that the Anaconda Company had provided a comparable facility for the Democratic delegation from Montana at the Los Angeles convention.

A comment on the role of the Anaconda Company, generally, in Montana affairs may be helpful. For many years the Anaconda Company, often in concert with the Montana Power Company, has maintained a position of preeminence in Montana both economically and politically. Over a period of more than forty years it has been able usually to block governmental action contrary to its best interest. Maintaining an effective lobby organization during state legislative sessions, Anaconda also has exercised an influential role behind the scenes in the Montana election process and has exercised influence over both political parties.

Recently the Anaconda Company occasionally has developed interests at variance with those of some conservative groups and organizations in Montana. One delegate complained that while a conservative Republican had no trouble dealing with the Montana Power Company, he found in the Anaconda Company an internationally minded organization whose interests were world wide in character and, because of its "bigness," often in conflict with interests of small businessmen and small and conservative mining operators in the state of Montana.

All delegates with whom this writer talked were of the opinion that the Anaconda Company in no way attempted to influence the course of any action by the Montana Republican delegation at the national convention. Perhaps it was unnecessary to exert pressure. Perhaps, also, the Anaconda Company has become subtle with maturity. Further, the company management probably assumed, with considerable justification, that the delegates could be depended upon to behave in a predictable fashion not unfriendly to its interests.

This study of the role of group pressures upon the Montana delegation to the Republican National Convention does provide certain conclusions about the nature of such pressures. In the first place, it is apparent from the data examined that delegates are far more concerned with the nomination of candidates than with the adoption of policies. Under these circumstances, the pressures to which delegates are immediately subjected are those representing the viewpoints of various candidates rather than the viewpoints of interest groups. When this is examined more closely, however, it becomes clear that inasmuch as the delegates reflect their own group affiliations, such pressures force them in time to support candidates who stand generally for their particular brand of politics. Thus, for example, the Montana delegation was sympathetic with the candidacy of Senator Goldwater because he could be identified more closely with the conservative coalition of the Montana Republican Party.

Furthermore, the pressures of interest groups are most likely to be exerted through the Resolutions Committee rather than through a state delegation. Interests recognize that this is their best opportunity for access. But delegations are not entirely ignored by interest groups. Interests in a state are concerned with the future prospects of the individuals who comprise the delegation. Moreover, the delegates themselves reflect the viewpoints of various interests with which their affiliations tend to identify them. Finally, a distinctive kind of pressure upon a state delegation may develop because of its position in the middle between the national and state platforms. The Montana delegation was caught between the opposing pressures of the coalition responsible for the national party platform and the coalition responsible for the state party platform. Such ambivalence inevitably produces party tensions fraught with peril if not satisfactorily resolved.

Inasmuch as interest groups must be concerned with all points in the political decision-making process, they cannot afford to neglect state delegations to national conventions. Their investment of time and effort at this point, however, is relatively minor compared with their pressure at other points. Significantly, those states which hold their state party platform conventions before the national convention afford the controlling interests within the state an opportunity at that point to secure favorable consideration. The delegation then selected is likely to reflect the basic alignment of interests within the party of the particular state, however much the delegation may depart from the peculiar brand of party philosophy being enunciated by the national organization and leadership.

9. Civil Rights and States' Rights: Georgia Democrats as a Conscious Minority

GEORGE F. BRASINGTON

Emory University

To Georgia's Democratic leadership—states' rightist by custom and conviction—political prospects in 1960 seemed dim, indeed. Once again, civil rights held the center of the stage and once again, the favored candidates ignored the south. To some disaffected Georgians, close associates of Governor Ernest Vandiver, even Lyndon B. Johnson of Texas, their erstwhile champion, had forfeited his claim to southern support by steering a moderate, conciliatory course as majority leader of the Senate. Accordingly, these leaders, acting with the tacit approval of the governor, proposed to draft their junior senator and former governor, Herman Talmadge, as a southern unity candidate. Brushing aside the senator's declaration of a personal preference for Johnson, the would-be drafters contended that a nomination campaign for Talmadge, even should it not be successful, could enhance his chances at the next convention and increase his influence in the Congress. Furthermore, with a sizable bloc of votes behind him at Los Angeles, the senator (and the south) would be in an excellent bargaining position in the event of close election balloting. The promoters of the Talmadge-for-President campaign approached the task which they had set for themselves with an abundance of enthusiasm and optimism. Gradually, however, as the formidable proportions of the proposed undertaking became apparent, the initial optimism moderated. On May 12, James H.

Gray, state chairman, had announced that plans were being completed for a pre-convention southern unity conference of ten or twelve states. Two weeks later the plans were amended to call for a pre-convention strategy meeting of six southern states. On the occasion of each announcement Gray declined to identify any of the states that were expected to participate in the proposed conference, nor would he name any politician outside Georgia who had committed himself to the Talmadge cause. Still later, on June 2, he disclosed that plans for the second meeting had been abandoned; instead, party leaders from the southern states would be invited to attend a strategy caucus at Los Angeles prior to the opening of the national convention. Gray stoutly maintained that, despite the difficulties they had encountered in planning for a conference, the Georgians were not discouraged in their efforts to secure regional support for their candidate. On June 17, however, Senator Talmadge requested that he not be considered for the Democratic presidential nomination.

The drastic reduction in the number of states which the Georgia party leaders had proposed to assemble in a display of southern unity was a sufficient indication that such unity could not be achieved under the Talmadge standard. According to the most generous estimate, the Georgian could be no more than the candidate of the deep southern states. Senator Talmadge realized this and declared that regional unity was paramount to all other considerations. In a televised statement that was reported by the Washington bureau of the *Atlanta Journal*, the senator said that his candidacy would "split the southern group, which would weaken our bargaining position." He once again endorsed Lyndon B. Johnson as the best qualified candidate. While he and Johnson had often disagreed, Talmadge continued, Johnson had helped the southern senators at the time of critical debates on civil rights. Talmadge proposed a curiously inverted quantitative determination of the acceptability of the leading candidates by citing a voting analysis prepared by the Americans for Democratic Action, "a highly radical organization." Senators John Kennedy and Stuart Symington had pleased the ADA with their votes 100 per cent of the time; Senator Johnson had pleased them only 58 per cent of the time. (Talmadge also noted with satisfaction that he and Senator Russell had pleased the ADA only 16 per cent of the time.)

Governor Vandiver had named the 66 delegates who would cast Georgia's 33 votes at the national convention before the collapse of the Talmadge movement in mid-June. He had carefully provided for any contingency by stipulating that the delegation would go to the convention officially uncommitted to any candidate. The delegates were all members of what might be called the Talmadge-Vandiver faction in Georgia politics; their political labels ranged from moderate to reactionary. As expected, neither of Georgia's most prominent liberals, Ellie Arnall, former governor, and William B. Hartsfield, mayor of Atlanta, was named to the delegation. Also as expected, the state's most militant segragationist, Roy V. Harris, former state legislative leader and editor of the *Augusta Courier,* a political weekly, was one of the 66. The delegation differed from those of recent years in only one arresting particular: of the state's twelve-man congressional delegation, only four, all representatives, accepted the places on the delegation that had been reserved for them and only one, John J. Flynt of the Fourth District, actually attended the convention.

Among observers of Georgia politics, the impression prevailed that the apparent indifference of the congressmen toward the national convention was a true index of sentiment within the state Democratic Party. Certainly the prospect of climbing aboard the Johnson bandwagon was not as emotionally appealing as that of driving a similar vehicle for Talmadge. To attenuate their enthusiasm even further, the delegates were aware that their loyalty to the party might be challenged in the credentials committee. Georgia's "unpledged electors law" of 1958 denies presidential and vice presidential candidates a place on the general election ballot, thereby relieving the state's electors from any obligation, legal or moral, to support the nominees of their party's national convention. Hence the Georgia delegates, like those of other deep southern states with statutory provisions for independent electors, were exposed to the charge that they could not offer absolute assurance of their support for the national ticket. The platform committee posed yet another unfavorable prospect for the delegation. During the spring, Negro sit-in demonstrations throughout the south had intensified the already clamorous demands for a strong civil rights plank. To some political observers, these were conditions that indicated a possible walk-out. Significantly, however, the state's leaders dismissed the possibility and affirmed that it was Georgia's intention to take part in the convention in good faith. Thus the "official" mood of the delegation was to be one of resoluteness rather than defiance. As many delegates expressed it, "we may be thrown out, but we are not going to walk out."

While the southern states encountered no hostility in the credentials committee, their views on civil rights were to be accorded a decidedly unsympathetic reception in the platform committee. Governor Vandiver had determined to counter the eloquence of the civil rights advocates by assigning to the platform committee the two most forceful spokesmen for states' rights in the Georgia delegation, James H. Gray and Charles J. Bloch. State chairman Gray, a native of New England who established residence in Georgia following World War II, is publisher of the *Albany Herald*. An intransigent on the issue of racial segregation and an orator of no mean talent, he has been in great demand for speaking engagements throughout the deep south. Macon attorney Bloch, who has long served as a legal advisor to Georgia governors, is a veteran defender of southern causes in the federal courts. He published an elaborate defense of "constitutional government" in a 1958 book, *States' Rights: The Law of the Land*, for which Senators Russell and Talmadge contributed laudatory comments. Both of these delegates were to achieve prominence in the convention before a platform would be adopted. Bloch, who viewed the platform committee as a "packed jury," acted to bind the southern members into a dignified bloc at the outset by persuading them to adopt the strategy of not questioning civil rights witnesses. The "silent sit-in of southern whites on the Democratic platform committee," as editor Eugene Patterson of the *Atlanta Constitution* described it, enabled the southerners to maintain their equanimity and hence to dispel the notion that the advocates of states' rights (and supporters of Lyndon Johnson) were a bunch of hot-heads.

The platform was still in the hands of a drafting subcommittee when the Georgia delegation assembled for its first caucus on the afternoon of Sunday, July 10. But Gray and Bloch, whose report to the delegates followed the opening roll call in the order of business, were already conceding that the civil rights plank, unlike that of the 1956 convention, would not accommodate the views of the party's southern membership. They assured the delegates that they would repudiate the expected "obnoxious" plank and that the southern members of the full committee would file a minority report on the platform for presentation to the convention. When their report had been concluded, and warmly praised by Governor Vandiver, Georgia's platform committeemen did not request instructions from the caucus; and no instructions were issued. Under the circumstances, they would have been superfluous.

It was agreed by sponsors and critics alike, that the panel of drafters submitted to the platform committee on Monday the strongest civil right plank in the party's history. Senator Sam J. Ervin, Jr., of North Carolina, a member of the panel, was acting as the chief spokesman and strategist for the sorely displeased, though hardly surprised, southern members of the committee. Ervin offered a motion to delete three sections of the plank—those that endorsed the Supreme Court's school desegregation decision, proposed that the Civil Rights Commission be made permanent, and declared that "the Attorney General should be empowered and directed to file civil injunction suits in federal courts to prevent the denial of any civil rights on grounds of race, creed, or color." The motion was defeated, as expected. At this juncture Georgia's Gray stepped to the fore, where he was to remain until the platform battle had been ended. There were other sections of the civil rights plank which were equally as pernicious from the southern viewpoint as those which had been the objects of Ervin's motion: the endorsement of "peaceful demonstrations for first-class citizenship," the pledge "to eliminate literacy tests and the payment of poll taxes as requirements for voting," and the proposal that a fair employment practices commission be established. Gray therefore read into the record of the committee a repudiation of the proposed civil rights plank as being "incompatible with the Constitution of the United States." Nine of the eleven former Confederate states endorsed Gray's statement (Tennessee and Texas were the exceptions), whereupon Gray and Bloch fervently set themselves to the task of drafting a full length minority report.

On Tuesday evening, amid the sounds of both applause and disappointment, Gray presented the southern minority report on the civil rights plank of the platform to the Democratic National Convention. His accent was that of his native New England and startled many who heard him, but his words were those of the deep south. The major proposition of the report, that the "radical" proponents of civil rights who assail the south are in reality bent on the destruction of "constitutional government," is manifest in the following exerpt:

> Increasingly, the loyalty of the people of the south to their party has been repaid with scolding and derision, pretending to invoke the Constitution of the United States. Those who are attacking the south have ignored the fundamental law of the land—and, in particular, the Tenth Amendment of the Constitution of the United States. Despite these attacks, the Democrats of the southern states have sent delegates to this 1960 convention whose aim was and is to unify the party and restore constitutional government in this land of ours.

The task of obtaining the final approval of the southern platform committeemen, in the form of their signatures upon the report, had fallen to Bloch, who moved about the floor from delegation to delegation. He even persuaded Tennessee, belatedly, to join the nine other states. Although the minority report was doomed from the start, it nevertheless represented a significant triumph for the Georgia delegation. After the disappointing efforts of the spring, Chairman Gray at last was the leader of a bloc of ten southern states, if only for an evening. Indeed, it was only when Governor Vandiver explained that it would be inappropriate for such a procedural matter as the presentation of a report, that the delegates abandoned a plan to stage a floor demonstration.

At the second (and final) caucus of the Georgia delegation, on Wednesday morning, the major item of business was the endorsement of a candidate for the presidential nomination, but the talk among the delegates was mainly about Gray's performance of the previous evening. Governor Vandiver, in a tribute to both Gray and Bloch, announced that the congratulatory messages from Georgia and throughout the south were voluminous. The delegates gave their platform committeemen an ovation. Representative John J. Flynt's nominating speech for Lyndon B. Johnson, though spirited, was somewhat anticlimactic. Georgia's support of the Texan virtually had been assured since June when Senator Talmadge had ended the favorite son speculation. Moreover, he had been warmly welcomed to the Georgia caucus on Sunday. Still, the circumstances were not those that evoke enthusiasm: Johnson had not been the first choice of the state leadership; an early ballot victory for Senator John Kennedy appeared to be a certainty; and the Georgia delegation was emotionally spent after the platform battle (which had been fought without the assistance of Johnson's Texas delegation). Flynt's motion was unanimously adopted, as prearranged, and Georgia cast 33 votes for Johnson that evening. But it was noticeable that most of the state's delegates sat out the Johnson demonstration.

Senator John F. Kennedy, whose political friends and supporters had been conspicuously active in the drafting of the national platform, won the Democratic presidential nomination on the first ballot Wednesday evening. On the following morning, Charles Bloch and Roy Harris, the veteran segregationists of the Georgia delegation, proposed that the state nominate Governor Vandiver as a favorite son candidate for Vice President. Their proposal, which would have placed Bloch on the rostrum to renew the attack on the civil rights plank, immediately drew the enthusiastic endorsement of a number of delegates. Meanwhile the Governor had been summoned to a conference with Senator Kennedy, where he told the presidential nominee that Johnson was his preference for the vice presidential nomination. However, even after Kennedy announced that afternoon that he had chosen Johnson to join him on the party's ticket, Roy Harris persisted in his support of a favorite son candidacy. Chairman Gray and state legislative leaders Frank S. Twitty and George L. Smith argued that it would be highly inconsistent to oppose Senator Johnson for Vice President after supporting him for President. Besides, Georgia should stand upon the minority report on the civil rights plank rather than seek to renew the debate. Vandiver listened to the conflicting counsels and chose the course of party unity.

When the invocation was delivered at the final session of the 1960 Democratic National Convention in the Coliseum on Friday, Governor Vandiver was already back home in Georgia. He had departed from Los Angeles without pledging his support to the Kennedy-Johnson ticket; and upon his arrival in Atlanta he still declined to do so. Like a number of other southerners, he appeared to be pleased that Johnson had been offered the vice presidential nomination and, concurrently, displeased that he had accepted it. He expressed a desire to learn "what the people think," which at least implied that he might use Georgia's "unpledged electors law" to withhold support from the convention nominees. Vandiver's only words of commendation were for the minority report, which he proudly identified as "the Georgia report" to which nine other states had subscribed. When pressed by an *Atlanta Journal* reporter for further information, he replied that Martin Luther King, Jr., (the Atlanta Negro clergyman who is a world-renowned champion of equal rights) had returned on the same flight. "He was a great deal more successful than the south was. I suggest you interview him."

Part IV:

State Delegations: Leaders and Followers

10. *"What Can I Do?"*: *Ohio Delegates View* *The Democratic Convention*

Aaron B. Wildavsky
Oberlin College

Although there is a great deal of descriptive literature dealing with the more glamorous aspects of national conventions, there is no account of how delegates view the convention. The purpose of this study is to show how individual delegates react to the convention environment, how they feel about it, and how they interpret what they see and hear. This is not merely a matter of curiosity. For the ways in which delegates adjust to the convention situation and perceive the events that take place within it affect their behavior. Of course, a delegate does not simply respond to an abstraction known as the convention. He acts within a specific set of political facts created by his state delegation which limits and shapes the kinds of things he does. It made a great deal of difference to the delegates from Ohio that they were pledged to John Kennedy in a primary vote and that this had occurred only after the Cuyahoga County (Cleveland) faction led by Ray T. Miller had threatened to enter the Senator in the primary against Governor Michael DiSalle. The astute governor, when he saw how the land lay, entered the primary as a favorite son pledged to Kennedy so long as he had a chance to win the nomination. When the Miller organization entered its own slate, the struggle was between a state and county apparatus both pledged to the same candidate; and the governor's ticket won by a margin of fifty-three to eight. This settled, they left for Los Angeles divided only by the equally vociferous claims of the factions to responsibility of Ohio's unity for Kennedy.

Adjusting to the Convention Situation

"Conventions are fun; they are attended by fun-loving Americans who enjoy themselves immensely. Anyone can see that this raucous, boisterous occasion is a happy one, for all but a few losers, and even they usually manage a smile." This is the accepted picture of national conventions. It is certainly not a completely false picture because many delegates do enjoy themselves at one time or another. But it fails to do justice to elements which induce anxiety among delegates and influence their behavior in many ways. The outside observer who asks them what they think is happening, how they feel about things, what they're doing, soon notices a troubled current beneath the surface flow of gaiety.*

The convention brings the delegates into a strange place in which they must participate, or appear to participate, in making an important decision in a terribly short period of time, under hectic conditions, where most of them never find out precisely what is going on and many are full of misinformation. "Kennedy's sure to win," a delegate insisted, "he's got the support of all the big labor leaders like Hoffa. . . ." "Can't find a G........ damn thing in this place," is the typical plaint of a delegate who finds it difficult to orient himself quickly, especially in Los Angeles which few delegates have visited before and where distances are great. It is not surprising, therefore, that some delegates develop an initial sense of not being in the right place, just at the time when events are moving so quickly that they need all the security of a familiar place to anchor themselves. "Do you think I ought to be at the Biltmore or some place?"**

---

*I wish to make it clear that my comments about the anxieties which delegates have do not imply criticisms of them, but rather are directed to the difficult situation in which they find themselves. I have no doubt that, as a group, the delegates would compare favorably with any cross-section of Americans in their interest, knowledge, and devotion to public affairs. Actually, I believe that the convention system is a superior mechanism for nominating presidential candidates, far better than any other alternative currently on the horizon. See my forthcoming, "On the Superiority of National Conventions," to be published by the *Review of Politics.*

**Most of the observations included here were made in the lobby of the Hotel Figueroa, the temporary home of the Ohio delegation, where I interviewed some 20 to 30 delegates a day for periods of five to twenty-five minutes during the week of the convention. The quotations all come from delegates unless specifically stated otherwise. They were written down immediately following the interview and were transcribed word-for-word as nearly as memory would permit.

Public mores invade private conscience and impose tremendous demands on the delegate. He should know what is going on, and if he doesn't, something is wrong with him. But on occasion he considers himself lucky if he can find out where he is supposed to be for formal party functions. "Do you know when we'll caucus?"

True, information is thrown at him from all directions but he hardly knows who or what to believe. One day in the papers a Kennedy victory is inevitable and the next it is doubtful and he is slipping. A Johnson staff man patiently explains why his candidate's victory is certain only to be succeeded by Kennedy and Symington people with different stories. One acquaintance says this and another says that. "If you know what's going on you're a better man than I am," responded a delegate who would feel insulted to give such an answer if he were asked about events in his county. "At home I know," said another delegate, "and here . . ." The comment trailed off with an expressive shrug.

A few delegates found it rewarding to go to convention headquarters to seek out their counterparts from other states, newspaper and television reporters, and candidate staff men. But only the most hardy come through unscathed. The more fortunate ones come back at least with conversation pieces and perhaps a word from a famous television personality who could be counted a celebrity. But for the most part these delegates found themselves crushed by the masses of people, uncertain of who to speak to (especially before delegates' badges were issued as identification) and subject to rebuff. "I never thought that Ed Murrow was such a sour type," said one delegate who felt he had been brushed off. "Don't go down to the Biltmore," a second delegate advised, "there's just a lot of people trying to find out what others are going to do."

Some delegates feel that they are important people back home. But at the convention the delegate often feels like "a little fish in a big pond" and worries about his status in his new environment. Why is he not consulted and why are his opinions not accorded customary deference by others? He may have only a few acquaintances among the other delegates and these may be political, not personal friends. Conversation may lag because his political acquaintances have different styles of life and do not share his interests in political issues, in horses, or in the weather.

There may be difficulty in locating people to talk to and a feeling of loneliness may develop. "Seems like everybody comes from someplace else."

The governor and his top aides are busy people, appearing and disappearing at odd moments and for mysterious purposes. All the delegate may get is a perfunctory handshake. If a delegate has budding feelings of inferiority—"I'm a small man," "what can I do?" "I don't expect to set any records," "little men don't change things"—these may be exacerbated by countless little indications that he is out of the know.*

It is in this context that the problem of getting a good seat at the convention or tickets for wives and friends takes on special importance. Many delegates come to regard the dispensation of these favors as indices of their status; that is, of the way others regard them. If a delegate finds himself in the back rows where it is difficult to see and hear, he may well consider this a sign of low esteem and a direct slap at his person. He can hardly believe that he got a bad seat by a random occurrence or that other people were just lucky in getting more tickets than he did. "Looks like my place is at the back . . ." one wistful delegate reported; and did not attend the next day's session because, as he put it, you could not very well enjoy the proceedings from that bad location. A good deal of state chairman William Coleman's time was spent trying to smooth over ruffled feelings of this sort. That these efforts were not always successful is indicated by the fact that the harshest arguments I heard concerned the distribution of tickets.

It is not surprising that delegates feel troubled when one considers that from their viewpoint the situation is highly unstructured—most of them have no formal role to play. Hence the nagging question of what a particular delegate is supposed to do may recur persistently without his being able to find a satisfactory answer. And if he does not ask himself that question, he feels that the people back home will casually, but insistently,

---

*There were numerous indications of delegate's seeking to compensate for feeling unimportant by building themselves up in the eyes of the listener: "When I go back to take care of my apartment houses;" "It won't be Kennedy who'll help the local ticket; I'll help my boys;" "my son's a brilliant boy and when I wrote the General about him, the General hopped right to it. . . ."

ask him precisely what he did, what his contribution was at the convention.*

The governor and a few party leaders are not subject to the same anxieties as the ordinary delegate; they have special ones of their own, for they have direct, personal interests in the outcome of the convention which less influential men do not share. The governor is but one of a number of men who are seeking the candidate's ear. In a fluid political situation the governor can hardly be certain that he will remain in the candidate's confidence or that other more ardent suitors will not usurp his place. The experience of others in past conventions may warn the governor that promises of future indulgences (usually more tacit than explicit) may be cast aside as the candidate's needs change. DiSalle's incessant chant to the effect that he was Kennedy's counselor had the sound of the lady who protests too much, especially in view of the fact that the governor's public preference for Vice President, Stuart Symington, was not chosen.

Mechanisms for Reducing Anxiety

As the convention provides an environment conducive to anxiety, so it also provides opportunities for adjustment. Anxiety induced by strangeness of place can be mitigated but not erased by familiarizing oneself with the surroundings. There is not enough time for that. Instead, the delegates immediately seek out familiar connections with the past. The cry goes out: "Are there Rotarians to make up a meeting?" and soon a quorum is found and a convivial group goes through the old ritual. Mayors breakfast together; Negro delegates converse and go off to a convention-wide meeting of their fellows; congressmen meet their associates from the Capitol; union members converse about their special policy interests; and delegates from the large counties seek each other's company. Still, some are left out.

Where lack of reliable knowledge is a source of concern, information costs may be cut by an acceptable stance which re-

---

*I am not suggesting that the delegates were free of troubled feelings before they came to the convention; obviously, like everyone else, they brought their strengths and weaknesses with them. Nor are the anxiety-provoking aspects of the convention necessarily unique. No doubt, delegates have gone to places which are strange to them before; they have probably had to make important decisions quickly; they may have been a part of events in which their role was not clear and yet they were expected to do something. It is the coming together of all these phenomena in the most famous of our political events that is significant.

quires the bare minimum of awareness. "We're supposed to be for Kennedy so what do I care about all these rumors." Or "I go as the Governor goes. That's all I need to know." It was a visible source of relief for some delegates to turn a question about what was happening into an explanation that they were morally committed to Kennedy. The more apathetic may say that "they don't tell me what's going on." "Who are 'they?' " "The big shots."

There are delegates with special contacts who do possess bits and pieces of information which enable them to feel knowledgeable. Negroes may nod wisely and say "yes," the civil rights plank is acceptable to their race; union men shake their heads and say "no," Johnson is not acceptable to labor; and a few with a line to the governor or Ray Miller or someone on the Kennedy staff generate confidence about Kennedy's chances, often mentioning what individual states are likely to do (right on Pennsylvania, wrong on California). Where the need to appear informed is great and the delegate or alternate lacks access to reliable information he may become an inside-dopester and trade on rumor and invention. He specializes in secret conclaves between shadowy figures behind-the-scenes, where evidence for or against is not likely to be forthcoming. One such person took me aside and whispered in confidential tones that (and this was off the record) he had secret information from the highest authority that Johnson and Kennedy were going to debate before a closed meeting of the Texas and Massachusetts delegations. He called people in Ohio only to learn that they had heard the story on TV and were preparing to watch the debate. More than one delegate discovered by telephone or mail that the people back home seemed to have better information than he did.

Some delegates see themselves as spectators. One says that he is present because "the convention is so interesting. I like to see the way in which things work out." Another feels that "political appeal is like sex appeal; don't know why but it's fascinating." Or he may take a scholarly stance and explain that he is a student of the subject and watches it with a sort of clinical detachment. Here is at once an explanation for what he is doing or not doing, a defense against involvement, since he is "really an observer like you," and a rationale to account for his not being terribly important, since his function is to follow whatever happens rather than work for a particular outcome.

Delegates who regard the convention as a vacation site have a set line for dealing with the problem of their personal involvement. They go to the races or Hollywood or Disneyland and justify it by asserting that what anyone does is of little or no importance. In that case, why not get some fun out of the trip. Of course, they could find out the trivial stuff that everyone else does, but it wouldn't count so why bother? "Take it from a man who knows, sonny, they're all wasting their time. Hey, Joe, put five bucks on . . ."

Men who are active on behalf of a candidate present a contrasting picture. They know who they are for and what they are going to do to help their candidate. They seek to locate and convince potential waverers. If this fails, they may call on someone who is in a position to influence the governors. The activists may go around button-holing delegates and putting in a good word for their man. They are realistic about it for the most part. "Who you are speaks more loudly than what you say. If you're the governor, this speaks loudly; if you are just one delegate like . . . [me] this doesn't mean much but occasionally it helps."

Virtually all activists were for Kennedy but there were a few deviants who had a special claim to fame. They were for some other candidate and they let everybody know it. "I'm going to switch on the second ballot regardless of what the governor does and I'll tell him so." (When the roll was called at the party caucus asking for preferences on the first ballot, this delegate told everyone that he would switch on the second.) After prophesying in the presence of reporters that Ohio would desert Kennedy on the second or third ballot, another deviant went on to tell of the slick trick he had pulled on a local political opponent and how he had told off a government official.

Active delegates appear to feel more self-assured because they are doing something and they have no trouble in explaining to themselves or their friends the significance of their participation in the convention. But what of the other delegates? Their chief claim to fame is that they are official delegates, important people by virtue of being chosen for this honor. Yet this is not quite enough; they have to do something. Convention speeches do not help the delegate meet his needs. The speeches may add to the reputation of the man doing the talking, but they do not enhance the delegate. Everyone at home can listen to the speeches, probably under more comfortable conditions. And this helps to explain why many delegates make no attempt to listen to them. The demonstrations, on the other hand, provide an opportunity for active participation ("did you see me on TV?") in a colorful event which the delegate can recount at home. The marching and the shouting not only serve to indicate support for a candidate but also may serve the function of reducing anxiety by giving the ordinary delegate a role to play.

Political advantage may be taken of the delegate's need to feel important. The task of a leader like Governor DiSalle is to convince delegates to attach their prestige to that of the state party, to assure them that a more significant role for the state enhances their individual importance. Indeed, the essence of the governor's remarks at party caucuses was that for the first time in many a year Ohio had a great role to play in determining the presidential candidate, and that this chance must not be impaired by a lack of unity which would make all their efforts worthless. In his appearance at the caucus, Ted Kennedy had a word along this line for everyone. On behalf of his brother, he wished to thank every individual delegate for the invaluable contribution they had made to John's success. John Kennedy was where he was because of Ohio and he would always remember, yes he would always remember, even after his election, that Ohio came in when he needed support the most.

In view of the preceding comments, the function which personal attentions like handshakes by leading candidates and pictures taken with prominent persons perform for delegates should be evident. Richard Nixon's practice of having a separate photograph taken of himself with every delegate, however exhausting and perfunctory this may appear, demonstrates a real appreciation of what this gesture means to many delegates.

The Delegate's Perceptions of the Convention

Most delegates share a few major political goals. They want to choose a man who can win the election, they want to get a claim on him (perhaps through their state party), they want to advantage their state party or faction, they want to keep the national party together if they can do so without too great a sacrifice of policy preferences. The information required to meet these goals—what the electorate will do, what the convention will do, what the effects on local candidates will be, what other party groups will accept—is never fully available to anyone, certainly not to the ordinary delegate. A great premium is thereby placed on the manipulation of information, for if a sufficient number of delegates and their leaders believe that a certain candidate is likely to win they may act on their conception of reality and bring about a self-fulfilling prophecy as others, observing their behavior, seek to get on the bandwagon. In a closely contested convention, the candidate who makes the picture of events favorable to the one shared by most of the delegates is likely to win. This is particularly the case in convention decision-making choices which must be made rapidly, under conditions of uncertainty, without an opportunity to test one's notion of reality against the outcome of events in time to change one's course of action. Even in the 1960 Democratic convention, where the nutcracker of opinion formed by all the public media of information insisted that Kennedy was going to win, the delegates evidenced considerable variations in perception. We may profitably pay attention to the process of perception even though, in this case, the convention did not go a sufficient number of ballots for us to observe the full political consequences of shifts in the delegate's perceptions of reality.

Will Jack Win?

The first great question, of course, was whether Kennedy would win the nomination. (In a convention without a strong front-runner, the question would be "who will win?") The range of responses may be graded in order of the degree of certainty. "It was all over after West Virginia. Kennedy had it sewed up before we came." "It's Kennedy before the end of the first ballot." "New Jersey will switch to Kennedy at the end of the first ballot. Meyner isn't strong enough to hold the delegation. Then Jack will win." Most predicted Kennedy would win on the second ballot; a few on the third. A sizable minority believed that if Kennedy did not make it on the first or second ballot at the latest, he was through. These were the delegates who speculated about where the delegation might go if Kennedy did not make it. (Johnson appeared to have the most support, followed by Symington and then Stevenson.) A few had serious doubts about Kennedy's ability to win the nomination because the other candidates would gang up against him, because of his religion or youth, because the old pro Harry Truman did not want him, or for some other definable reason. But most of the doubters just felt that the convention was so unpredictable (at least for them) that you just could not know. "With 4,000 delegates around anything can happen," was a typical comment. The number of delegates certain that John Kennedy would win increased after Ted Kennedy informed them that Pennsylvania would give most of its votes to his brother and this was confirmed later that day. The number of doubters increased after the Stevenson demonstration occurred and after stories about how Kennedy was slipping began to circulate. If perceptions were this far apart when so many signs pointed to Kennedy, one can imagine what the case would be when no one candidate had emerged as the overwhelming favorite.

A Religious War?

Yet most delegates clearly had some idea that Kennedy was going to win and the question of who was expected to win did not occasion as much comment as it might have at other conventions. Often, a delegate would brush right past this question and ask what I thought Kennedy's chances were in the election or add that he wished Kennedy's chances in the election were as good as those for the nomination. This was the way the delegates had of bringing up what was troubling them most—the Catholic issue and its effect upon Kennedy's electoral chances. There was more comment on this than anything else although I never introduced the subject. Religion, for the delegates, was an especially painful topic because the very mention of it violated deeply held norms of what was proper behavior in public life. Religious conflict was un-American, disgraceful, violated the Constitution, against our way of life, and "I shouldn't even be talking about it." Having brought up the subject himself, a Negro delegate flared up to say, "don't you tell me discussion of religion is not right; segregation isn't right either but it's a fact of life."

Before they arrived at the convention the delegates began to collect personal impressions on which to base an opinion on the impact of the religious factor. "I talked to a trainman . . . he was a Mason and he said that he had spoken to a hundred Masons in the past few days and none of them would vote for Kennedy because in the past the Pope had said some nasty things about the Masons." An automobile trip brought a delegate in touch with members of the Holiness sects. These fundamentalists would not vote for Kennedy, he was sorry to say, but there was one ray of light. A Jehovah's Witness had told him that he would vote for Kennedy since it seemed to be God's will that America have a Catholic President.

The memory of the Al Smith campaign in 1928—"that was not so pretty"—was strongly imprinted in the minds of many older delegates who feared "a religious war." "The Kennedy people say that Smith was 25 years ago but I don't know," one perplexed delegate said. "People are different now," said a delegate. "I think their children have inherited that disease," another replied. His apprehension was increased when, like other Ohio delegates, he saw anti-Catholic signs and demonstrations at the Biltmore Hotel where the theme was that America must not be ruled from Moscow or Rome.

A very few delegates were of the opinion that Kennedy was using the religious issue for his own benefit. One delegate had the sneaking suspicion that the Kennedy people put up [anti-Catholic] signs to gain sympathy. Another had a Catholic friend in Texas who asserted that the Church had tried to pressure him into supporting Kennedy. Without doubt, the religious issue brought some delegates to a more vigorous defense of Kennedy than might otherwise have been the case, as they demanded, "it's time we practiced what we preach [about religious freedom]." Many questions by the interviewer about the approach used by the Johnson staff men who visited the Ohio delegation revealed that none of them tried the traditional tactic of claiming that Kennedy could not win. Why not? "That," in the words of a Johnson man, "would have been interpreted to mean a reference to the religious issue."

An antidote to scattered attacks on the influence of Kennedy's religion was humor. "I'm more afraid of the Republicans than I am of the Pope," retorted one Protestant delegate. Upon being informed that if Kennedy became President "the Pope would move into the White House and bring his wife and children too," a delegate gleefully reported, "that's how much they know about it." Humor was the weapon of Catholic delegates who declared that the Pope would certainly not enter the White House until Kennedy had cleaned it up.

Who's Making All That Noise?

Of lesser concern but nevertheless of considerable interest to the delegates was the Stevenson demonstration on the second day of the convention. To be sure, those who look upon the convention as a vacation ground had no reaction because they were not there. The small group actively working for Kennedy were totally unimpressed. "It was all in the galleries as far as I could see." "They don't vote in the galleries." "Who is there to impress? The people demonstrating outside the convention hall were all from California." "I saw a fellow who said he was a Texan for Stevenson but he never saw Texas." The whole thing was "bought and paid for" or it was "a lot of hullaballo" presumably signifying nothing. Any candidate would have gotten the same, an activist asserted, and pointed out that the loser always had to make more noise as evidenced by the southern shout on the platform vote. There are always a few delegates who claim to know how it was all done. "I stood by [Senator Mike Monroney] while he directed it." Or, the "tickets were given to the Stevenson people the day before yesterday." Delegates who looked on the convention largely as spectators, particularly those who had not been to three or four conventions, were visibly impressed. "Remarkable, never saw anything like it." "It was disturbing—something in it— must have been spontaneous." They felt that Kennedy was definitely weaker now but since they were pledged to him the only speculation concerned what might happen on the second ballot.

Perhaps the most revealing comment came when a woman delegate, at a convention for the first time, revealed that she had applauded loud and long for Stevenson. She admired him and he had led the party for two elections. "But," she said, embarrassed, "I didn't know anyone would think I was actually going to vote for him."

What the Governor Wants

At the first Ohio caucus on Monday morning, Governor Di- Salle sought to head off any possible defections from Kennedy. Beginning with a gesture toward the delegate's sense of self- importance—no commitments would be made on behalf of the delegation until it took action; it would be kept informed—the governor reminded them that they were pledged to Kennedy. Anyone with contrary ideas had an opportunity to file a separate slate. A moral commitment was all that was asked for but there was nothing more important in politics than the man who gives his word and keeps it. There was no way, continued the governor, of getting a man to keep his commitment. All the leadership asked was that the delegate tell them what he was going to do and give his reasons in caucus. Ending with a magnanimous gesture, the governor declared that he could not remember who had voted for whom at the last convention, but it was important that the delegation stay together.

There was remarkably widespread agreement among the delegates on the governor's position. He was thought to want a cabinet post in Washington. Why? "Well, we know he does." "DiSalle likes it in Washington." "He has complained about the low salary he gets as governor." In order to accomplish this purpose, he had to deliver the delegation to Kennedy. And this would also serve to solidify his position as head of the state party.

Defections?

With possibly one or two defections, it was assumed that all of Ohio would go for Kennedy on the first ballot. But after that, there was much less certainty. The range of responses to a question about defection on the second ballot went from none to twenty; few felt able to venture a prediction on the third ballot, an eventuality which appeared too remote to contemplate. The hard-core Kennedy supporters would stick with him, most delegates thought, and the governor would sway party officials and state employees. Beyond that, no comment.

Yet, strangely enough, many delegates were convinced they could predict something about how DiSalle would behave if Kennedy dropped out. At all costs, he would try to keep the delegation united under him. If he could not persuade all, as was likely, he would "try to figure out which way the wind was blowing" and move in a direction where the preponderance of delegates would support him because he was, in fact, following them.

The immediate problem was the first ballot and here Representative Wayne Hays of Ohio drew much comment by his well-publicized wavering in the direction of Lyndon Johnson. Reactions varied with the type of delegate. Spectators concentrated on the moral problem as the following conversation reveals: "Are we pledged?" "Morally." "He has none, the way he was talking last night." "Hell, this is a free country." "He's an exhibitionist." Said an inside dopester, "he's been promised something," hinting that he knew what but was unwilling to say. The groups of delegates who worked in Congress or had some previous experience there, however, were quite explicit in offering an explanation. "Last night I heard that Speaker Rayburn said, "I'm going to be speaker for ten years and I have an awfully long memory." Another delegate responded, "sure, Rayburn and Johnson have leverage over congressmen. Of course, they can't take you off committees once you are on." And a third delegate in that circle added, "but the speaker can make it tough." And in a manner to give notice that he was speaking only in a semi-serious way, the delegate said that "Hays might find it tougher to go overseas on those jaunts and live high on those counterpart funds." The activists were blunt: "He better watch out." Their conclusion, however, was that Hays would talk big but that he would have to honor his commitment to Kennedy on the first ballot in order to avoid stirring up resentment within his home district. Amidst muttering about freedom on the second ballot, Ohio voted solidly for Kennedy on the first and there were no more.

No Strife, No Excitement

Aside from a few strong words about possible defectors, there was little serious dispute in the delegation. With both the DiSalle and Miller slates committed to Kennedy, there was no open disagreement among them except, perhaps, in vying for their candidate's favor.* When the Miller faction caucused on the opening day, they decided that since they were outnumbered six to one, they would attend the regular state meetings and create no difficulties. While they were all Kennedy supporters, Miller told his group, they should show courtesy to other candidates and listen to them respectfully.

Courtesy appeared to be the watchword and there was little invidious comparison of the candidates within the delegation. The delegates would say, "we have four good men and there's nothing wrong with any of them." Enthusiasts for Kennedy were by no means as numerous as his supporters and there was not too much stress on his attributes. Mention was made of Kennedy's war record, his courage, and, above all, his will to win. But there was also a defensive attitude with praise negatively

---

*The one jarring note came on a move to replace the aging Albert O. Horstman as national committeeman because he had done little with the job in the past four years. Governor DiSalle was quoted in the press as saying that "Horstman worked and contributed heavily when there wasn't any real Democratic Party in Ohio. Now he wants another term and I think he should have it."

stated. "He's smart even if he didn't write that book himself."
"Any religion a man has is a good thing." "People don't realize
that in the 1920's men had to work before finishing school, began
their careers in their thirties. Today they finish in their twenties,
and get a lot of experience by the time they're thirty."

Lyndon Johnson's "ability to get men to work together"
counted heavily with his partisans, while he was not quite
liberal enough for others or at least they thought this sentiment
would block his nomination. Most of the Negro delegates, especially those with congressional contacts, were favorably inclined toward Johnson although not actively. "I know him. He's
a practical southerner. He knows that things can't go on the
way they are." Symington had some support but excited virtually
no interest except as a vice presidential nominee. There was
even less support for Stevenson who was admired in a general
sort of way and then disqualified. "He's a good brain, but the
pros are against him because he lost twice." "A smart man, but
he's got the taint of an appeaser on him." One delegate had a
special theory about why Stevenson was doomed to defeat.
"You gotta be married to succeed today . . . a lot of women
voting . . . everyone knows about Stevenson's divorce. Knew a
single fellow who ran for office and, oh, the stories they told
about him. He lost."

The platform occasioned virtually no comment whatsoever
from anyone. Negroes noted with satisfaction that it met their
desires and that was all. A question about the platform did serve
to embarrass some delegates, and one replied that he did not
know but, in any case, the delegation was bound by the unit
rule and would follow the governor. Of course, there was no
unit rule, but if one could believe that there were, and that the
decision belonged to someone else, then one need not feel guilty
about an excusable lack of knowledge concerning the platform.

The relative lack of controversy within the delegation, as well
as the dullness of the first two days' proceedings, were a source
of disappointment to some delegates. After this came up spontaneously a few times, I began asking delegates if they felt this
was so and why. The Kennedy activists rejected the question as
unimportant, saying that "the convention will be fine with me
so long as it comes out all right." Some delegates, however, tried
to find a reason for it. "This one's not as lively as the previous
conventions I've been to. At previous conventions many states

had candidates they were really for. Not now. Many people who will vote for Kennedy are not really for him. It is just that other candidates all have something wrong."

Missionaries

There was one dedicated band of men who manifested unflagging interest in the affairs of the Ohio delegates—the candidates' staff members assigned to the delegation. They haunted the hotel rooms and the lobby, zealous in the service of their man. Taking no chances, the Kennedy staff was there radiating confidence in all directions. "Let's get it over on the first ballot. Why waste time. Let's begin work on the election. Jack's over the top now." Listening to him, a delegate suggested that it "might be better for the party if it [the balloting] went further; no charges of rigging, then." But he made no impression. On Wednesday morning, with more talk of defection than usual, a Kennedy staff men arrived breathless announcing, "I'm worried about a couple of defections."

At the Monday caucus, a wealthy businessman representing Lyndon Johnson listened to Ted Kennedy say that brother Jack was beyond the necessary 760 mark. "The way he talks, it's all over," he muttered. Undaunted, he proceeded to demonstrate to the delegates surrounding his seat why Johnson would be a certain winner in the election. He would win all the southern and border states and then he'd need only 61 more electoral votes. Furthermore, Johnson would win the nomination by switches on the third ballots, since Kennedy would fall short on the first and no one else had enough strength. On Tuesday several delegates reported visits from Johnson men in their hotel rooms. Johnson was, it appeared, the most mature, best qualified, most harmonious candidate, and certain of victory, too. Hope still burned bright on Wednesday as the Johnson representatives spread the word that Maryland was wavering (it was bound by primary law). There would be plenty of moves toward Johnson on the second ballot, they assured their listeners, but they did not expect any on the first in view of Ohio's previous commitment to Kennedy.

A representative from Symington's headquarters was in evidence, but he followed his candidate's lead by playing his hand in a low key. His pitch was: "Let the people vote. We don't want six or seven politicians to decide." Naturally, Ohio delegates were pledged to Kennedy on the first and he respected that. But on the second there would be defections. In fact, he wanted to give everyone a chance, Johnson and Stevenson, too, so that there would be an open convention.

Adlai's man did not show up until early Wednesday morning, tapped me on the shoulder and inquired, "do you know who's supporting Stevenson here?" Discovering that I was not a delegate and the nearby representative of the city police vice squad (sent to watch for pick-pockets and prostitutes) could not help him either, he found some delegates. An hour later he was full of confidence and figures: 14 for Stevenson on the second, plus 23 more his side had to speak to. "The trouble with Stevenson," one of his small group of Ohio supporters later said, "was that he started too late."

A Final Word

Wednesday afternoon saw the second Ohio caucus addressed by prominent speakers. Lyndon Johnson stated that he came, not to convert but to give the delegates a chance to size up another candidate. He stressed the success of Democratic Congresses, his liberalism, and his mature judgment as "a trustee for you and your children." A delegate in the crowd commented, "effective, but no matter what happens he can't be nominated." Stuart Symington seemed apologetic about talking so much on defense —but it was his committee—and dared anyone to have a better voting record than his. Mike Monroney spoke for Stevenson stressing the gravity of the world situation, the need to find a man of sufficient stature to handle it, and the delights of a Stevenson-Kennedy ticket.

Chairman Coleman popped up to say that he was sorry there were not sufficient tickets to go around and that some alternates were "seated in the peanut gallery." If the alternates would take badges labeled "demonstrators," that might get them on the floor. If that did not work the same strategem tried the day before would be used—a shuttle system for badges with page boys as messengers.

Governor DiSalle appeared for his final word before the voting. All the candidates had been heard and there was not one who would not make a great leader. For the first time in 40 years Ohio was trying to build a cohesive party. Now, the delegates were being bombarded with telegrams. But they must adopt a correct measure and compare the number of telegrams with the number who voted for them in the primary. There was no reason why Ohio should not present a large undivided vote on the first ballot, and for the first time in many years become a force in the nation. Kennedy would be the nominee and he would know that we were there first with the most.

Had there been a series of ballots during which several of the favorites dropped out, it is possible that delegates in search of a candidate might have been swayed by the personal appearances and the arguments of the staff men. As it was, in no case did I observe these speeches change a vote or an intended vote looking toward a possible second ballot. Rather, those who were positively in favor of a particular candidate were reinforced in their opinions and those without strong feelings were unmoved. The Kennedy activists were impatient. "Oh, what's the use of more talk. Jack's got the vote."

By and large, the delegates were happy with Kennedy's nomination. They could all live with it. Most of them were for him in preference to others even if they did have some uneasy feelings. Few had any strong feelings against him. There had been some excitement at last—the demonstrations—and there was visible relief that the big decision had been made.

Who'll Be Vice President?

Speculation about the vice presidency ran wild. Not that the delegates thought they would have a choice; Kennedy admittedly had the right to choose the man if he wanted to. But it was fun speculating about who Kennedy would pick, a game fraught with no dangers, in which all could participate on an equal basis of ignorance. Virtually everyone thought Symington was the logical man. His record was good on defense, labor, civil rights, and farm legislation. He came from a border state, was Protestant, and he had offended no one. Moreover, he had Governor DiSalle's support. Johnson was counted out, not because of his attacks on Kennedy which everyone accepted as part of the political game, but because the congressional specialists kept insisting that he would be a "damn fool" to give up the powerful job of Senator majority leader. (I mention, only in passing, the delegate who thought DiSalle would be the vice presidential candidate, but added "I don't know if he'll accept it.") The Johnson nomination surprised everyone but no one was in a disposition to argue much, considering it Kennedy's prerogative. Placating the south made some sense, a Negro delegate said. "You got to give something to get something."

Satisfaction

Looking back at their convention experiences, most of the delegates were pleased. Their surroundings seemed more familiar, partly because they knew their way around a little better and partly because they had drifted into some acquaintanceships. Kennedy's active supporters had the satisfaction of seeing their man nominated. Party leaders and officials had the satisfaction of seeing the state delegation emerge unified. A county chairman was delighted. "Ohio is in very good shape, came out for Kennedy first. This means federal patronage and it will help local patronage, too. You know, there are governors and governors. Not much patronage under Lausche. People have to decide whether they want a two-party system. Now, at least, we have a state party." Those who had come to watch the workings of politics might have preferred to see one more ballot but they felt they had learned a lot and had observed the fascinating Kennedy apparatus at work. The men with the real, the true inside story would wow the folks back home with an account of what really happened. Everyone enjoyed the demonstrations.

There was noticeably more banter: "Watch out, here comes a trend." "How about lunch?" "It's about time, I've been living on rumors all week." "How come Kennedy won?" "You can't stop something with nothing." "Hear about the policeman who found a dead horse on Figueroa Street? He moved it to Flower Street because he couldn't spell Figueroa." On that note, the delegation left its hotels and went back to Ohio.

Conclusion

The Ohio delegation did not come close to running the gamut of convention experiences. The continual splits, indecisions, waverings, pressures, and hence the bitterness, recrimination, and even tears of the California delegation were not felt by Ohio. Had the Ohio delegation been unpledged, divided, without effective leadership, we should have been able to observe more closely the impact of events upon the delegates and the significance of their responses for decision-making. Had the convention gone several more ballots, the ways in which the delegates acquire different perceptions could have been clarified as well as the consequences of their views of reality upon the eventual nomination. There is no reason to blink at the facts: one cannot study decision-making at a convention when the decision has been determined before the delegation arrived.

Yet the task of the political scientist is not solely to explain how and why decisions get made. His task is also to identify and analyze other phenomena—like perception and adjustment—which impinge on the process of decision. There can be little question that, in this connection, the varying perceptions of the delegates and their different ways of adjusting to the convention environment are important. In some respects, therefore, the fact that few major decisions were made at the convention was an advantage. Undistracted by the added excitement of a closely fought convention, we have had an opportunity to examine underlying factors which (though operative at all conventions) might otherwise have been obscured.

11. Hoosier Republicans in Chicago

"Why should I pay $500 for my seat as a delegate and incur a total expense of probably $1200 only to come and have somebody tell me what to do? —Overheard in the Indiana delegation.

DAVID R. DERGE
Indiana University

Some observers have serious doubts about whether a four or five-day, television-oriented national convention can be a deliberative decision-making body. The modern convention, with well over a thousand voting delegates, is too large to be deliberative in the sense that a legislative body is meant to be. Seventy-two to ninety-six hours seem hardly adequate to assure the identification of a reasonable number of alternatives, to fully consider these alternatives and their expected consequences, to make a free choice among the alternatives, and to set up a communications system to support the foregoing activities.

With the advantages of telecommunications and rapid travel which were not available in prior times when conventions may have provided the only reasonable approximation to party deliberation, the necessary elements of deliberation have been decentralized and extended over a longer period of time, producing party decisions with more popular control and sober judgment than the convention can hope to provide. In this sense the "open" convention marked by uncertainty, confusion, and hasty decisions is pathological rather than normal. It manifests a breakdown or stalemate in the longer and less spectacular process of reaching consensus within the party through decentralized deliberation and must offer little comfort to those critics who value responsibility within the party and the party's decision-making apparatus.

This does not mean that the modern national convention is without function. It serves important political needs. The convention formalizes and legitimizes for the American public the decisions reached through the longer process. It girds the party psychologically for the struggles of the campaign, and provides the symbols of unity for disparate party groups. It focuses American political life on the election of a President. It gratifies loyal party workers who class a national convention with homecomings, weddings, funerals, and other gala events. The Republican convention of 1960 performed these functions handsomely. But it was not a deliberative body.

The Chicago Story

The Indiana delegation did not need to transport itself to Chicago to make decisions. The significant decisions either had been made before the convention started, or were made by others before the delegation had much chance to become involved. The delegation was committed to the nomination of Richard M. Nixon by a presidential primary and by personal preference, and this was known to all. Further, the delegation was committed to Nixon to the extent that it would accept his designee for the vice presidential nomination even if he should be Henry Cabot Lodge. Finally, the delegation issued a statement about the forthcoming platform after its sole pre-convention meeting in July. At this time the delegation went on record for a conservative platform which would not attempt to out-promise the Democrats, and one which would preserve the integrity of the states against what delegates viewed as a threat of federal encroachment. Most delegates could examine the final draft of the platform only a short time before they were asked to approve it by voice vote on the convention floor.

This is not to say that the Indiana delegation found all of these key decisions pleasing. Many in the delegation had hoped for a midwestern vice presidential nominee and had little enthusiasm for Lodge. They reasoned that a midwesterner would strengthen state and national tickets in what Hoosiers have always considered the most important section of the country—the midwest and more specifically, Indiana. The conservative base of Indiana Republicans did not mix well with some features of the platform thought to be leaning too far to the left. Grumbling about the platform was heard in Indiana ranks throughout the convention. Ex-Senator William Jenner came close to expressing the sentiment of the delegation when he commented in caucus that "the Republican party is just a little bit pregnant with New Dealism, and you ladies know you can't be just a little bit pregnant."

However, all of the talk within the delegation about a midwestern vice presidential nominee and a conservative platform took place against the background of a strong and irrevocable commitment to Nixon. This commitment embraced, directly or indirectly, all convention decisions and emasculated Indiana's role as it did that of most other states.

The Indiana delegation drifted into a something less than festive convention city on Sunday and Monday. The governor firmly presided over formal caucuses on Monday, Tuesday, and Wednesday. While some delegates may have thought that they were in Chicago to settle important questions, the atmosphere of the caucuses was not that of a deliberative body debating alternatives and reaching meaningful decisions. The first of the two open caucuses was called to hear a report from Indiana's representatives on the platform committee. Since the committee was still in session, and no one claimed to have seen a copy of the platform, there was only general discussion and no decision. The delegation did not take a decision on the vice presidential nomination because Nixon had not revealed his preference.

The Tuesday caucus went in much the same way. After some general discussion about the platform, the governor stated that "the platform is to be one on which the presidential candidate can wage his campaign," committing the delegation to whatever the platform committee reported. The delegation agreed to postpone until Wednesday further discussion of vice presidential candidates since Nixon had still not revealed his preference.

The Wednesday caucus was closed and each delegate and alternate was given the opportunity to express his views on the vice presidential nomination. The purpose of the caucus was twofold: first, to allow the delegation to let off steam on an issue which had been causing some discomfort, and had left some delegates with a frustrated and powerless feeling; second, to determine what the delegation would do in the unlikely event of an "open" nomination, which few really thought would happen. Nearly everyone spoke out. Discontent was expressed over the impending nomination of Lodge, with various delegates urging support for Morton, Judd, Goldwater and others. This session produced the wistful statement that should the nomination be thrown open the Indiana delegation would conduct "lightning" caucuses on the floor of the convention to determine where its 32 votes would go. When asked what would happen if Nixon picked his running-mate, the governor publicly stated that "when the decision is made Indiana will accept it whatever it is. Indiana has been in Nixon's corner for a long time and will continue to be."

Thus, the delegation as a group made no meaningful decisions during its stay in Chicago. The governor was active during the convention in support of a conservative platform and a midwestern vice presidential nominee. He attended governors' meetings, talked with Nixon and his advisers, and made public statements. But it seemed to observers that all of his efforts had the ubiquitous qualification that he, and the delegation, would accept Nixon's decisions and would support them on the floor of the convention. They did just that.

One Hoosier wryly appraised the delegation's deliberative and decision-making activities as follows: "Where did you go? Out. What did you do? Nothing." But the Indiana delegation did more than fret about the inexorable forces at work in the convention. Much as religious orders retreat to a different environment to refurbish the soul, the Indiana Republicans underwent a heartening reintegration in Chicago. It was not a notably optimistic group of politicians in the first days of the convention, but a spirit of optimism, conviction, and unity developed before the day of adjournment.

The business of state politics went on unabated by the convention. While Indiana Republicans became sincerely enthused about a national victory in November, they were keenly aware that this happy event would be a Pyrrhic victory if political fortunes within Indiana failed. There are few Hoosiers with political ambitions extending beyond the state boundaries and to most political survival is measured in terms of maintaining control in Indiana. The party loyal threw themselves into a state party function. Numerous candidates for state executive offices and the Congress played no important role in delegation activities, but got in five good days of campaigning. More than five hundred Hoosiers came to visit with one another and attend convention sessions. The Indiana hospitality room at the Palmer House was well supplied with county chairmen, women's clubs, and candidates running for public office back home. These people generally discussed national nominees and platform in terms of what effect they would have on state and local Republican tickets. Political fence-mending kits were in evidence. Republicans were seen exchanging generous measures of cordiality which might have been in shorter supply had the encounters taken place back in Bippus, or Santa Claus, or Russiaville. This cannot be discounted in a state noted for its intra-party factional battles.

Most of the convention's formal business and social activities seemed calculated to truss up the sagging elements in the party and to send away uplifted and inspired delegates. Conservatives went away thinking that they had served warning on the prodigal factions of their party and had laid the groundwork for a renascence in coming years. Liberals went away feeling that the party is still in good hands. Practically everyone left with the conviction that Republicans had a good chance of staying in the White House. Such convention functions might be ridiculed by solemn editorial writers, but they were good for the party, and for Indiana Republicans.

Characteristics of the Indiana Delegation

Assuming that conventions may sometimes be called upon to deliberate and make decisions, do delegates seem to be equipped by background and experience to perform these functions? A short analysis of the Indiana delegations to the 1960 conventions may provide some evidence on this question.*

---

*Data on which statistics in this section and other parts of the paper are based were gathered on survey forms sent to delegates of both parties. The sample size for the Republicans is 57 per cent, and for the Democrats 65 per cent. Because of these sample sizes, the conclusions should be treated as tentative.

TABLE I

OCCUPATIONS OF CONVENTION DELEGATES

	Republicans Per cent	Democrats Per cent	Experienced labor force, Indiana 1950 Per cent
Professional	19	48	7
Manager, Official, Proprietor	42	24	8
Farmer and farm manager	6	5	9
All other occupations	33	23	76
Total	100	100	100

As measured by occupation both delegations were much alike —biased toward high socio-economic status. As indicated in Table I, 61 per cent of the Republicans were professionals, managers, officials or proprietors, while 72 per cent of the Democrats fell into these high status occupations. Entrepreneurial occupations were more heavily represented among Republicans; the professions among Democrats. There was more upward social mobility in evidence among the Democratic delegates. One fourth of the fathers of Democrats were professionals, managers, proprietors or officials in contrast to about one-half of the fathers of Republicans. One-fifth of the Democrats came from working class families but this was the case for only about one-twentieth of the Republicans.

High status is also reflected in the educational backgrounds of the delegates. College attendance was reported by 85 per cent of the Republicans and 78 per cent of the Democrats. One-third of the Republicans and one-half of the Democrats held advanced or professional degrees. In a state where the median number of school years completed is 9.8, the delegates clearly came from the highly educated sector of the population.

Many delegates had extensive political experience in the management of party affairs, competition for public office, or both. In the Democratic delegation, 60 per cent had run for public office, 37 per cent successfully. Only 35 per cent of the Republicans had been candidates and 24 per cent had held office. Most of the running for office in both groups had been on the local and county level. Salaried political appointments to public office had been held by 21 per cent of the Republicans and 45 per cent of the Democrats. Thus, the Democratic group included more competitors for, and holders of, public office than the Republican group.*

The skeleton of Indiana's party system is the party committee structure which manages most of the political activities in the state. Many of the delegates to both conventions had occupied key positions in this structure. One-fourth of the Democrats and one-fifth of the Republicans had served at least one term on the highest party council, the state central committee. Delegates who had served at least one term on a county committee made up 67 per cent of the Democratic delegation and 56 per cent of the Republican delegation.**

A sharp contrast develops between the two delegations when party involvement is defined in terms of performance for the party during campaigns and the undertaking of the necessary chores of winning elections.

TABLE II
WHICH ACTIVITIES HAVE YOU PERFORMED FOR YOUR PARTY

	Republicans Per cent	Democrats Per cent
Managed Campaigns	35	73
Gave Speeches	35	85
Contacted Voters	71	90
Distributed Literature	50	73
Other	47	45

As Table II indicates, more than twice as many Democrats undertook management of campaigns and speech-making, and Democrats have a significant edge in routine work of contacting voters and distributing literature. Most of the "other" activities reported by Republicans related to the raising and soliciting of funds. The "other" activities reported by Democrats ranged widely but did not concentrate on fund raising. To the extent that the two delegations can be compared on political activities,

---

*A significant minority in both delegations came from a family background of high political involvement. Parents of 45 per cent of the Democrats and 40 per cent of the Republicans had held either an elective public office, a party office, or both.

**This is in interesting contrast to another group of Indiana politicians, the members of the General Assembly. Only 29 per cent of the 1959 General Assembly had ever served on a party committee, 41 per cent on the state central committee. There is reason to believe that the party managers and office-seekers come from two different groups within the state, and that the overlap between the two is not great. Some delegates present interesting exceptions to this rule.

it appears that the Democrats were more heavily involved in both party management and other facets of party work.

All Democrats and 85 per cent of the Republicans had attended at least one state party convention, which in Indiana nominates candidates for state executive offices and the United States Senate, and writes the state party platform. About four out of ten in both delegations had been to at least one other national convention as delegate or alternate, and several more had attended as spectators. Thus, the mysteries of political conventions were not new to either group and many members of both delegations went to the 1960 conventions with an extensive background in the lore and operation of nominating politics.

In summary, Indiana provided the two national conventions with more than ordinarily seasoned politicians. Many were experienced in the management of party affairs and had themselves run for public office. On the whole they were highly educated and were drawn from high socio-economic strata. These groups could hardly be called cross-sections of the citizenry. On the contrary, one might say that they had been skimmed off the top. Judged by personal background and political experience, the delegates to both conventions appear to be fully capable of any decision-making required of them. This is a tribute to Indiana's selection process which is firmly under party control. It seems doubtful whether any other method of selection would have produced a more comely group of politicians.

Why Delegates Go To Conventions

What causes an individual to undergo the considerable expense and lost time resulting from a national convention?* Indiana Republican and Democratic delegates were asked to explain why they chose to attend the 1960 convention and while each answer was different the following general classification can be made.

---

*Indiana Republicans were assessed $500 by the party for a delegate's position, and $300 for an alternate's position. Furthermore, all delegates and alternates were required to meet all convention expenses without party assistance.

TABLE III

WHAT LED YOU TO SEEK TO BE A DELEGATE OR ALTERNATE TO THE
1960 NATIONAL CONVENTION?

	Republicans Per cent	Democrats Per cent
General interest in politics and desire to participate in as many phases as possible	35	45
Desire to have a part in nomination of party's candidates and/or writing of the platform	33	23
Desire to further the interests of a particular candidate designated by the respondent	9	18
Honor and recognition which derives from attending convention	6	5
All other responses	17	9
Total	100	100

Findings in Table III suggest that less than half of the respondents in both parties *specified* that they went to the conventions with the hope of playing a decisive part in the nomination of a particular candidate or, in general, to be instrumental in the convention's decisions. It seems reasonable to presume that more than half of both delegations would have made the trip even if they had the foreknowledge that the convention's important decisions would be made without benefit of consultation with delegates. Most of these people, in the words of one delegate, "have been hooked by the political habit." The writer is inclined to believe that less than half, and possibly only a fraction, of the Republican delegates expected that they might make a significant impact on decisions. If this is correct, most Republican delegates were not disappointed to discover that their job was to legitimize decisions made by others.

Sources of Information for the Delegation

Again assuming that conventions may be called upon to deliberate and make decisions, it is appropriate to examine the sources of information on which delegates might base their actions. Republican and Democratic delegates were asked to rank, from most useful to least useful, their sources of information about trends and developments in the nomination of candidates and the writing of the platform. The following pattern emerges from the responses.

TABLE IV

RANKS AND MEAN SCORES OF INFORMATION SOURCES*

	Rank		Mean Score	
	Republicans	Democrats	Republicans	Democrats
Leaders of the Indiana Delegation	1	1	5.1	4.8
Caucuses of the Indiana Delegation	2	4	4.7	3.5
Other members of the Indiana Delegation	3	3	3.6	3.8
Television, newspapers, radio	4	2	3.3	4.2
Delegates from other states	5	5	2.5	3.2
Other sources	6	6	1.7	2.4

*Based on interval scale score obtained by assigning weight of 6 to source the respondent counted most useful, 5 to next most useful, and so on.

Table IV indicates that the delegation leadership was the most useful source of information for both Republicans and Democrats, but that Republicans seem to have relied more heavily on this source. Caucuses of the Republicans were relatively more useful than those of the Democrats. Both groups reported that contacts with delegates from other states were among the least useful sources of information, but Democrats rated these relationships higher than Republicans did.

Conversations with Republican delegates revealed that few of them had established contacts outside their own delegation. Out-of-state contacts which did occur were mainly on the leadership level and information about the activities and plans of other delegates, sparse as it was, came to the rank and file through the leaders. When Republican delegates and alternates are considered separately some variations appear. Alternates found caucuses slightly more useful than delegation leaders as sources of information, and they relied more heavily on mass media.

About one-sixth of the Democrats mentioned candidates, or headquarters of candidates, as important sources of information, while none of the Republicans counted these as important. This difference no doubt reflects the greater sense of competition in Los Angeles and the use of channels of communications by candidates to further their interests.

The mass media played a significant role in informing delegates about convention developments. Two-fifths of the Democrats and one-fifth of the Republicans stated that television, newspapers and radio comprised their most useful source of information. It should be noted that comments on mass media tended to be extreme, ranging from "clearly the most useful source" to "completely undependable and distorted."

No systematic effort was made to determine how much, in absolute terms, the Republican delegates knew about what was going on in the convention. However, subjective impressions gained from talking with Republicans and spending two sessions on the convention floor led the writer to conclude that the average delegate knew little more about the unfolding of events than the alert television viewer and newspaper reader.

These findings on sources of information and impressions about the average delegate's understanding of convention activities are not surprising. Consider the problems of establishing a system of communications for the brief period of four or five days to serve 1300 people scattered over several square miles in temporary quarters. A great majority of these people do not know one another. There may be competition or blockage at the input points of the system as different sources of information attempt to convey different impressions or withhold necessary data. Add to this the inclination of those who could use the information to cut themselves off by spending long hours listening to speeches and being otherwise inaccessible.

It probably makes little difference that an elaborate communications system designed to inform all delegates about all things did not exist in Chicago. The primary tasks of the convention were to register decisions already made about the nominees, and to approve a platform which by its own nature and the structure of the convention could not be examined and debated in full. A sophisticated communications system would have been superfluous.

Communications Patterns within the Delegation

One might hypothesize that members of a deliberative decision making body would ordinarily communicate among themselves. We have already seen that there was little useful inter-delegation contact. We now turn to communications within the delegation. Republicans and Democrats were asked to report the relative amount of discussion they had with each of their fellow delegates concerning the nomination of candidates and platform provisions. The three categories of response were "frequently," "occasionally," and "infrequently, or not at all."

In view of the size of the delegations and the limited time they spent at the conventions, one would not expect each delegate to have had frequent discussions with all other delegates. Even so, the findings indicate a smaller volume of communications than anticipated. In a group of 32 delegates, the average Democrat spoke frequently with nine others, and occasionally with 14 more. Correspondingly, the average Republican and Democrat spoke infrequently, or not at all, with a majority of his colleagues. There were considerable differences among individuals. One Democrat reported frequent discussions with 41 other delegates, and a Republican with 22 others. There were both Republicans and Democrats whose communications were limited to occasional conversations with only a small fraction of their delegations. In no case did a Republican or Democrat have frequent discussions with more than two thirds of his colleagues. Variations in communications were greater for the Democrats. With more extremes of very active and very inactive delegates, the differences in communications patterns probably stem from the fact that the Democrats had more than twice as many voting delegates as the Republicans did.*

More significant were differences between Republican delegates and Republican alternates. The average delegate spoke frequently with nine other delegates or alternates, but the average alternate spoke frequently with only four other delegates or alternates. The delegate sought out other delegates more than he sought out alternates. The alternate, on the other hand, communicated more often with delegates than with other alternates. In all, communications initiated by delegates accounted for more than two thirds of the total for the group. As might be expected, the most sought out delegates were the state party leaders and those not sought out occupied no important position in state party affairs. The exceptions to this pattern were rank and file members who were most vigorous in their opposition to going along with Nixon on the vice presidential and platform matters.

Reflecting the transfer of state political patterns to a national convention, the Republican communications behaviors were different for a long-time party worker and sometime office-seeker on the one hand, and the person whose main contribution to the party had been financial and whose experience in

---

*Coefficient of variability for communications scores was .523 for Republicans and .622 for Democrats.

party work had been limited. Each of these groups communicated primarily with itself and less with the other. The ten members of the Republican delegation with the highest communications scores included the governor, state chairman and vice chairman, a United States senator, an ex-United States senator, an ex-governor, the national committeewoman, and three of the powerful congressional district party chairmen.* The ten with the lowest scores had never been on an elective party committee or run for public office, although three had served on finance committees. After examining the communications scores, the writer concludes that a rank order of these would correlate nicely with his perception of the political pecking order within the state. In this sense, the Republicans interacted in Chicago in much the same way as they do at home.

Summary

This paper has examined the behavior and characteristics of the Indiana delegation to the 1960 Republican National Convention, with some comparative statements about the Indiana Democratic delegation. Because of the nature of the Republican convention and certain commitments made by the Indiana delegation prior to the convention, the Indiana Republicans made no meaningful decisions in Chicago. However, when the convention is viewed as a device for psychological conditioning and as an extension of state politics, Indiana Republicans appear to have derived considerable profit from it.

Both Indiana delegations were largely comprised of high-status, well-educated individuals. Many of them had extensive backgrounds of involvement in party management and competition for public office. Evaluated in these terms the delegations were suited for political decision-making. However, it is doubtful whether most delegates went to the conventions expecting to play a decisive role in choosing among alternatives.

Both delegations ranked the delegation leadership as the most useful source of information about convention developments. Contacts with delegates from other states were infrequent and not very useful. The mass media contributed significantly to

*The communications score was determined by the frequency with which respondents reported having discussions with the delegate, with each "frequent" conversation scored 2, and each "occasional" conversation scored 1.

the delegate's understanding of his convention, particularly in the case of the Democrats. The average Republican probably knew little more about what was happening than the person who followed the convention closely on television and in the newspapers. No communications system was developed to keep the delegates well-informed.

Communications within the delegations were less extensive than expected, with most delegates maintaining no contact, or very infrequent contact, with most other delegates. Interaction patterns among Republicans in Chicago appeared to closely resemble those established prior to the convention.

In general, the writer concludes that national conventions are better fitted for legitimizing decisions reached through a longer, decentralized process than for undertaking deliberate decision-making.

12. The Role of the California Republican Delegation
HOUSTON I. FLOURNOY
Pomona College

California's delegates gathered in Chicago for the 1960 Republican National Convention secure in the knowledge that their favorite son, Richard Nixon, was by all odds the almost inevitable choice of the convention for the presidential nomination. However, so little did they contribute to the major business of the convention, the California delegates might just as well have given Nixon their proxies and watched the convention on television. In addition to saving transportation and convention costs, they would probably have had a much better idea of what was going on in Chicago.

The decisions which were reached at the convention were primarily made through the Nixon headquarters at the Sheraton-Blackstone Hotel and did not appreciably involve the California delegation, symbolically far uptown and relatively isolated at the Drake Hotel. To the extent that California's presence was considered at all, it was the accurate presumption that the delegates would support whatever Nixon wanted. Their real function was to supply part of an unqualified base of support for Nixon's actions. They ratified his decisions; they did not advise nor intimately participate in shaping them.

Actually, with the presidential nomination virtually pre-determined, the only major actions for the convention were to select

Nixon's running mate, and to draft and adopt the platform. California's relationship to these actions was appropriately illustrated by the way Nixon proceeded to choose Lodge to complete the ticket. No member of the California delegation was invited to the midnight conference of party leaders which Nixon called to survey the potential vice presidential alternatives. The only other Californians present were two key members of his personal staff, administrative assistant Bob Finch, and press relations assistant Herb Klein. Nixon and his personal assistants presumably represented California's interest in the conversations, without requiring any assistance from the party leaders within the delegation. When Lodge was chosen, California perfunctorily accepted him without dissent.

To be sure, many of the individual delegates from California had been interested in other vice presidential candidates prior to the Nixon announcement. There had even been a California movement to support Senator Morton's nomination. National committeeman Edward Shattuck, national committeewoman Marjorie Benedict, state chairman Georgia Milias and other members of the California delegation spearheaded a California Republican Committee for Thruston Morton for Vice President. With the understanding that Morton was one of the acceptable possibilities, this committee had circulated a statement to all the delegates and alternates in Chicago to seek their support for Morton. However, as Shattuck told the California caucus after Henry Cabot Lodge had been named by Nixon, the whole Morton movement had been conducted subject to the Vice President's own decision. It had been their intent to indicate to Nixon the popular support for Morton among the convention delegates. It had been their hope that the indications of Morton support would encourage the Vice President to designate Morton for the nomination. It had never been their intention to support Morton against Nixon's ultimate choice.

Of course, every member of the California delegation did not accept the vice presidential choice with equal enthusiasm. Indeed, precautions were taken in the delegation's caucus to ensure that there would be no opposition to Lodge's nomination. It seemed apparent that the leaders of the California delegation feared some resistance to Lodge might erupt. Wounds incurred by the supporters of Senator Taft during the 1952 convention might be sensitive to the nomination of the man who led the victorious Eisenhower forces. At the caucus, Senator Kuchel immediately recognized Herbert Hoover, Jr., who appealed to friends of the former Ohio senator to support Nixon's choice. He cited his close association with the late Senator Taft; the fact that his father had given Taft his first job; the fact that Hoover had always had the greatest respect and admiration for Senator Taft; but also the fact that he had come to know Lodge through their association within the State Department; and that he admired and respected Ambassador Lodge for his great work at the United Nations.

It seems improbable that Hoover's statement was necessary to quell any important revolt within the California delegation. Possibly his comments made the Lodge nomination more palatable to a small number of the delegates. In any case, no open opposition developed. A unanimous voice vote carried the endorsement of the California delegation.

On the other hand, the caucus discussions of the platform did produce open dissension. The pre-convention announcement of the Nixon-Rockefeller meetings in New York initiated some disquiet within the California delegation. At California's Sunday caucus before the opening of the convention, Congressman Glen Lipscomb, a California delegate on the resolutions committee, made a commitment that there would be "no dictation" of the platform—an obvious reference to the Nixon-Rockefeller agreements.

On Wednesday morning, Lipscomb and Mrs. Ruth Watson presented the completed platform to the caucus. Lipscomb emphasized that there had been no dictation to the platform committee and that the platform had been worked out for the best interests of the nation. This was a platform for the whole country, and not for a particular district. Furthermore, while he urged the delegation to approve its terms, he specifically reserved his right as a candidate for Congress to disagree with particular portions of the platform's content. Earlier that same morning, Vice President Nixon had also addressed the California delegation, putting considerable emphasis upon the necessarily wide range of views within each party of a two-party political system. He had cautioned the delegates to remember that the differences within the Republican Party were infinitesimal compared with the differences within the Democratic Party or between the two parties.

Despite the urgings of Lipscomb and Nixon, the controversy over the civil rights plank which had plagued the platform committee also provoked open division within the California delegation. Discussion focused on the specific language of the civil rights plank. What was the meaning of the platform's support of "the constitutional right to peaceable assembly to protest discrimination *in* private business establishments?" Was it the intent of the platform to support demonstrations within private industrial and manufacturing concerns? Did this plank support interference with the rights of an individual to manage his own business? Did this language refer to *"discrimination"* in business establishments or *"assembly"* in business establishments?

Caspar W. Weinberger made an attempt to clarify the meaning of the language by noting that the platform merely supported the "constitutional" right to peaceable assembly and therefore could not and did not support any acts of assembly or demonstration which were not legal. Admittedly the constitutional limits of peaceable assembly were unclear, but Weinberger insisted that there could be no intention to support illegal activities. Despite this interpretation some members of the California delegation thought that the platform should be amended to make the permissible limits of such demonstrations more specific.

Their concern raised the question of procedure for casting California's votes in the event there was an effort to amend the platform on the convention floor. Senator Kuchel made it clear that any endorsement of the platform by the caucus would not bind the individual members of the delegation should a contest develop. Their votes would be polled on the convention floor and accurately reported.

The delegation ultimately voted to approve the platform, even though the delegates had neither seen nor heard the complete text. No amendments were actually proposed in the caucus, but a motion to table approval of the platform was made and defeated with only 11 delegates standing to vote against platform approval. After Senator Kuchel made a very strong appeal on behalf of the civil rights plank, the leadership of the delegation overwhelmingly supported the platform and the Vice President's wishes. Neither they, nor the bulk of the members, wanted any action of the California delegation to embarrass the Vice President or to undercut his efforts to secure a platform of his own choosing. Clearly, however, had a floor fight developed there would have been a number of California votes which would have supported changes in the platform.

Of course, considering the method by which the delegates were selected, it would have been surprising if the delegation had contained any serious group of dissidents. The delegation was placed on the primary ballot by a committee supporting Vice President Nixon; the composition of the delegation was cleared through the Vice President's office; it was unopposed in the primary; and it was informally bound to support Nixon except for the remote possibility that he might release them. It was, in short, a handpicked delegation of persons who were either to be recognized for supporting the Vice President or to be drawn more closely into the Nixon for President effort. Furthermore, the 1958 election had eliminated all the opposing or competing party leaders of any substantial power within the state party.

The formerly powerful figures of Knight and Knowland had been swept from office in a landslide, and although Knight was a member of the delegation, he clearly did not have any significant part in the proceedings. Former Senator Knowland found his place at the press table rather than at the head table. While Senator Kuchel remained as the only major statewide Republican office-holder, he had consistently supported Vice President Nixon, and would have had little independent power within the delegation to challenge Nixon had he wished to do so.

As a whole, there were few public office-holders who might have had an independent power base within the delegation. Only two of California's Republican congressmen and only five of California's state legislators were delegates. Rather than being composed of various power factions within the party—a common factor in the past—the California delegation was a composite of organizational and regional elements of the party, with a strong representation of prominent financial backers of party causes.

The only group of delegates who participated very closely with the Nixon drive for the nomination was a group of personal friends and staff assistants of the Vice President who were also members of the delegation. Stanley McCaffrey, who had joined the Vice President's staff from the University of California a few months before the convention, proved to be a key channel of information between the Nixon operation at the Blackstone and the California delegation. It was through McCaffrey that most indications of the Vice President's feelings, intentions, and desires were communicated. (McCaffrey had the same role during the proceedings of the Republican State Convention and the Republican State Central Committee in Sacramento after the national convention.) Jack Drown, by virtue of his close personal association with the Vice President, was involved more deeply in the Nixon organization than most members of the California delegation. Ray Arbuthnot and Warren Brock, who had undertaken a survey of agricultural areas of the country to assist the Vice President's efforts to cope with the farm problem, also spent considerable time at the Nixon headquaters in the Blackstone.

The California Young Republicans were very active around the periphery of the Nixon efforts in Chicago. The Young Republican group, headed by Mrs. Virginia Savell, had the specific responsibility for operating the Nixon Hospitality Center in the Conrad Hilton Hotel. The YR's also participated in organizing the traditional "spontaneous" demonstration for the Nixon nomination on the convention floor. While these activities hardly affected the ultimate result of the first ballot voting for the presidential nomination, nonetheless they were a part of the "required" Nixon convention activity.

Other California delegates were kept busy with the "housekeeping" functions of the delegation itself. George Milias handled the onerous task of distributing the guest tickets. Mrs. Benedict was in charge of the delegation's credentials, and Mrs. Cecil Kenyon operated the delegation's hospitality room at the Drake Hotel. Such responsibilities consumed a considerable amount of time and effort on the part of several delegates, but they were hardly crucial to Nixon's nomination.

Summary

This report on the activities of the California delegation was initially designed to analyze the role of a delegation in support of its home-state candidate for the nomination. It was assumed that such a delegation would constitute an integral part of the candidate's efforts to secure the nod. It was anticipated that the leaders of the delegation would be active in the candidate's organization; that they would be an important factor in the convention's deliberations.

Perhaps the relatively uncontested atmosphere of the Chicago convention produced unique results. Perhaps the vice presidential office offered alternative courses of action which are peculiar to that office. Perhaps Nixon's undisputed position within the California Republican Party produced a deviation from the assumed norm. In any case, these assumptions about California's part in the Republican National Convention were not borne out by the proceedings in Chicago.

The role of the California delegation at Chicago, as a delegation supporting a presidential contender, was primarily to "stand and wait." The Nixon organization in Chicago did not depend upon contributions from individuals within the California delegation. The party hierarchy of the G. O. P. in California had virtually no role in nominating Nixon. They were a part of the general mass of support within the delegation, counted upon to support the Vice President, but not relied upon to participate in any of the top-level decision-making, nor brought into operation to contact or influence other delegations.

California's seventy votes were important to Nixon in the total need for nomination, but few of the seventy individual delegates had more than a passing connection with the fundamental activities of the convention.

13. Decision-Making in a Small Delegation: Idaho Republicans

ROBERT J. HUCKSHORN

University of Idaho

The Idaho delegation to the 1960 Republican National Convention arrived in Chicago uncommitted to any candidate and undecided as to the stand to be taken on the nominations and issues with which it would be confronted. Selected by the state convention in April, the 28 delegates and alternates represented virtually every political hue in the Republican spectrum. Their disunity was manifest prior to the convention and their divergent opinions had not been reconciled upon their return to Idaho.

From the beginning it was obvious that the delegation would have fewer decisions to make since the convention had generated little conflict. Even so, a study of decision-making was feasible because it was only necessary that the members of the delegation believe that decisions would be required of them and that their actions would affect the convention's outcome. Since decision-making is a function of beliefs, the fact that the Idaho delegation merely ratified decisions made by others is of little consequence in the study.

Most of the members of the Idaho delegation believed that the national convention was a deliberative body, duly constituted for the purpose of deciding upon candidates and principles to be presented to the people in November. With the expectation that their decisions could be registered at the proper time during the convention, many members of the Idaho group consciously attempted to evaluate the candidates and issues, and to make decisions on the basis of that evaluation. Others in the delegation reached conclusions but cherished only a glimmering hope that they would be called upon to record them. Nevertheless, the decisions were made and the process by which they were arrived at is analyzed here.

Most of the delegates and alternates were interviewed during the first two days of convention week. At that time, a majority of them believed that decisions would be required of them. This was apparent in the interviews and in the statements made during the first two caucuses* Furthermore, as the week progressed, the positions and the arguments of the delegates shifted as new decisions were individually arrived at.

Four areas of concern were believed by most of the members of the delegation to require decisions of them. Foremost among these was a controversy over the action of the state convention in resolving to bind the delegation under the unit rule. The other three, as could be expected, were the nominations for President and Vice President and the adoption of the party's platform. Each of these areas of action is treated separately below and a concluding section analyzes the patterns of decision-making which were evident in the delegation.

The Unit Rule: Quest for a Decision

Although the Republican Party does not allow use of the unit rule in its national convention proceedings, recent Idaho conventions have bound the state's delegations to vote as a unit. None of these efforts was sanctioned by the national convention and under the rules of the party they could be voided if challenged by a minority delegate from Idaho. The question of legality was

---

*The author attended the Republican State Convention in Twin Falls and all caucuses of the Idaho delegation at the National convention in Chicago.

never discussed during caucus proceedings and, indeed, there was no evidence that any member of the delegation actually realized that the unit rule was prohibited under the rules of the national party.

The matter first arose in the opening caucus on the Sunday afternoon prior to the convention when the chairman, Governor Robert E. Smylie, was asked whether or not the delegation was bound to vote as a unit. He replied that it was not, but corrected himself when reminded by a party official that the state convention had resolved to recommend that the delegation operate under the unit rule. The subsequent controversy revolved not around the question of legality, but whether the word "recommend" actually constituted a binding instruction to the delegation. In subsequent caucuses the question also arose as to which of the delegation's actions would be affected by the resolution if agreement were reached to use the unit rule.

The supporters of Senator Barry Goldwater raised the question of the unit rule in the second caucus on Tuesday morning and argued that by its use they were being denied their votes. They maintained that a resolution in the form of a "recommendation" was not binding upon the group, but left to the delegation the decision as to whether to vote as a unit or not. Although he was not a member of the Goldwater faction, Senator Henry Dworshak spoke against use of the unit rule and stated that had he known it was to be invoked he would not have permitted his choice as a delegate. He strenuously argued the desirability of allowing each delegate the opportunity to vote according to his own beliefs.

The leader of the minority then moved that the rule apply only to choice of candidates and not to the platform, but after a moment's consideration withdrew the motion since he did not wish to be bound to the majority choice of candidates. After an inconclusive discussion the delegation took no formal action with regard to the unit rule in the second caucus.

The Wednesday caucus immediately became embroiled in the controversy over the unit rule and several motions were offered though all were withdrawn. An apparent desire to avoid a showdown vote on the matter finally led the delegation to authorize the chairman to cast Idaho's fourteen votes in Richard Nixon's behalf, but with the understanding that the vote was not cast as a unit.

The final caucus, on Thursday morning, ratified the choice of Ambassador Henry Cabot Lodge as the vice presidential nominee. The necessity for a decision on this matter having passed, the unit rule controversy remained unresolved at the conclusion of the delegation's business.

Candidate Decisions and Platform Principles

The Idaho delegation generally was enthusiastic over the choice of Vice President Nixon as the party's nominee for President. A number of delegates cherished the hope that they would have an opportunity to register their votes for Senator Goldwater for either position on the ticket while others supported Governor Nelson Rockefeller or Senator Thruston Morton as the vice presidential nominee.

Immediately after the state convention in April, a poll of the newly selected delegates revealed that most of them supported Nixon for the presidential nomination, although two delegates indicated their support for Goldwater and three professed to be undecided.

During the first two days of convention week each delegate and all but one alternate were interviewed to determine their choice of candidates and the process by which they had arrived at their decisions. An additional effort was made to ascertain the candidates with whom the delegation members found themselves in ideological agreement. The results of these interviews revealed a distinct difference in political philosophy between the delegates and the alternates and each segment of the delegation is, therefore, treated separately.

Among the fourteen voting delegates, eleven stated a preference for Nixon as the presidential candidate although five of that number expressed themselves as ideologically oriented toward Senator Goldwater and his conservative program. With the three Goldwater supporters, for whom the Arizona Senator was an obvious ideological choice, the eight constituted a majority of the voting delegates who identified themselves as conservatives, although most of them found Nixon an acceptable candidate who they believed could win the election in the fall.

The thirteen alternates who were interviewed showed a much greater affinity for liberal Republicanism. Twelve of them favored the Vice President as the candidate to head the ticket and one expressed the hope that Governor Rockefeller could be prevailed upon to accept the party's nomination. When questioned as to their philosophical preference the alternates displayed a more pronounced sentiment for liberal candidates. Only three expressed agreement with Goldwater while four favored the policies espoused by Rockefeller and the rest aligned themselves with Nixon, generally believing him to be a liberal Republican. Two of those who agreed with Rockefeller were equally enthusiastic about Nixon and tended to equate the political programs and beliefs of the two men.

The same division was apparent in the vice presidential choices of the delegation members. One half of the Idaho delegates favored Senator Thruston Morton of Kentucky as the party's vice presidential choice. Senator Goldwater was the favorite of four delegates while two favored Rockefeller and one was for Lodge. All of those supporting Morton alleged that his conservatism was a major factor in their decision. Among the delegates there was more second choice support for Ambassador Lodge than for any other candidate, although Morton, Goldwater, Rockefeller, Senator Everett Dirksen and Congressman Gerald Ford all had scattered support.

Again the alternates were more likely to favor liberal candidates for the second spot on the ticket. Of the thirteen interviewed, seven favored Rockefeller and three favored Lodge, generally because the two men represented liberal beliefs. Two of the alternates supported Morton and one favored Goldwater. In terms of second choice candidates, seven alternates named Lodge, most of these seven giving first preference to Rockefeller. Here too, it was apparent that the alternates were seeking more liberal candidates than were the voting delegates.

Discussion with the members relative to platform principles is more difficult to analyze, but again seems to demonstrate the same disparity between voting delegates and alternates. The delegation's representative on the platform committee was Congressman Hamer Budge, a member of the conservative wing of the party. Budge played a key role in the platform deliberations of the Idaho caucuses, representing as he did the group's only contact with the drafters of the document. Many members of the delegation expressed their willingness to accept the views of the congressman on platform matters. The delegates, however, were considerably more outspoken than were the alternates in their desire for a conservative platform and they were also more eager to oppose planks which they regarded as too liberal. The alternates were much more likely to express themselves in favor of a liberal party program or "one which Nixon can run on." There were no demands for a conservative platform among the alternates, although three of them agreed to the platform as drafted on the basis of Congressman Budge's qualified recommendation.

Apparently this ideological bi-polarization of the delegation could have come about in two different ways. That is, there may have been a deliberate attempt on the part of the committee which made the choices of delegates and alternates at the state convention to place the conservatives in the voting positions on the delegation, or the distribution could have been mere coincidence. Of the two, the latter explanation is the more plausible. During the meetings of the selection committee at the Twin Falls convention, there was no discernible effort to determine either the candidate choices or the philosophical beliefs of the applicants for the delegate-at-large positions. The political beliefs of some of them, such as the leading elected officials, were well known but that was not the case with the majority of the applicants. Indeed, the major consideration in choosing the delegates-and alternates-at-large was that of geographical location rather than personal political beliefs or candidate support. Furthermore, four delegates and four alternates were elected on the floor by the respective congressional district caucuses and no questions of this sort were raised in either caucus. It seems obvious, therefore, that the "liberal-conservative" distribution in the Idaho delegation developed solely by chance.

Patterns of Decision-Making

The decisions reached on the two nominations and the platform were all accomplished by unanimous votes of the fourteen delegates and with apparent unanimous agreement of the alternates. In some cases the delegate's vote obviously did not coincide with his convictions. By and large these decisions were reached before the convention or during the early days of convention week. From interviews with the members of the delegation and from their statements in caucus, there appeared a series of decision-making patterns which the members had either consciously or unconsciously employed.

The first of these decision-making patterns was one of leadership influence. The delegation was officially headed by Governor

Robert Smylie but leadership was voluntarily shared, to some extent, with Senator Dworshak, Congressman Budge and state chairman Ray Robbins, all of whom were delegates-at-large. The superior experience and political knowledge of these officials created a disposition on the part of some delegation members to follow their leadership in reaching the necessary decisions at the convention. This was particularly true of those delegates who, prior to the convention, professed to "an open mind" with regard to the nominations and platform.

Governor Smylie was the delegation's major link with the convention organization and with Nixon headquarters. He reported his views on the candidate races on two occasions, saying in each case that Nixon was the obvious winner of the presidential nomination. In the Tuesday morning caucus he reported that the vice presidential choice had narrowed to Morton and Lodge. In the final caucus on Thursday morning he discussed the post-nomination meeting of top party leaders with the Vice President in which the choices for a suitable running mate had been sifted. He said that he had assured Nixon that Senator Morton would be the favorite choice in Idaho but that Ambassador Lodge was certainly acceptable as a nominee. Immediately after the post-nomination meeting in Nixon's suite at the Blackstone Hotel, Governor Smylie met with the leaders of the Goldwater faction and informed them of the Vice President's choice of Ambassador Lodge. As a result, when the Thursday caucus convened, the supporters of the Arizona Senator not only supported Lodge but moved that the delegation give him its unanimous approval. This action did not, of course, mean that the group had abandoned Senator Goldwater but merely that they recognized the inevitable. Their attitude of resigned acceptance of Lodge was summed up by the following statement made to the press after the Thursday caucus:

> I don't think much of it (the Lodge nomination). The people with my viewpoint accomplished what they wanted by showing that the conservative element can act as a brake. Goldwater knew all the time that he didn't have a chance, but he came out as the biggest man in the convention. His star is launched.*

Because of the Governor's contacts and the information which

---

*Lewiston Morning Tribune, July 29, 1960

he furnished, a number of delegates were willing to follow his lead in those actions they were called upon to record.

Senator Dworshak spoke only once in reference to candidates. During the Wednesday caucus he reported on a meeting of ten Republican senators the consensus of which had been that Nixon should be permitted to choose his own running mate. His statement, in conjunction with similar expressions from Governor Smylie, seemed to quiet discussion within the delegation of an "open" convention and of "tests of strength" for one candidate or another.

As previously stated, Congressman Budge represented the delegation's contact with the platform drafters and the influence which he had in that regard has already been indicated.

A second pattern of decision-making was based on the delegates' philosophical beliefs. Most of the members of the delegation were willing to identify themselves as liberals, moderates or conservatives and in so doing they ordinarily associated themselves with the respective programs of Rockefeller, Nixon or Goldwater. A number of these delegates apparently chose the candidate for whom they wished to vote on the basis of that individual's program or political convictions. Those who supported Senator Goldwater were particularly outspoken in their devotion to principle rather than "political expediency." Some of them stated publicly as well as privately that they preferred a man with whose principles they could agree regardless of his potential as a winning candidate. The same disposition was professed by some of those who supported Governor Rockefeller. It is, accordingly, evident that these decisions were born of political philosophy or of strong convictions.

The platform served as the focal point for the decisions reached by a third group of delegates. This small group of individuals usually expressed greater concern for the various stands to be taken in the platform than with the choice of candidates to head the ticket. Sometimes their interest was concentrated on one specific plank and sometimes on their desire for a "conservative" or "liberal" statement of party principles. Two members of the delegation indicated that their interest was concentrated on the platform because it presented the only real opportunity for them to record their own decisions in as much as the nominations were, in their opinion, a foregone conclusion.

Congressman Budge actively sought his position on the platform committee in order to work in behalf of a conservative statement of party principles, and in view of the lack of candidate contests, he probably looked upon the adoption of the platform as the most important decision to be made by the convention. Some delegates revealed an interest in particular platform planks. A number of delegates, including one physician, were particularly concerned with the platform references to medical aid for the aged. Others expressed special concern for the farm or water resources planks. Although each of the delegates who fits within this third pattern of decision-making showed an interest in the candidacy of particular individuals, their avid interest in the deliberations of the platform drafters was the factor which set them off from the remainder of the delegation. Their interest in the nominations was only secondary in regard to their decision-making.

Edmund Burke's theory of "the imperative mandate" was transferred by some delegates to the arena of the political convention and constituted a fourth basis for decision-making. Five members of the delegation indicated that the effect of the group's actions upon their "constituents in Idaho" was a matter of utmost importance to them in reaching their decisions.

Concern with "constituent" reaction was particularly apparent among those who supported Senator Goldwater and there were repeated references, both in caucus and interviews, to the "constituents" represented by these delegates. These members represented the "delegate" theory of representation in the true Burkeian sense of the word even though they served in a national political convention instead of a deliberate legislative body. In every case these members of the delegation indicated that this concern represented an important element in the decisions which they reached.

Finally, there was some evidence that delegate support sometimes accrued to the candidate with whom the delegate was personally acquainted or whom he had previously met. All of the members of the delegation met Vice President Nixon on Wednesday morning after it had become quite apparent to all that he would be the party's nominee. That particular meeting did not, therefore, affect any decisions. Nine of the members of the delegation had not previously met any of the candidates for either position on the ticket, and the four delegation leaders and one other delegate were acquainted with all or most of them.

Five of Senator Goldwater's supporters for either office had previously met him and two of them described themselves as "personal friends" who had met none of the other candidates.

Governor Rockefeller was personally known to two of his supporters on the delegation and in each case was the only candidate known to them. Senator Morton was also known to two of those who preferred him as the vice presidential nominee.

Some of the delegates, who fit within this fifth pattern, freely stated that an important element in their choice of candidates was the factor of personal acquaintance. Furthermore, Congressman Gerald Ford and Senator Everett Dirksen both picked up one or two supporters for the vice presidential nomination after they or their spokesman appeared before the delegation to appeal for support. Although certainly not a major factor in delegate decision-making, these occurrences seem to indicate the validity of the assumption that personal acquaintance created a bond between some delegates and the candidates to whom they gave their support.

Conclusions

Here, then, were the discernible patterns of decision-making in one small delegation. None of these paths was followed exclusively by any member of the delegation since many elements entered into each decision. Nevertheless, many of the delegates and alternates could be readily identified with a particular pattern among the five indicated.

The fact that none of the delegation's decisions was crucial to the convention's outcome was a source of irritation and frustration to some of the delegates. The obvious tailoring of the convention to fit television programming was a further source of complaint and convinced some of the delegates that the national convention, as presently constituted, is in serious need of reevaluation. These anticlimactic frustrations probably attend every low conflict convention; a contested convention in 1964 would certainly relieve some of the anxieties about the present nominating process.

14. Decision-Making in a Small Delegation: South Dakota Republicans

CHARLES O. JONES

Wellesley College

South Dakota is one of sixteen states which use the presidential primary to select delegates to the national convention. Despite the democratic intent of this device, South Dakota Republican voters had no choice, on July 7, 1960, but to vote for the single slate of delegates and alternates which had been selected by the Republican State Central Committee working with the national committeeman and committeewoman. The real election of those delegates and alternates, therefore, occurred when the national committeeman informed them that their names would appear on the ballot. In this sense, 1960 was typical of recent primaries since there have been but two contests in the South Dakota Republican presidential primary since 1932.

The selection committee relied on several criteria in determining who would go to the Chicago convention. First, the congressional delegation (two senators and one congressman) was excluded since it was felt that they would attend anyway as special guests. Second, there was an attempt to represent various geographical sections and varying economic interests in South Dakota. Third, party service was rewarded. As the national committeeman noted, "we decided to give these out to people who had worked for the party." Fourth, one Republican who was critical of the selection process observed that defeat as a candidate was used to keep one man off, but the committee included two others who had been recently defeated for high public office. Finally, it was helpful to have known some of the party leaders. One delegate, for example, was included at the request of the 1960 gubernatorial candidate.

The result was a delegation which was essentially leaderless; that is, the state's most important party figures were not members. The only delegates who could conceivably be labeled party leaders were Joe Foss, a former governor who now spends relatively little time in South Dakota in his capacity as Commissioner of the American Football League, and L. R. Houck, a former lieutenant governor.

Several of the more important state party leaders did attend the convention, however. Senators Karl Mundt and Francis Case, and Congressman E. Y. Berry were guests of the convention.

National committeeman Carroll Lockhart, national committee-woman Kathleen Christianson, and state party chairman Glen Rhodes attended in their capacities as members of the national committee. Among those absent were the 1958 and 1960 gubernatorial candidates.

This report intends to discuss the South Dakota delegation's activities by examining the relationship between state party leaders and the convention delegation. A small-state delegation such as South Dakota obviously will not be near the power centers of a nominating convention. If they deny themselves the communication with power centers which their state leaders are likely to have, they place themselves that much further from some knowledge of what is being decided. Eventually, of course, whether they include leaders in the delegation or not, they will be forced to turn to their state leaders when faced with decisions. Though there were few decisions for delegations to make in Chicago, the South Dakota delegation's activities tend to support the analysis above.

The South Dakota delegation had a total of five caucuses—one in South Dakota and four in Chicago. The pre-convention caucus in South Dakota was organizational. The delegation selected Joe Foss as chairman and several delegates to serve on committees at the convention.* The convention city caucuses were concerned with the three important decisions of any national nominating convention: the presidential and vice presidential nominations and the platform.

Presidential Nomination

The delegation had stated no presidential preference on their nominating petitions and so none appeared on the ballot** According to the national committeeman, no special effort was made to make this a "pro-Nixon" delegation. In their pre-convention caucus, however, the delegation unanimously voted to endorse Vice President Nixon. This endorsement was a preference only and not a pledge.

During the week end before the convention, Vice President

---

*Two delegates were selected to serve on the resolutions committee, and one each on the credentials, rules, and permanent organization committees.

**South Dakota law requires that delegates and alternates either state their preference on their nominating petitions or state that they have no preference.

Nixon met with Governor Rockefeller to discuss platform compromises. This meeting resulted in renewed activity by the "Goldwater for President" enthusiasts—sparked by Senator Goldwater's criticisms of the platform agreement between Nixon and Rockefeller. The South Dakota delegates and alternates began arriving in Chicago on Sunday, July 24, and were greeted at their hotel (the Morrison) by the noisy pro-Goldwater sentiment of various southern delegations who were quartered there. The "Goldwater for President Headquarters" was also located in the Morrison Hotel.

Discussions in the South Dakota headquarters on Sunday clearly indicated that the Nixon endorsement was being reconsidered by several delegates and alternates. There had been sentiment for Goldwater in the South Dakota delegation before the Chicago convention but it was directed to supporting him for Vice President. In Chicago some South Dakota delegates favored joining the movement to support him as a candidate for President. Pro-Goldwater letters and telegrams flooded the delegates' mail boxes. One delegate said that he had received 25 letters favoring Goldwater the day he left Chicago. At least two South Dakota families had made the trip to Chicago at their own expense for Goldwater.* All in all, the South Dakota delegates (many of whom would find Goldwater conservatism attractive under any circumstances) were being deluged with pro-Goldwater sentiment.

The first caucus in Chicago was held on Sunday at 9 p.m. The meeting was chaired by national committeeman Lockhart in the absence of Joe Foss. Lockhart suggested that no firm commitments be made in the absence of the chairman. An alternate immediately raised the question of whether there should not be some reconsideration of the previous endorsement of Nixon since events over the week end had changed some delegates' opinions. Lockhart answered that the delegation was in no way bound by the pre-convention endorsement of Nixon and no retraction need be made. Two delegates supported this view. Another delegate announced that Goldwater might let his name go before the convention as a serious contender for the nomination, in which case there would be several votes for him in the South Dakota delega-

---

*One delegate drove to Chicago with one of the pro-Goldwater couples. Though the delegate was moderately pro-Nixon before the convention, he was strongly pro-Goldwater upon arrival at the convention.

tion. It was this delegate's opinion that it was best to await further developments before announcing a commitment. The meeting adjourned without taking definite action, but it was apparent that many delegates were disenchanted with Nixon. Another caucus was scheduled for Tuesday, July 26.

Between the Sunday and Tuesday caucuses, there was informal discussion among certain delegates about the Goldwater nomination. At least six delegates said they would vote for Goldwater if he were to let his name go before the convention as a serious contender, and two or three delegates were determined to vote for him in any case. At 9:40 on Tuesday morning the delegation was asked to meet Vice President Nixon in the Sheraton-Blackstone Hotel. The caucus (scheduled for 10 o'clock) was rescheduled to follow the meeting with Nixon. The Nixon meeting (to which only delegates and alternates were invited) turned out to be a combination "pep" talk and marathon picture-taking session.

The Tuesday caucus, which had promised to be exciting, indicated that the delegation would support Nixon. Chairman Foss was in charge of the meeting and attendance was high. Important state party leaders such as Senators Mundt and Case, Congressman Berry, and national committeeman Lockhart were present. Though there had been some opinion among delegates that this should be a closed caucus, the delegation voted unanimously to allow the press to attend.*

One of the pro-Goldwater delegates opened the meeting by announcing that Goldwater apparently would let his name be introduced only as a favorite son candidate, but that the delegation that should keep flexible in case Goldwater changed his mind.**
Chairman Foss reported on a conversation he had had with Senator Goldwater on Monday to the effect that the Senator did not wish to cause any difficulty at the covention. A telephone call from Goldwater headquarters during the caucus confirmed Foss' assessment of the situation. This appeared to be the first

---

*The press was asked to leave while the delegation discussed the subject of a closed caucus. The fact that the press had complained about being excluded from the Nixon meeting was important in the decision to allow them to attend the caucus.

**That is, the pro-Goldwater delegates wanted to vote for Goldwater if Rockefeller announced that he was a candidate. One of the Nixon delegates observed that if Rockefeller were to announce, Nixon would need the South Dakota support even more.

instance of direct contact between the South Dakota delegation and Senator Goldwater. Foss' statement had a "cold water" effect on the whole Goldwater discusssion. Previously silent pro-Nixon delegates asserted that Nixon was certain to receive the nomination, and divided support from the South Dakota delegation would make it difficult for the state party in November.* Goldwater delegates retorted that some conservative protest to the platform agreement was necessary. It became evident, however, as the presidential nominations drew near, that a large majority of the South Dakota delegation would support Nixon. Senator Goldwater obviated any decision on the part of individual delegates by withdrawing his name before the balloting and South Dakota's fourteen votes were cast for Nixon.

In conclusion, the Goldwater 'flurry" might be explained as a result of the following factors: (1) the Goldwater headquarters and leading supporters were located in the Morrison Hotel and several South Dakota delegates were in contact with this headquarters; (2) Goldwater's conservatism was naturally attractive to many South Dakotans; (3) those South Dakotans supporting the Goldwater movement did not have accurate information or solid contacts either with the power centers at the convention or with the Senator himself. The party leadership did not support Goldwater and, after allowing the pro-Goldwater sentiment full expression, was able to swing the delegation back to Nixon.

Vice Presidential Nomination

The vice presidential situation was complicated before Nixon's announcement preferring Ambassador Henry Cabot Lodge. In delegate interviews conducted by the author before the convention, it was apparent that the delegates had not made up their minds. There was considerable support for Goldwater but many other names were mentioned as acceptable. Lodge was not among these. One of the alternates had suggested that the South Dakota delegation support Senator Karl Mundt on the first ballot.** Senator Mundt had joined his colleague, Senator Case, in supporting

---

*That is, Republicans would have to explain why they refused to support Nixon in Chicago.

**The chairman of the Minnehaha County Republican Party wrote each of the delegates suggesting they support Mundt since he was well liked in the South and would help the ticket in the midwest.

Secretary of the Interior Fred Seaton, however, and did not encourage his own candidacy for Vice President.

The vice presidential nomination was not discussed in the Sunday caucus but the author's conversations with delegates and alternates indicated support for Senators Goldwater and Morton and Secretary Seaton. State party chairman Rhodes said that in his opinion the delegation would vote for Seaton on the first ballot.

In the Tuesday caucus the delegation spent considerable time on the vice presidential nomination. Chairman Foss noted the importance of awaiting Nixon's decision. He said that any number of candidates might be chosen and the delegation should do no more than discuss the possibilities. One member reported a rumor that Lodge was definitely favored by Nixon. This announcement was met with groans from the delegation. Several delegates voiced their disapproval of Lodge—indicating that Lodge would find little support in their home areas and they could not support him in good faith. Only one delegate announced support for Lodge. Chairman Foss then asked the delegates to indicate vocally which candidates they favored. Congressman Judd (a possibility only after his keynote speech), Senator Morton, Congressman Halleck, and Secretary Seaton (in that order from most to least enthusiasm) received favorable responses. One member raised the question of supporting Mundt on the first ballot. Senator Mundt responded that the delegation might consider the benefits of placing his name in nomination only if Nixon refused to name a vice presidential candidate.* Senator Case had earlier made a short speech favoring Secretary Seaton under similar circumstances.

In summary, the overwhelming majority of delegates were opposed to Ambassador Lodge as the vice presidential candidate but were unwilling to commit themselves to any other candidate. The decision, as with the presidential nomination, was to await developments.

On Wednesday, July 27, the author participated in discussions where Senator Mundt convinced pro-Goldwater, anti-Lodge delegates of the need to support Nixon's choice for vice president. In

---

*Senator Mundt was referring to the benefits which might accrue from a television appearance for his reelection bid in South Dakota. Joe Foss was to have nominated him and then Mundt would make a withdrawal speech.

an interview after such a discussion, a pro-Goldwater delegate expressed the opinion that the delegation should vote for Lodge if Nixon wanted him. This opinion contrasted sharply with the anti-Lodge opinion expressed on Tuesday by the same delegate.

Senator Mundt, himself, had to be "won over" to Lodge. Nixon called a meeting of Republican senators on Wednesday. As Mundt reported it, Nixon asked which of the vice presidential candidates would benefit Republican senators in their reelection bids. Mundt favored Judd and presumed that the rest of the midwestern senators would agree with him. Senators from Kansas, Iowa, and Idaho, however, reported that Lodge would help in their states. Both Mundt and Lockhart told this story later to delegates as an illustration that Lodge was not totally unsatisfactory to the midwest.

Nixon's choice of Lodge was announced early Thursday morning. By Thursday afternoon the delegates seemed resigned to the fact that Lodge would be the candidate. State party chairman Rhodes called several delegates together in an informal caucus to report on his breakfast meeting with the Midwest and Rocky Mountain Chairman's Association—a meeting called to explain why Lodge was chosen. Those delegates who were present (six or seven) accepted the reasoning grudgingly. After the meeting several delegates expressed disgust because of the insignificant role that they were playing and suggested that they might return home before the final session of the convention. That evening, South Dakota gave her fourteen votes to Ambassador Lodge.

The Platform

The plaform was a center of controversy in Chicago but the South Dakota delegation played a small role in this controversy. The two South Dakota delegates on the resolutions committee were Goldwater conservatives. Their efforts were directed to obstructing acceptance *in toto* of the Nixon-Rockefeller platform agreement. Their actions reflected the sentiment of many South Dakota delegates (though they did not formally consult with the delegation in their actions on the platform).

Discussion of the platform in caucuses was minimal since delegates did not have copies of the completed platform until Wednesday. The farm plank was of most concern to the South Dakota delegates and Senator Mundt reported (at the Sunday caucus) that it was a plank which South Dakota Republicans could live with, but he was not enthusiastic about it.

In conclusion, the delegation had little direct information about the platform, and appeared not to have a great deal of interest in it: that is, the details of the completed platform were printed in the Chicago daily newspapers so that interested delegates could know what was being adopted. None of the delegates, however, was willing to speak about the platform in the absence of the representatives on the resolutions committee. Most delegates were willing to accept (not necessarily "support") the platform if the farm plank was reasonable. Senator Mundt assured them that it was.

State Party Leaders and the Delegation

The lack of decision-making in the South Dakota delegation presents a problem in attempting to analyze the relationship between party leaders and the delegation. The only decisions which were made were those to postpone positive action until more information was available. Possibly the lack of information itself allowed the delegation to believe that there were decisions to make since adequate information would "cue" them to ratify Nixon's nomination and his choice for Vice President. Delegations which were in close communication with Nixon headquarters probably had less to discuss and decide than did the South Dakota delegation.

Of the six non-delegate leaders attending the convention, it seemed evident that Senator Karl Mundt was the most important. Several delegates told the author that they considered Mundt the most important and influential man in the South Dakota Republican Party. In addition to the respect that a two-term senator might naturally expect, however, Mundt appeared to have influence because he was seeking reelection. Senator Mundt was trailing his Democratic opponent in an early poll. Delegates were concerned about this situation and were anxious to do whatever they could in Chicago to ensure Mundt's reelection. Finally, Mundt had access to information and to national party leaders by virtue of his leadership position. He was called on often in caucuses to clear up specific matters.

The other members of the congressional delegation, Senator Francis Case and Congressman E. Y. Berry, played small roles in the delegation's activities. Senator Case left Chicago on Tuesday after making a token "pitch" supporting Secretary Seaton for

Vice President and did not return. Congressman Berry attended only the last third of the Tuesday caucus and had little apparent influence beyond informal discussions with delegates. In general there was evidence to indicate that the congressional delegation considered it a mistake to exclude them from membership on the convention delegation, but they reacted differently. Senator Mundt could not afford to alienate the delegation. Senator Case and Congressman Berry could afford to stay in the background since the former was not up for reelection and the latter was considered safe in his reelection bid.

State party chairman Glen Rhodes had some influence but was reluctant or not interested in using it. It seems fair to suggest that Rhodes was not vitally interested in the national picture and therefore did not participate enthusiastically in convention activities. Rhodes' influence came because he had access to information rather than because he wished to convince the delegation to make a specific decision. The meeting of the Midwest and Rocky Mountain Party Chairman's Association is a case in point. Rhodes returned from this meeting with information about the vice presidency but did little except report the reasoning which had been explained at the meeting.

The busiest man in the South Dakota headquarters was national committeeman Carroll Lockhart. He undoubtedly had influence because of his position, his access to information, and his affable personality. He was unquestionably liked by all members of the delegation. His fairness in chairing caucuses and his energy in handling all administrative matters for the delegation commanded the respect of everyone connected with the South Dakota delegation. It is likely, however, that the delegate who suggested "Lockhart probably would have influence with the delegation, but I don't know how much he would use it," was accurate in his evaluation because Lockhart seemed personally indisposed to exert leadership.

The national committeewoman, Mrs. Kathleen Christianson, had little apparent influence on the delegation—directing most of her attention to the scheduling of ladies' events.

Over-all Impressions

Several factors stand out in an evaluation of the South Dakota delegation's activities at the Republican National Convention. First, the delegation which was selected included only two important party leaders and only one of these ever attended a Chicago caucus. Chairman Foss presided at the Tuesday caucus but former lieutenant governor Houck was on the resolutions committee and was absent during the two most important Chicago caucuses. The delegation was split between Goldwater and Nixon for President and among several candidates for Vice President. In filling the need for some leadership, the delegation relied on the chairman the one time that he attended and turned to Senator Mundt. Mundt's position was important for two reasons: (1) he was up for reelection; (2) he had access to information on the platform and nominations.*

Second, much of the activity in the South Dakota delegation seemed to result from a lack of information about (1) what was going on; and (2) the delegates' expected role in a convention of this type. Thus, the Goldwater enthusiasts had been impressed by demonstrations of support for Goldwater in the Morrison Hotel but were unsure as to whether Goldwater himself was willing to be considered a serious candidate. They had no contact with the Senator. Much of Goldwater sentiment melted when Chairman Foss reported on his conversations with Senator Goldwater. This direct contact with Goldwater was, of course, impressive to the delegates.

The same was true in regard to the vice presidential nomination. The delegation was willing to support almost any candidate except Lodge and a few said they intended to oppose Lodge in any case. In at least two instances, Senator Mundt convinced such delegates of the need to support Nixon's choice.

Third, despite the early fervor about conservatism, Goldwater, the Nixon "sell-out," and the like, delegates were able to accept what happened at the convention because they were less interested in the national ticket and the national platform than they were in South Dakota politics. Thus, many delegates were anxious to work for a conservative platform and conservative candidates but if they were not successful it would not deter them from similar attempts at the state level. In the author's many discussions with delegates and alternates, they were able to discuss South Dakota politics with understanding and interest. National politics was less familiar. They were not sure of the relation of

---

*It is possible that any delegation is more "leaderless" if the party does not control the governorship of the state. South Dakota had a Democratic governor in 1960.

national political decisions to South Dakota politics nor of their own roles in relation to national politics. Where they felt that it was necessary to have some information about this relationship, they relied on party leaders. And what party leaders had to tell delegates about their relationship to national nominating politics frustrated them.

A final overall impression, therefore, suggests that the South Dakota delegation was essentially leaderless and had limited access to the centers of decision-making at the convention. As the convention proceeded, they were able to establish lines of communication, principally through their chairman who had contacts with national party leaders and through party leaders who were not members of the delegation. Once these lines of communication were established, it was apparent to the South Dakota delegation that they had little to do except ratify the decisions which were made by presidential candidate Nixon.

15. *Freedom and Constraint in the Indiana Democratic Delegation*

KARL O'LESSKER

Wabash College

One-ballot conventions have the virture of concealing a good deal of intra-delegation stress and strain: the factional disputes that may erupt within a delegation, if the nominating process wears on too long, remain dormant, known only to insiders and their confidants. This seems especially true of the 1960 Democratic Convention, where, if rumors floating around at the time had any substance, many a delegation would have split noisily open as early as the second ballot. The case of Indiana is instructive: under the terms of its presidential primary law the delegations had no choice but to vote for Senator Kennedy on the first ballot; but it was clear long before the Convention opened that something like half the delegates planned to cast their votes for other candidates on the second and subsequent ballots.

Now from the point of view of the academic observer, the really interesting question about Indiana's delegation was not so much whether a number of members *wanted* to defect from Senator Kennedy as whether they *would be able to*—whether, that is, they possessed enough individual autonomy to vote as they pleased after having discharged their legal obligations. In order to determine this it is not enough to see that the total delegation vote is divided among, say, three different contenders; for it is always possible that such a division is a token not of the individual delegate's freedom but of a falling out among party leaders in the state, with each leader exercising firm control over the particular delegates beholden to him. Thus even if there had been a second-ballot split, it would still have been necessary to interview individual delegates to try to determine why they voted as they did. Accordingly, I conducted post-Convention interviews with ten of the state's 66 district-selected delegates (that is, excluding the national committeeman and committeewoman, who are members ex officio and have ½-vote each); this represented a sample of slightly over 15 per cent of the entire delegation, selected with reference to the geographical area and type of community from which they came. In addition, I had numerous lengthy conversations with two of the alternates (who are personal friends), who were able to confirm much of what the ten delegates themselves told me. Before presenting the interview findings, however, I must first sketch enough of the background of pre-Convention and Convention activity to make what follows intelligible to non-Hoosiers.

One of the more striking characteristics of the Indiana political situation in early 1960 was the fragmentation of power within the Democratic Party. It had not elected a governor for eight years; and although Democrats had won by historic pluralities in the senatorial and other statewide elections of 1958, no single leader had come even close to mastering the diverse factions of which the party is composed. As a consequence, political power rested among a number of individual strongmen and local district organizations, none of whom appeared at all willing to abandon the prerogatives of independence unless and until the Party should have elected its gubernatorial nominee, State Senator Matthew B. Welsh. It was in this connection of fragmented power that the presidential primary of May 3, 1960, was held and, a month later, delegates to the National Convention chosen.

The primary itself was the object of considerable interest throughout the nation, for it was one of the few which could be viewed as a "straight fight" between Senator Kennedy and Vice President Nixon: the only other candidates on the ballot were, for the Republicans, a Negro attorney named Frank Beckwith, whose candidacy was by his own admission merely a symbolic gesture of racial pride; and, for the Democrats, perennial candidate Lar Daly, of Chicago, and one John H. Latham, an almost wholly obscure Hoosier. Thus it was thought that the results of the primary would in some degree indicate the relative strengths of Kennedy and Nixon, uncomplicated by other preferences on the part of the voters.

The outcome (considered surprising in some quarters) might have had a substantial impact on the behavior of the Indiana delegation in Los Angeles if the convention had gone to a second ballot. For although the Democratic candidates drew a slightly larger combined vote than the Republicans (433,000 to 422,000), Nixon outpolled Kennedy by some 50,000 votes; a full 23 per cent of all those who voted Democratic cast their ballots for the utterly frivolous candidacies of Latham and Daly, while Nixon on the other hand lost less than 5 per cent of the Republican vote to his opponent.

In any other presidential primary, this sort of large-scale defection from the leading candidate would doubtless have been interpreted simply as a sign that substantial numbers of the faithful preferred other contenders to the one whose name was on the ballot. But given the fact of Kennedy's religion and the further fact of Indiana's historic ties to the Ku Klux Klan, a great many commentators immediately suggested that the deviant 23 per cent was primarily an expression of anti-Catholicism, and as such could be expected to carry over into the November election. Whether or not this interpretation is correct, the *Indianapolis News* was surely making a reasonable estimate of Democratic sentiments when it reported that "Kennedy's showing here weakened his chances to keep a majority of the state's 34 Democratic national convention votes after their first ballot obligations are discharged." It is clear, in other words, that as a result of the primary a substantial number of Democratic politicians throughout Indiana began to develop grave doubts about Kennedy's ability to carry the state in November. Those doubts were to show up even more strongly at the party's state convention six weeks later, when, according to another newspaper report, "Johnson supporters were gleeful over a poll conducted at the convention which showed that Kennedy would hold only 10½ of Indiana's 34 votes on the second ballot. . . . Senators Lyndon B. Johnson of Texas and Stuart Symington of Missouri will have 11 each of the second ballot with ½ vote for Stevenson and one vote uncommitted."

The next step in the pre-convention process was the selection of delegates, which took place—formally at any rate—in congressional district caucuses held the night before the state convention of June 21. As it happened, the selection proceedings were openly contentious in only one of Indiana's eleven districts; in all others the district leaders had apparently made their selections well in advance of the formal caucuses. But in the Eleventh District (Indianapolis and adjacent townships), something of a fight was made by Johnson supporters, who wanted to get at least one of the Majority Leader's admirers on the district slate. By previous agreement among organization potentates, however, the delegates whose names were offered to the caucus were known to favor Kennedy and Symington only; and these, after a Johnson man's motion for a secret ballot had been rejected, were officially chosen.

In no other district was the selection of delegates the occasion for a struggle; and, so far as I have been able to determine, in only two other districts (both industrial and strongly committed to Kennedy) was the question even raised as to whom the potential delegates would support after the first ballot. Thus the great majority of delegates appear to have gone to Los Angeles wholly unpledged beyond the legally determined first ballot.

During the convention itself the Indiana delegation acted as a unit only twice (apart from its attendance on the floor.) It held a preliminary breakfast caucus on the opening Monday, during which housekeeping details were the only item on the agenda, and a longer caucus the following Wednesday, which heard speeches from Senator Kennedy and representatives of Johnson, Symington, and Stevenson. Immediately after the speeches, however, the delegation chairman, Congressman Ray Madden, declared the caucus adjourned, in an obvious move to forestall expressions of anti-Kennedy sentiment; these, according to rumors heard at the time, could conceivably have led to a bolt from Kennedy even on the first ballot, and despite the presumably binding nature of the primary-enforced commitment. In any event, the threatened defections never occurred; the potential defectors contented themselves with waiting hopefully, but vainly, for a second ballot.

As regards the vice-presidential selection of the following day, there seems to have been little or no serious displeasure among

Indiana delegates on the naming of Senator Johnson—although it is fair, I think, to say that in an open contest such as took place in 1956, Senator Symington would have received a substantial majority of the state's votes. In fact, however, the delegation was never polled on the question of accepting or rejecting the selection of Johnson, and may be said to have acquiesced with good grace when the voice-vote was declared to have carried by the required two-thirds.

We come now to the post-convention interviews.

The principal questions I asked were these: If there had been a second ballot whom would you have voted for? What considerations led you to favor that candidate over the others? Were you under any obligation to consult some other member of the delegation before making your decision? What do you think the role of the individual delegate *ought* to be? How satisfied are you with what you personally were able to do as a delegate? And finally, how do you feel about the primary in Indiana? Each of my respondents answered these questions fully and frankly; and equally impressive, so it seems to me, was the degree of near-unanimity I encountered on many of the answers, revealing what indeed may be elements of a genuine consensus among Democratic politicians in the state.

One area of agreement among the respondents stands out in interest and significance. Eight of the ten delegates interviewed expressed the general conviction that he was, and by rights ought to have been, a free agent in deciding how to cast his vote in the presidential balloting (after, of course, the primary-determined first ballot.) Each of these eight emphatically denied that he was, or would have been, "bossed" by anyone. Indeed, their expression of this view sounded positively Burkeian in its insistence on the right and responsibility of the individual delegate to make up his own mind, not only about whom to vote for but, interestingly enough, about what criteria to use in reaching that decision. One especially articulate county chairman from a small rural county put it this way: "Look, if I want to vote for the man I personally figure will make the best President, that's up to me. Or if I want to vote for the man my people back home want me to vote for—no matter what I think of him—I can do it. Or if I want to go up to a Matt Welsh [the Democratic nominee for governor] and say, 'Matt, who do you want me to vote for?' well, that's my decision to make. The point is, there's nobody going to tell me I *have* to do it one way or the other. I make my own living and I'm my own man in politics."*

Now let me emphasize that this was the typical, not the unique, view. Seven of the eight delegates who took this position were self-employed, while the eighth was a local government official; none expected to profit monetarily from a Democratic presidential victory in November. As regards the two delegates who did not claim to have freedom of choice during the convention (one a union official, the other a county official), neither seemed to believe that he *should* have been free to go his own way. Instead, both pointed to the inescapable necessity for solidarity within an organization; both insisted they had won their place as delegates precisely because, being members of their respective organizations and having taken part in the decision as to whom to support, their loyalty could be counted on. "What's the point of having an organization," one asked, "if it doesn't act like an organization?"

As I reported earlier, only three of the state's eleven districts appear to have selected delegates on the basis of whom they could be depended on to support for the nomination; the two respondents whose views I have just described came from two of those three districts. Is this to say that all delegates from the other eight districts would have made a second-ballot choice independent of any outside influence? By no means. Some, to be sure, would have done so: four of my respondents asserted that their second-ballot vote would have been decided strictly on the basis of their own judgment as to the relative attractiveness of the candidates (the process of forming a judgment would of course include attention to the views of friends within the delegation, but would not include mere deference to the views of others who happen to be more highly placed.) But of the four remaining non-committed respondents, three indicated that they would have sought, and probably deferred to, the wishes of gubernatorial nominee Matthew Welsh or persons known to be close to him. This they explained on the grounds that Welsh and

*This and subsequent quotations, while not absolutely verbatim, are nevertheless close enough in tone and content to the respondents' words to merit being put in quotes.

When I asked this county chairman whether he could be his own man if he had to depend on a state job, or at least on the expectation of one, he laughed and said, "Brother, I wouldn't be in politics if I had to make a living out of it!"

his associates would have the most at stake in the November election and were entitled to the delegates' support in attempting to get all the help they could from the national ticket. Moreover, as one of the three added, "Welsh is the head of our party now. I think he deserves to be listened to on things like this."

The fourth district respondent in this group stated that he would have sought the advice of his district chairman, the reason for this being that his chairman certainly knew more than anyone else about sentiment in the district and would thus have the surest judgment as to which candidate would run the strongest. Asked what he would have done if there had been open disagreement between his district chairman and Senator Welsh, he replied that this was not even a possibility in view of the close relations between the two men. Was there any chance that his own view and that of his chairman would have conflicted, and if so how would he have voted? "I'll tell you the truth," he answered. "I just didn't feel strong enough myself. But for that matter, neither did the chairman. I don't see how we could have gotten into a real fight about it."

A question arises at this point concerning the willingness of these four respondents to defer to the views and wishes of persons more highly placed in the party hierarchy: surely a delegate cannot be said to be "free" when he holds an inner commitment to defer to someone else's judgment? The answer here, I believe, is that there is a distinction between deference freely granted and deference coercively exacted, between the man who says, "I'll follow your lead because I want to," and the man who says, "I'll follow your lead because you'll ruin me if I don't." And even though at the deepest level of analysis this distinction may fail to hold, yet I think we must concede that, since each of us has undoubtedly felt the distinction to be meaningful in terms of his own personal experience, it can only be arbitrary to deny its meaningfulness for delegates to a political convention. Those, therefore, who chose without consideration of potential penalties or rewards to defer to the wishes of others, acted as free agents in doing so.

Returning to the interview material, a further question dealt with the delegates' views as to their obligations to the voters in their districts: to what extent did they attempt to discover candidate preferences among local partisans, and how far would they have been guided by that information if they had had to make a second-ballot choice? Several respondents in answering this question took pains to point out that they were not elected by the general public but were instead chosen by the district leadership, and that they were therefore not responsible to the voters as a whole. On the other hand they all agreed that voter preference at home would have been a factor in their own decision-making. "I wouldn't have been doing anybody a favor," said one, "nominating a guy who couldn't lick Dick Nixon." Each, moreover, had what he considered to be a reasonably accurate picture of the general sentiment in his district, though none had made any special effort to discover it. (Not surprisingly, most of the delegates had a much clearer idea of whom the people did *not* want than of whom they actively preferred.) But in general, my respondents were far from considering themselves as mere instruments for recording the will of the lay public; though I should add that in no case did a delegate tell me he would have voted for a candidate whom he later described as being unpopular in his district.

The final question I shall report on here dealt with the respondents' view on the Indiana presidential primary, which had bound them to Senator Kennedy on the first and only ballot despite his somewhat less than spectacular showing in the May 3rd contest. With only one rather tentative exception, each declared himself opposed to the law and in favor of its speedy repeal. To be sure, there was considerable variation in the fervor with which each delegate condemned it; but it is notable that three of those who opposed it had had Kennedy as their first choice for the nomination (as did the one delegate who liked the primary "pretty well" to begin with.) The consensus centered on two major points. First, a presidential primary is almost certain to be unrepresentative in that rarely if ever will all the serious contenders enter it. This means that the voters who prefer one of the non-running candidates are faced with the choice of either helping a candidate they like less or, by not voting at all, giving a minor boost to the candidate of the opposition party. How then is the delegate to interpret the results in his district? As regards the 1960 primary, what could he conclude about the 23 per cent of the Democratic voters who chose Latham or Daly in preference to Kennedy? Would they simply refuse to vote for Kennedy if nominated in November.

The second point had to do with what the delegates felt regarding their own competence for choosing a nominee. Most took the position (with all due modesty) that they probably were better judges of who would make a good candidate than were the voters, and should thus be permitted to exercise their special competence in the matter.* A common thread running throughout the comments of the nine respondents who disliked the primary is what we might call "pride of place." Each, though in varying degrees, was obviously proud of having been selected to speak for Indiana at the convention; hence it is not surprising that an institutional device which deprives the delegate of an important measure of autonomy is looked upon with resentment and misgivings.

It would be wrong, however, to suppose that hostility towards the primary is a function simply of injured pride. On the contrary, I found a quite genuine concern about the distortions in the picture of public opinion which are produced by primary contests in which only one or two names appear on each party's ballot. And when I asked my respondents whether they would like to see the law changed to make subsequent presidential primaries non-binding in their results, all agreed that, while this would be an improvement over the present law, most such contests would probably continue to produce more confusion than clarity, and are thus eminently dispensable.

The one delegate who thought the primary law a good one made his case on the grounds that the people have a right to be heard on so important a matter as choosing a presidential nominee. Asked whether he thought the 1960 primary, with only Kennedy entered, gave the voters much of a choice, he readily admitted that it did not, but then went on to point out that this was the fault of Kennedy's opponents, not the law. And he further observed that, in light of the importance of primary victories in Kennedy's drive for the nomination, future contenders would not be likely to let very many states go by default. He conceded, nevertheless, that it might be just as well to amend the present law to make primary results non-binding on the delegates; but he had not as yet entirely made up his mind on that point.

Taken at face value, the interviews clearly indicate that most of the Indiana delegates would have been free to vote as they

---

*It should be noted that I am not here agreeing or disagreeing with the views of my respondents (nor did I attempt to push them in the questioning). I am merely reporting what they told me.

pleased after the first ballot. But the hard question remains, how likely is it that the delegation leaders would have been content to permit so many delegates to retain that freedom of action on later, crucial, ballots? Put another way, were my respondents being overly sanguine in supposing that they could have exercised as much decisional autonomy as they believed they had? A persuasive answer to either question would require two kinds of information: first, whether the leaders themselves, individually or collectively, were willing to refrain from putting pressure on the delegates responsive to them; and second, what sanctions the leaders could have applied, had they wanted to, in order to force the delegates to vote for a particular candidate. Regarding the first, I am frankly unable even to guess at an answer; certainly it would depend upon the temperament, character, leadership philosophy, and so on, of the men in question. The only hard datum I can offer on this point is the testimony of the one district leader who was included among my respondents. When asked how far he would have gone in attempting to get the other delegates from his district to vote as he would on later ballots, he replied that he "probably" would have talked it over with them but would definitely not have tried to coerce anyone— the reason being that "there are more things involved in keeping our organization together than just getting everybody to vote the same out in Los Angeles." But while this answer is suggestive (and I shall return to it a little later), I do not claim that it must be representative of the views of all, or most, other delegation leaders.

Regarding the question as to what sanctions the leaders could have applied had they wanted to, this is equally difficult to assess by virtue of the fact that different leaders would possess different kinds of sanctions and different delegates would have different powers of resistance. But this much, I think, can be said, and it goes to the heart of the entire problem; given the multiplicity of cross-pressure and interests, of lurking jealousies and antagonisms which are endemic in any situation of fragmented political power, it is reasonable to suppose that the leaders would be rather more chary of attempting to impose their various wills on presumed confederates than would a leader whose power extends virtually unchallenged over the mass of his subordinates.

This surely is a part of what the district leader quoted above had in mind when he spoke of the requirements of holding an organization together. Implicit in his remarks is the understanding that the risks of alienating the support of one's followers must be weighed against the importance of the objective one wishes to achieve. And the degree of risk, I would suggest, is inversely proportional to the amount of power which the leader holds within the total political context (that is, the Democratic party of Indiana.) Put in rather more homely terms, the little man needs each of his few friends a good deal more than the big man need each of his many. Now I think it is fair to say that in Indiana in 1960 the state political situation loomed far more importantly in the eyes of most politicians than the national situation. Conversations throughout the state lead me to believe that most Democrats were more concerned with electing Welsh as governor than with carrying Indiana for Kennedy (or for whomever else the nominee might have been). Consequently, the balloting in Los Angeles must have struck many leaders as being secondary in importance to the necessity of keeping their respective organizations strong and happy; and this factor, too, would have militated against their attempting to coerce those delegates responsive to them. In other words, the objective to be achieved—the nomination of a particular presidential candidate—must have counted for even less as against the risk of alienating their followers.

The conclusion would therefore seem to be that the delegates who believed themselves to have been free to vote as they chose at Los Angeles were almost certainly justified in that belief. And this unusual degree of freedom, we must suppose, was to an important extent a consequence of the fragmentation of power within the Democratic Party of Indiana in the summer of 1960.

16. The Michigan Democratic Delegation: The Role of a Delegation Chairman

ROBERT L. SAWYER

Central Michigan University

During the past twelve years the party system in Michigan has evolved from a modified one-party system into a vigorous two-party system. On a statewide basis, the Democratic Party now occupies the position of first major party in Michigan. The Michigan Democratic Party's rise to power was coincident with the administration of Governor G. Mennen Williams, who first led the party to victory in 1948. Election to six consecutive terms in the governorship had clearly established him as the number one leader in the Michigan Democratic Party. It was to be expected, therefore, that the governor would lead the Michigan delegation to the 1960 Democratic National Convention as he had done in 1952 and 1956.

The 102 delegates and 50 alternates of the Michigan delegation were chosen at a state convention held in Grand Rapids on May 7, 1960. Immediately after the state convention, the delegation caucused for the purpose of organizing for the national convention. The caucus first named Governor Williams as the delegation chairman and then proceeded to the election of the other officers of the delegation. These included four vice chairmen, four secretaries, a treasurer, a parliamentarian and two sergeants-at-arms.* The office of first vice chairman of the delegation was given to Neil Staebler, who had held the office of Democratic state chairman since 1950. This office, which ranked second in importance, resembled and complemented that of the delegation chairman to a large extent.

The state convention which chose the national delegates adopted a resolution committing the delegates to the support of the governor's candidacy until such time as he should release them. The strategic objectives of the Michigan Democrats were revealed in the provisions of the "favorite son" resolution which obligated the delegates to support Governor Williams for any office which he might seek. Thus, without closing the door to the presidential nomination, Michigan Democrats indicated that they were quite willing to accept the second position on the national ticket. Since the delegation was not polled at the first caucus, there is no accurate record of the second choice of the delegation at that time. The prospects for Senator Kennedy

---

*This caucus also elected a set of officers for the alternates and selected the delegation's representatives on the committees of the national convention. At the first caucus in Los Angeles, the delegation elected the national committee members from Michigan and several "honorary" vice chairmen and secretaries. A number of the working committees were appointed by the leadership. These included: spectator seats, delegate liaison, publicity, convention arrangements, credentials, delegate kits and assignments, governor's reception, trailer, general office staff, historian, information center, pages, and transportation.

appeared bright, however, for a professional poll conducted at that time showed him to be a strong favorite among Democratic voters in Michigan.*

Governor Williams's decision to support Senator Kennedy was announced on June 2, following a conference between the two men at the governor's mansion on Mackinac Island. Also present at the conference were Neil Staebler, state chairman; Thomas Quimby, national committeeman; Mrs. Margaret Price, national committeewoman; and Mrs. Mildred Jeffrey, alternate national committeewoman and director of community relations for the UAW. All of these party leaders went on record in support of the governor's endorsement of Senator Kennedy, and the endorsement was favorably received among the delegates.

At the second caucus which was held on the campus of Michigan State University in East Lansing, on June 18, the governor made his major appeal on behalf of Senator Kennedy. This was the only caucus at which there occurred an extensive discussion of the presidential candidates.**

The discussion of presidential candidates was opened by Governor Williams who spoke at length on behalf of Senator Kennedy. In general, the governor's speech reiterated the points that he had made in previous press releases and communications to the delegates. The three main lines of argument were: (1) that Kennedy was *knowledgeable;* (2) that Kennedy was a *real liberal;* and (3) that Kennedy was a *winner.* In connection with the first line of argument, Williams stressed Kennedy's experience in the public service and his grasp of foreign affairs. He dwelt at some length upon two of Kennedy's books, *While England Slept* and *The Strategy of Peace,* citing these as evidence of Kennedy's knowledge and intellectual acumen. The governor then reviewed various aspects of the Kennedy record on domestic issues. This was done with the apparent objective of demonstrating Kennedy's liberalism and, in that regard, particular emphasis was placed upon civil rights. Moreover, the governor predicted that Kennedy could be nominated without the votes of southern

---

*The percentages were: Kennedy—63.0; Stevenson—22.2; Humphrey—7.4; Symington—5.6; Johnson—1.8. The press also reported that the "general impression" at the state convention on May 7 was that Kennedy would get the "bulk" of Michigan's support.

**Certain other routine business, including committee reports, was transacted at this caucus. But this was relatively unimportant compared to the discussion of the presidential candidates.

delegates and, consequently, would be under no obligation to compromise in the field of civil rights.

Following the governor's speech, some nineteen other delegates spoke briefly. Of these, four expressed no commitment, ten spoke for Kennedy, four spoke for Adlai Stevenson, one spoke for Stuart Symington, and one declared his continuing loyalty for Governor Williams. Several of the Kennedy supporters, including some prominent labor leaders, expressed a strong attachment to Adlai Stevenson. But a conviction that Adlai could not win, and the desire to unite the liberals in opposition to Senator Johnson's candidacy, had caused these one-time Stevenson adherents to cast their lot with John F. Kennedy.*

At the conclusion of the discussion, an "unofficial" vote was taken. Alternates as well as delegates were included in the poll. 42 of the 152 members of the delegation were absent. The results, in terms of one-half votes, were as follows: Kennedy—84; Stevenson—10; Symington—8; abstaining—8. Despite its obvious limitations, this vote proved to be quite accurate; a subsequent telephone poll of all the delegates—alternates excluded—revealed a similar number of votes for Kennedy.

The vote received by Senator Kennedy in the June 18 caucus was within one half of a vote of that which Michigan gave to him during the presidential balloting on the floor of the national convention. But the caucus proceedings indicated that much of the Kennedy support was not yet "firm" as of June 18. The discussion in the caucus indicated that a number of the delegates desired additional information in regard to Senator Kennedy's position on civil rights, an issue of paramount importance in the Michigan Democratic Party.

Immediately after the June 18 caucus, Governor Williams arranged for a conference between Senator Kennedy and a group of Michigan Democrats who were keenly interested in civil rights. This group, consisting largely of prominent Negro leaders, journeyed to Washington and spent several hours discussing civil rights with Senator Kennedy. Party leaders report that the meeting was highly successful. All of the Michigan leaders came away convinced that Kennedy was a strong liberal and that he had a

*Two of the most important of the labor leaders in the delegation were August Scholle, state president of the AFL-CIO, and Leonard Woodcock, a vice president of the UAW. Some 44—29 percent—of the 152 delegates and alternates were reported to be trade union members.

keen interest in the field of civil rights. While this meeting may not have resulted in a large number of conversions, the observations of those who attended indicated that it played a crucial role in the reinforcement of the pro-Kennedy sentiment among an important segment of the Michigan delegation.*

Except for a flurry over the vice presidential nomination, the events at Los Angeles proved anticlimactic for the Michigan delegation. When the Michigan delegation met in caucus on Thursday afternoon, interest in the vice presidential nomination ran high, indeed. The questions delegates directed to the leadership were both hopeful and fearful: hopeful of a Williams nomination and fearful of a Johnson nomination.

The party leaders answered that they did not know, as yet, who the vice presidential nominee would be. They indicated, however, that they did not believe that it would be Senator Johnson. Governor Williams, reporting on a recent meeting with Senator Kennedy and other top party leaders, stated that he had taken a strong stand against the nomination of Senator Johnson. He stated, further, that he "suspected" that the vice presidential nominee would be either Senator Symington or Senator Jackson.

As for himself, Governor Williams said that he would accept the nomination if offered to him but he was not "pushing" for it. State chairman Staebler stated that there were alternative approaches to the strategy of the presidential campaign and that Governor Williams's nomination would "make a great deal of sense" if one of these approaches was followed.

Governor Williams left the caucus early to attend a high level meeting about the vice presidential nomination. The caucus continued its discussion for another half hour and then adjourned to await further information relative to the vice presidential nomination. A close examination of the remarks made by party leaders toward the end of the caucus indicates that they were realistic enough to recognize the possibility of a Johnson nomination. Remarks relative to alternative approaches to campaign strategy, as well as suggestions that the delegates should not be too doctrinaire in their thinking, indicate that the leadership was trying to prepare the delegates for all eventualities. However, neither the leaders nor the delegates were quite prepared for the an-

---

*This meeting occurred between the June 18 caucus and the telephone poll of the delegates which is discussed in the text. Sixteen of the 152 delegates from Michigan were Negroes.

nouncement made by Senator Jackson shortly after the adjournment of the caucus.

The Michigan delegation was rather widely dispersed when
Senator Jackson announced that Kennedy had selected Johnson
as his running mate. Moreover, communication was probably re-
tarded by the fact that many delegates departed for the convention hall shortly after the announcement was made. At any rate,
two hours or more elapsed before the delegates were assembled
in emergency caucus at the convention hall. This caucus, at
which Governor Williams and the state chairman presided jointly, was conducted in a highly emotional atmosphere. The leaders
were obviously surprised and disappointed at the turn of events.
The delegates appeared to be even more disconcerted: women
were in tears and men shook their heads in solemn disbelief. The
leadership apparently perceived that circumstances were not conducive to effective deliberation. Accordingly, and after the delegates had had some time to give vent to their disappointment,
a strategy committee was appointed to work out a plan of action.

As it turned out, the task of the strategy committee was simply that of deciding what to do in the face of a *fait accompli*.
When the time arrived for the nomination of the vice presidential
candidate, it was evident that Michigan would stand virtually
alone in any roll call opposition to the nomination of Senator
Johnson. This information was obtained, in part, through a delegate liaison operation in which each Michigan delegate had
reported on sentiment in the state delegation to which he had
been assigned. The strategy proposed, therefore, was that Michigan should cast five votes for Johnson, and the remainder against
him, in the event of a roll call vote. In the event of a voice vote,
the delegation was to shout a vigorous "no"—which they did!

At this point it is appropriate to inquire into the causes for
Michigan's strong reaction to the Johnson nomination. In the
first place, there was the practical question of Johnson's vote-
getting ability in Michigan. Governor Williams had stated, prior
to the convention, that he did not believe that "Johnson could
carry Michigan." Although the preceding remark was made in
reference to Johnson's presidential candidacy, the same strategic
considerations would apply to the vice presidential nomination.

Another, and probably more important, reason for Michigan's
opposition to Johnson lay in the delegation's disappointment
over its failure to capture either the vice presidential nomination

or the national party chairmanship. Although Governor Williams and Senator Kennedy had been careful to deny that any "deals" had been made, Williams' endorsement of Kennedy gave rise to immediate speculation that the governor might be chosen as Kennedy's running mate. There was widespread speculation, also, that either state chairman Staebler or national committeeman Tom Quimby might be chosen to head the Democratic National Committee.

This kind of speculation was to be expected in view of the role which Michigan Democrats played in the Kennedy nomination. Senator Kennedy, himself, had indicated that he considered Governor Williams' support to be of special importance "because of his example to the other uncommitted liberals of the nation."

The third reason for Michigan's reaction to the Johnson nomination is probably the most important and it is related to the one discussed immediately above. The loss of the vice presidential nomination to Johnson meant more to the Michigan delegation than the mere loss of a "plum" for their chief, for the nomination had been lost to the man who represented the conservative image in a contest which had been characterized in Michigan as a struggle between the forces of liberalism and the forces of conservatism.

Despite his opposition to the nomination of Senator Johnson, Governor Williams had stated, prior to the convention, that he would support the nominees of the convention. Thus, the closing session of the convention found him on the speakers' platform, along with the losing presidential aspirants, pledging his full support to the ticket and urging all Democrats to do likewise. If there was any anti-Johnson sentiment left among Michigan Democrats on November 8, 1960, it was not sufficient to prevent the party organization from turning out a popular majority for Kennedy. For the first time since 1944, Michigan gave its twenty electoral votes to the Democratic presidential candidate.

17. The Decision-Making Process in the Pennsylvania Democratic Delegation
SIDNEY WISE
Franklin and Marshall College

Introduction

Three facts stand out in reflecting on the behavior of the Pennsylvania delegation to the Democratic National Convention of

1960. Most striking is the extent of purely state and local considerations which dominated the actions and attitudes of the delegates. Time and again the topic of which candidates should be supported was discussed within the framework of how the candidate would fare in the specific district of the delegate who was talking.

Secondly, one recalls how advantageous it was for the Pennsylvania delegation not to be confronted by the problem of caucusing for a second ballot. The extent of the harmony which was generated by a one-ballot convention meant that it was possible for the party to enter the campaign with a great degree of unity.

Second and third ballot caucuses might well have generated splits in the delegation along urban-rural lines which would have undoubtedly been along Protestant-Catholic lines as well. One very influential and responsible delegate has stated that had there been a second ballot, the vote for Stevenson would have gone to 45. On a third ballot, he claimed, the Stevenson total would have been 65. This same delegate also said that he and several other delegates who were willing to go along with voting for Kennedy despite their enthusiasm for Stevenson made specific inquiries about a second ballot. The inquiries were to the question of whether Governor Lawrence would feel that his posture as head of the delegation would be threatened if, on a second ballot, these delegates were to vote for Stevenson. The answer that came back was that the governor would appreciate first ballot votes for Kennedy but would not interpret second ballot votes for Stevenson as a personal repudiation.

The third item worth recalling is that there was only one occasion when the platform was specifically and formally mentioned before any considerable number of delegates. On the Sunday prior to the opening of the convention a luncheon was held for the delegates and alternates from southeastern Pennsylvania. Bill Green was toastmaster and in his remarks paid tribute to Governor Lawrence, expressing confidence that the delegates would respect his leadership in the days ahead. The meeting ended with Green's announcement that as one of the state's delegates to the platform committee he was about to leave for a session at the Hotel Biltmore where he would "fight for a strong civil rights plank." This was the extent of the references to the platform before any formal meeting of the delegates.

During the film presentation of the platform, I asked Green

what procedures he felt the Pennsylvania delegation would follow if the platform controversy were to necessitate a roll call of
the states. His reply was that if a roll call were necessary on
the platform Governor Lawrence would simply announce that
Pennsylvania's 81 votes were for the platform. In other words,
there would be no caucus on the platform.

Organization

The Pennsylvania delegation to the 1960 Democratic convention consisted of 162 delegates with 81 votes. Of these, 42 were
delegates-at-large selected by the state committee. The remaining
120 delegates were selected in party primaries, four from each
of the state's 30 congressional districts.

The selection process was not marked by any significant controversy. On many occasions Governor Lawrence stated that the
delegates-at-large were selected without regard to any identification with any of the candidates for the nomination. A study of
the list confirms this statement, for the delegates-at-large so
obviously included the *de jure* leadership of the party that the list
seems to have written itself.

The typical situation in the congressional districts was that
the candidates for the posts of delegates and alternates were
selected with the cooperation of local party officials, but again
with little regard to commitment. In a few situations there were
contests and in a few situations the non-organizational candidates
campaigned on the basis of a pledge to support a specific candidate.

The organization meeting of the Pennsylvania delegation was
held on June 1 in Harrisburg with nearly 242 delegates and alternates in attendance. The only important items of business in
this rather ceremonial meeting were the selection of Governor
David L. Lawrence as chairman of the delegation and the unanimous approval of the governor's appointments to the four national convention committees. The governor then made a statement disclaiming any interest in attempting to get a "unit rule."
He stated at that time and many times afterward that he was
uncommitted, and that he would express no preference until the
delegation had an opportunity to listen to all of the candidates in
Los Angeles.

On the first day of the convention (Monday, July 11) the
Pennsylvania delegation held its long-awaited breakfast caucus.

The delegates were addressed by Senators Kennedy, Johnson, Symington, and Monroney, the latter speaking on behalf of Governor Stevenson. This part of the caucus was public. The delegates then moved to another room where the recommendations and balloting took place. This part of the meeting lasted for 90 minutes.

The only other time the delegation caucused was on Thursday morning. This meeting was very brief, with the delegates merely expressing their confidence in any discussions that Governor Lawrence might participate in with respect to the selection of a vice presidential nominee. Both meetings were chaired by Governor Lawrence. Indeed, the governor's stature in the party is such that any other arrangement was inconceivable.

Throughout the convention the atmosphere among the delegates was one of relaxation. The sign at the entrance of the Huntington-Sheraton in Pasadena had read "Welcome Delegates from Pennsylvania, Canal Zone and Virgin Islands." Once the delegates from this important state overcame their pique at this bracketing and at their being housed some 16 miles from the convention site, they discovered that their isolation was splendid. The swank surroundings made for conviviality and socializing. But the first newspaper headlines which the delegates saw said that the convention was over before it started and nothing in the Pennsylvania atmosphere seemed to refute the contention. This meant that convention details were only a small part of the chit-chat. One often had the feeling that the delegates were really at a $100 dinner in Harrisburg, greeting each other with the easy amiability of politicians about to settle a minor patronage problem. A great deal of business was undoubtedly transacted in the crowded lobbies, but it was the business of the Pennsylvania Democratic Party. The easy access to the top leaders of the party, the frequent and lengthy bus rides to and from the Sports Arena, and the hotel's several swimming pools all added to the extra-convention politicking.

One had the impression that the delegates were convinced the conclusion was determined and so overwhelmed by the proceedings that their attention often turned to a discussion of state politics or the diversions of Los Angeles. Absenteeism was frequent and extensive. If the delegates had the feeling that the convention posed only a handful of problems and that these problems had, to a great extent, been resolved by events that had unfolded prior to their arrival in Los Angeles, this is not a suggestion that the delegates did not have an accurate picture of the proceedings or that the proceedings were unimportant.

Some delegates did express frustration. These delegates undoubtedly came to the convention in the hope that their individual votes would be courted. The Stevenson delegates most frequently expressed the discomfort of being overwhelmed. But the overwhelming majority of the delegates accepted the rumored judgment of the leadership that a first ballot vote for Kennedy was politically astute.

The Leaders and Their Problems

The sole division of any significance among the delegates was on the choice of a presidential nominee. For some time, the delegates had been waiting to hear Governor Lawrence's position, though the governor had "met the press" and "faced the nation" without expressing anything more than his very high regard for Stevenson and his high regard for the many other candidates.

When Governor Lawrence spoke to the caucus on behalf of Kennedy he again underscored his personal affection for Stevenson but, in essence, contended that Kennedy could win. While he expressed an appreciation of Stevenson's decision not to seek the nomination, Governor Lawrence said that Stevenson's unwillingness to encourage his supporters made it extremely difficult to urge his candidacy at this time. He then pointed to the string of Kennedy victories in the primaries and insisted that the Democratic Party could not deny the nomination to a candidate who had compiled such a record.

The tensions within the caucus were definitely Kennedy v. Stevenson. Following the governor's speech, the caucus was addressed by former governor George Leader, whose home in York County is in the heart of the state's "bible belt." Leader spoke enthusiastically on Kennedy's behalf, despite his well-known affection for Stevenson. Indeed, while asking for Kennedy support, he told the caucus that he "would not be able to sleep tonight" if he did not feel that a Kennedy victory would mean that Stevenson would be Secretary of State.

Senator Joseph S. Clark added that he felt that Senator Kennedy could win and that the party "should be united" and "work hard." He also conceded that he had shared some of the misgivings about the Kennedy candidacy but that he was now convinced that Kennedy would be an excellent candidate.

The next speaker was Miss Genevieve Blatt. As Secretary of Internal Affairs, Miss Blatt had long been identified with Governor Lawrence. She had been raised in Allegheny County politics, and enjoys a considerable reputation as a politician, having even received more votes than Governor Lawrence in the election of 1958. Her comments were on behalf of Stevenson. She spoke with emotion and conviction, insisting that if so many political leaders were personally convinced of Stevenson's qualifications, then they should nominate him. She temporized her endorsement with the comment that her remarks were only her own and that the delegates would probably do well to follow the lead of Governor Lawrence.

The only other comments at this important caucus were those of Henry Leader, who said that he was not following his brother's lead and would vote for Stevenson, and the vehement denial by Emma Guffey Miller, long time national committeewomen, that she had ever told the *Pittsburgh Post-Gazette* that Jack Kennedy could not win.

As the time for the voting approached, the atmosphere was tense, not because of any doubt as to how the voting would go, more perhaps because many of the delegates were not quite certain of why they were voting as they were. One of those who had spoken on Kennedy's behalf expressed the hope that the delegates from the rural counties would recognize that Kennedy was destined to get most of the state's votes and that they should also vote for Kennedy on the first ballot so that Pennsylvania would not appear to be split on religious lines on the first ballot. These comments, bristling with political logic, added to Kennedy's count but they also added a further note of uneasiness. Incidentally, no speeches were made for Johnson or Symington despite rumors of their strength in Pennsylvania.

The voting was by voice. First the delegates-at-large, the real professionals, were called on. Then the delegates.

The results:

Kennedy	64
Johnson	4½
Meyner	1½
Symington	1
Lawrence	½

The morning after Senator Kennedy was nominated, the delegation caucused again. But the function of this caucus was to listen to a report from Governor Lawrence that he would be among those consulted by Senator Kennedy in selecting a vice presidential candidate. Many of the delegates expressed satisfaction at the recognition which Senator Kennedy had accorded Governor Lawrence and Pennsylvania by this invitation.

During the entire convention only one incident of misgivings could be described. On Tuesday evening, Senator Clark was quoted as saying that if Senator Kennedy did not win a first ballot victory, "we should all reconsider our positions." The news of Clark's statement swept through the delegation. The reaction was instantaneous, particularly on the part of Representative William Green. Within a very few minutes, Robert Kennedy was amiably walking among the delegates, chatting at length with Governor Lawrence and posing for pictures with Mayor Richardson Dilworth and Green. The fact that Dilworth was standing with Green served to isolate Clark. For many years the names of Clark and Dilworth were synonymous with the reform movement in Philadelphia. Whether Dilworth chose to remain with Green (and therefore Kennedy) because of intentions to run for governor with Green's support in 1962 or whether his zeal for the Kennedy candidacy was genuine can only be a matter of speculation. What is certain, however, is that an incipient revolt was quickly choked off by swift floor work made possible by excellent communication. "As a result of Senator Clark's activities, Kennedy will have more Pennsylvania votes on the first ballot than we expected," Green told the *Philadelphia Inquirer*. And the next morning, two of the Stevenson delegates announced for Kennedy.

The reason why the decision to support Kennedy went as smoothly as it did is relatively simple. Pennsylvania is an organization politics state. In this sense, the party can be contrasted with, say, the California Democratic Party. Once the lines of support had been clearly established among the leadership of the party, it came as no surprise at all that the delegates would follow, for the delegates were overwhelmingly organization men.

18. The Presidential Convention as a Stage in the Struggle for Political Leadership: The New York Democratic Delegation

BERT E. SWANSON
Hunter College*

Politics is business. We figure Senator Kennedy for a winner who will help the local ticket. My first preference is Lyndon Johnson but party considerations come first. DeSapio, who is in trouble back home, and Michael Pendergast are the real leaders. Sure, we have Governor Harriman as the Honorary Chairman and Mayor Wagner as the chairman of the delegation—we had to give Harriman a place of distinction and the mayor just wants publicity and is only protecting his own political future in New York City.**

The national presidential convention is a proper place to study influence, the influential and the influenced. The delegates, individually and collectively, have gathered together under one roof and label to make a set of explicit and implicit decisions. The decisions involve high stakes of negative sanctions and/or rich rewards for the participants. The delegate has an opportunity to participate in the distribution of these sanctions and rewards. He is in a position to persuade and be persuaded. It is obvious, as in virtually any large-scale organization, that all the members do *not* equally hold the power necessary to change the attitudes and behavior of their fellow delegates. However, the delegates do *share* power with one another in the making of convention decisions. Yet the tradition of the American convention system has convinced some observers that the large urban states with their strongly organized party hierarchies are controlled by a single boss or a small tightly-knit handful of power-hungry men who dominate not only their own delegations but the convention as well.

This report on the New York delegation, the largest contingent (226) of delegates and alternates with 114 votes, is, then, a study of influence, the influential and the influenced. This study attempts to explore the conditions and exercise of influence within the delegation, the influence of the New York dele-

---

*The writer wishes to acknowledge the assistance of Eleanor Main, Hunter College.
**This statement was made by a New York delegate in the Ambassador Hotel, Los Angeles.

gation on the convention as a whole, the ways in which New Yorkers went about affecting the final outcome, and the anticipated and unanticipated consequences of their convention activity. The leadership of the delegation will be examined, particularly the role of Mayor Robert Wagner of New York City as he projected himself into national politics.

The decisions made by the New Yorkers in Los Angeles had a prologue. We shall examine two phases of the convention decisions: (1) the pre-convention phase—selections of delegates, the skirmish for leadership positions, the delicate negotiations carried on with the leading presidential candidates and the efforts to gain early commitments; (2) the convention phase—caucus decisions, general support given to the various candidates, the contact with other states, and the public display of leadership.

PRE-CONVENTION

Factionalism

The New York Democratic Party was rife with factionalism as it began to prepare for the 1960 presidential convention. Unity of presidential politics is a rarity in New York. Only in 1936 was the party united in recent times, and then only on a second term for Franklin D. Roosevelt. In 1932 the party was split between Alfred Smith and Roosevelt. In 1940 and 1944 there was considerable opposition to Roosevelt's third and fourth terms. The party differed in 1948 on Eisenhower and Truman, in 1952 and 1956 on Harriman versus Stevenson. In addition, the Democrats have suffered a series of important defeats. The Republicans carried the state for Eisenhower in 1952 and 1956. They elected Nelson Rockefeller in 1958. They elected Senator Jacob Javits in 1956 and Senator Kenneth Keating in 1958. In fact, in 1960 only one Democrat, Comptroller Arthur Levitt, held a statewide elective office.

The recent defeats at the polls have led to a bitter struggle for power within the party. In New York City, and particularly in the Borough of Manhattan, this struggle resulted in the formation of the Committee for Democratic Voters, an "insurgent" or "reform" group poised againt Tammany, the "regular" organization. The insurgents rode a reform wave which launched a general attack against the "bossism" of Tammany. Behind this attack lay the frustration not only of the defeats at the polls but also of the apparent local orientation of the regular party organization and its lack of enthusiasm for Governor Adlai Stevenson in 1952 and 1956. The insurgents also complained about the 1958 Buffalo party convention decision which selected New York District Attorney Frank Hogan to run for the United States Senate instead of former Air Force Secretary Thomas K. Finletter. Carmine DeSapio, Tammany's leader, insisted on Hogan as a loyal member of the organization as well as a necessary component on an ethnically balanced ticket.

The insurgents were partially successful in their attack on "Boss" DeSapio. After the party primary of September 1959, they had seven active clubs in Manhattan which cast 3-5/6 of the 16 votes on the county executive committee. Manhattan was the primary battleground, since no insurgent club existed outside the county. Again in the spring primaries of 1960, the insurgents won four out of six contests—one congressional, one state senatorial and two assembly races. At the same time, Representative Adam Clayton Powell repelled any danger to his political domination of Harlem, threatening to support a Republican presidential candidate in 1960 and a fusion mayoralty candidate in 1961 unless the Negro voters were given greater consideration in decisions which affected their interests. The anti-Tammany expression at the polls led to demands that DeSapio resign as chief of Tammany and not seek reelection as National Democratic Committeeman, or at least that he should be deprived of any control over the New York delegation at the national convention.

Factionalism within the New York Democratic Party, then, represents a wide variety of differences. The regulars mainly perceive "politics as a business" where it is more important to retain control of party machinery than to advance certain social or political policies. The regular tends to focus primarily on the local nature of politics. He is concerned about matters in his assembly district, the level at which his club is organized, and about party affairs in his county. The insurgent, on the other hand, views politics as a necessary evil to obtain good government with businesslike practices. His whole attention is directed to policy issues such as international relations, disarmament, housing, education, and juvenile delinquency. This policy orientation pervades so much of insurgents' thinking that they even attack the regulars who frustrate their policy objectives. For example, they have linked DeSapio with the "slum lords" and the inadequate housing in the city. This issue orientation also has led the insurgents to be concerned mainly about presidential politics, for they seek solutions to the city's problems on the national rather than the local level. The insurgents also differ from the regulars on the basis of access to political power positions and status within the party. Only within recent years have certain ethnic groups been allowed entrance into the once Irish-dominated Democratic Party. Ironically, DeSapio represents the acceptability; while the Negro has partially "arrived" with the elections of Congressman Powell and Borough President Hulan Jack. The Jews are gradually securing their place in the party, too. Meanwhile, the young professionals must wait patiently for their opportunity to seek elective offices. These still are reserved for the loyal senior club members. Women also find it difficult to become integral working members of the party. They are given positions involving headquarters work, but they are frequently left out of critical policy-making.

The United Democratic Leadership Team of Harlem, led by Congressman Powell, seeks recognition for the Negro and solutions to his particular problems—housing, education, employment, and political access. Powell's strategy has been a flexible one. At times he chooses to remain allied with the regular organization; an exception occurred when his own purge was initiated in 1958 by DeSapio. This purge itself was in response to Powell's support of Eisenhower in 1956. The Powell faction markets the Negro vote as a commodity in exchange for the highest return in solving the problems of Harlem. He threatens the regulars, who control party patronage, with joining any other group—insurgents or Republicans—in order to gain more power and status for the Negro.

Selecting the Delegates

The National Democratic Committee allocated 114 votes at the national convention to the state of New York. The state committee decided to select two district delegates, each with a full vote, from the state's 43 congressional districts. An alternate delegate was also chosen for each district delegate. The method of selection was through a statewide party primary held in June. The remaining 56 delegates, known as delegates-at-large, with a half-vote apiece, were chosen by the state committee. Forty-three

were chosen from the congressional districts upon the recommendation of the county chairmen. If a congressional district was
made up of more than one county, then the county chairmen from
the district would reach an agreement on who should represent
the district. Eleven additional delegates-at-large were chosen
among important personages throughout the state such as party
leaders and public officials. The national committeeman (De-
Sapio) and committeewoman (Representative Edna Kelly) completed the list of delegates. The state committee also selected
a list of 27 alternates-at-large.

The insurgent Committee for Democratic Voters, led by Mrs.
Eleanor Roosevelt, former Senator Herbert Lehman, and former
Air Force Secretary Thomas K. Finletter, took issue with the
decision to have the state committee appoint delegates-at-large.
They feared that domination of the regular organization by
Michael Prendergast and DeSapio would result in an unrepresentative delegation. They argued that all delegates should be
elected in the June primary. The state party leaders ignored their
request and proceeded with the preparation of the selection
process. The insurgents, on the other hand, were ill-prepared to
compete with the regular organization for delegate positions in
the primaries.

As in past convention primaries, there were very few contests.
The small number of contested races (20) can be attributed in
part to a state election law provision which forbids a candidate
to express his presidential preference on the ballot. Eleven contests were in Brooklyn, where the regulars were the victors by
overwhelming margins ranging from two-to-one to twelve-to-
one. Three were in Manhattan, where the insurgents lost two
races by better than three-to-one, but almost defeated regular
John J. Merli, who has been mentioned as a possible successor to
DeSapio. (Congressman Powell successfully defeated his opponents in Harlem.) Upstate regulars, however, were defeated
in two of four contests. It should be noted that an open primary
fight between insurgents and regulars was averted by a compromise in the 17th congressional district where Thomas Finletter
and former Postmaster General James A. Farley were allowed to
run uncontested.

A major controversy developed over the state committee's
designation of the delegates-at-large. Prendergast and DeSapio,
in a retaliatory mood after the insurgent primary victory in Man-

hattan, chose not to include insurgent leaders Herbert Lehman and Mrs. Roosevelt in the delegation. Prendergast charged that their disapproval of the method of selection by the state committee meant they were not interested in becoming delegates and they had not expressed their desire to be delegates. A small handful of insurgents on the state committee made several futile moves to place the names of Lehman and Roosevelt on the delegate list. At most the insurgents were able to muster a mere 14 votes out of the more than 300 votes on the state committee. So crushing was the Prendergast victory that he did not use the 196 proxy votes in his possession. At the conclusion of the meeting Prendergast issued an "open declaration of war" against the insurgents, saying:

> . . . I am aroused, aroused because I think and care too deeply for the Democratic Party to see it harmed by a destructive force masquerading as a reform movement.

> And I am not going to stand idly by any longer and see good, able, decent people forced into undeserved defeats in primaries on election day because the electorate was confused, misguided, and lied to, and our people slandered.

> Nor am I going to stand by and see our great mayor, our other city and state officials, and our party officials suffer unwarranted irresponsible attacks.

> From this day forward I say to each and every one of you precinct workers—block captains—district leaders—town leaders—come out of your clubhouses—your offices—come out and carry the fight with everything at your disposal—fight fire with fire—propaganda with facts—slander with the truth and if necessary, revert to the philosophy of our ancestors of an eye for an eye.

The ringing applause had hardly died when a reaction of disbelief set in against the rebuff to Senator Lehman. The *New York Times* lamented, "the elder statesman of the party, the pilot of many victories, the wise counselor of old, the conscience of the party's better days, was dropped." Others joined in denouncing the "arrogance" of the state Democratic leaders who would end Lehman's long attendance since 1928 as a delegate to the party's convention. Mayor Wagner unsuccessfully attempted to intercede prior to the state committee action. He later publicly stated that he would press for a reversal of the decision at the Albany pre-convention caucus to be held the following week. In addition, as one close observer put it, "the Jews were raising hell with Sharkey in Brooklyn." Joseph Sharkey, Brooklyn county chairman, sparked the move within the party hierarchy to reconsider the Lehman decision.

In the meantime delegate-designees State Comptroller Arthur Levitt and Franklin D. Roosevelt, Jr., offered to resign to make way for Lehman. The insurgents had asked Roosevelt to resign. Prendergast spurned both offers and challenged the sincerity of the Roosevelt gesture. This rejection further encouraged the speculation that the Lehman decision was legally irreversible. At the closed Albany caucus, however, an unexpected move by Prendergast produced a unanimous resolution favoring the appointment of Lehman as a delegate-at-large. Prendergast further announced that he personally would step aside to make a place for Lehman. He thus took full responsibility for the Lehman decision, despite the contention of the *New York Times* that "it would be fatuous to credit the party leadership with a sudden seizure of nobility." Lehman closed the affair by conditionally accepting the delegate position upon "the understanding that I will be completely free to cast my vote and to raise my voice as my conscience dictates."

Let us examine the results of the selection process of the New York delegation. Over 85 per cent of the delegates held positions in government or were active participants in the Democratic Party. Better than a quarter were appointed public officials serving on boards and commissions or as civil servants. A sixth of the delegates served as county chairmen or vice chairmen. Another sixth were elected public officials at various levels of government. Better than half of all the 63 county chairmen participated in the Democratic convention. It is interesting to note that they served primarily as delegates rather than as alternates. The district leaders, on the other hand, served primarily as alternates.

The prominent role of the lawyer in politics is again confirmed upon examination of the occupations of the New Yorkers. Nearly a third of the delegation were lawyers, while nearly another quarter were businessmen. There was a higher proportion of lawyers among the elected district delegates and attorneys than among the delegates and alternates-at-large. The very few housewives were chosen as alternates.

The role of women in convention politics was greatly limited. Only one-eighth of the total New York delegation was composed of women. And three-quarters of these served as alternates. Certainly if the number of women in the delegation is any measure of influence in policy-making, there is substance to the charge of former state vice chairman Mrs. Eleanor Clark French that women in general, and she in particular, were used for routine matters and not consulted on policy-making.

Election of Leaders

One of the first acts of the New York delegation was to elect leaders. While the state had no favorite-son nominations for president, it had an embarrassment of riches in those eager and willing to serve as leader of the delegation at Los Angeles. Former Governor Averell Harriman sought the chairmanship because he was titular head of the party, having held the highest elective position in the state. State Comptroller Arthur Levitt wished to be chairman because he held the highest elective position and he was laying the foundation of his probable 1962 gubernatorial campaign against Governor Nelson Rockefeller. State chairman Michael Prendergast felt he should be chairman because he was the acknowledged leader of the state party organization. The claim of Mayor Robert F. Wagner, Jr., to be chairman was not so clearly defined. The Wagner administration had encountered setbacks during the recent past; evidence of inefficiency and corruption had been uncovered. Governor Rockefeller had appointed a state commission for the purpose of investigating the operations of the city government; this later developed into a charter revision effort, and there were rumors of a possible "fusion" ticket in the forthcoming mayoralty election of 1961. Mayor Wagner also hoped to disprove the adage that in New York City "the office of mayor is the end of a career, not an office which leads to higher posts."[*] Nevertheless, Wagner viewed himself as the most popular Democrat in the state and as a mediator in the insurgent-regular factional fight, as well as the person to pick up the mantle of leadership if DeSapio fell.

The skirmish for leadership positions began when Mayor Wagner stated in 1958 that he was "the titular head of the Democratic Party in the city." Then in the spring of 1960 he made a series of mystifying public comments which pleaded for unity in the party under his leadership. He sidestepped public identity with the insurgents, yet as Francis Adams, former po-

---

[*]Wallace S. Sayre and Herbert Kaufman, *Governing New York City* (Russell Sage Foundation: New York, 1960), p. 697.

lice commissioner and one of the leaders of the insurgent movement, said, Wagner in due time "would be found on the Lord's side." Wagner defended his "friend" DeSapio and his leadership's great "appeal to the voting loyalty of our people." Yet two weeks later Wagner refused open support to DeSapio's continuance as national committeeman; he was reported to feel "that a diminution of Mr. DeSapio's political importance would be helpful in unifying the New York City Democratic organization."

Wagner's fence-straddling position produced both friends and enemies. The Liberal Party, a potent third force in New York City politics, decided to bypass DeSapio at the Los Angeles convention and seek the counsel of Mayor Wagner, whom they regarded as the spokesman for the Democratic party. Wagner began to lose friends among the insurgents for not vigorously taking up their battle cry. The insurgents, led by Herbert Lehman, began to point out certain "inadequacies in matters of major civic importance, such as housing, integrity in government and boss influence in city affairs . . . I want him [Wagner] to have a much better record as mayor than he has made in the past couple of years." Lehman hastened to add, "of course, I want to see Mr. DeSapio out as national committeeman, but it would never enter my head to criticize the mayor's administration in order to force or induce the mayor to act against Mr. DeSapio in that capacity." The regular party members remained publicly silent during the initial stages of the leadership fight.

A week before the Albany caucus when the leaders were to be selected, Mayor Wagner made his first public bid to take over as leader of the delegation. He announced his availability to serve as chairman of the state delegation. By now it was known that DeSapio, reacting to the Wagner threat, favored former Governor Averell Harriman. Other party regulars such as Sharkey of Brooklyn and former Postmaster General Farley tended to support Wagner. However, some leaders questioned the desirability of Wagner as head of a delegation which might later bargain over his nomination for vice president.

When Wagner arrived in Albany for the caucus, he expressed his "anger" at reports that Prendergast was scheduled to become caucus chairman. He felt that he had been relegated to the role of figurehead. He was overheard telling DeSapio, "I don't want to be chairman. It's a big joke." DeSapio and Prendergast ushered the mayor into the state committee headquarters where a hurried conference was held to "clarify" the situation. The mayor was assured that "he would be the real chairman and head of the delegation." The "clarification conference" resulted in a unique leadership arrangement for the New York delegation. Three chairmanships were agreed upon: Averell Harriman would be honorary chairman, Robert Wagner would be delegation chairman, and Michael Prendergast would be caucus chairman.

Within the hour the New York delegation ratified the triumvirate arrangement. They had reelected DeSapio as national committeeman, with only two negative votes and several abstentions. The mood of unity within the caucus was continued when it resolved that Lehman should become a delegate.

Selecting a Presidential Candidate

New York's 114 votes were highly prized by all the leading presidential candidates in the Democratic party. They all made ceremonial visits to New York. All were properly introduced by Mayor Wagner to the party leaders at Gracie Mansion, the mayor's residence, or to the voters of New York at party rallies. Each candidate had supporters in New York.

After the West Virginia primary, however, the Kennedy forces pressed their advantage with the New York leaders. Senator Kennedy not only was a consistent and regular visitor to the state but he had recruited several important party leaders in his cause. The party leaders included DeSapio, Prendergast, Wagner, Charles Buckley (Bronx county chairman), Benjamin Wetzler (state party secretary) and upstate county chairmen John Stillman and Peter Crotty. DeSapio, Prendergast, and Wagner held back during the early spring consciously attempting to maximize the reward to New York of joining the Kennedy drive. This meant not only the proper timing of their public announcements in support of Kennedy, but also the proper preparation to bring a sufficient proportion of the 114-vote delegation along with them.

Each New York leader desired certain favors. It was rumored that DeSapio was interested in the post of Democratic national chairman, Wagner in a cabinet position such as Secretary of Labor or head of the newly-proposed Department of Housing and Urban Affairs, Prendergast in the dispensation of federal patronage for New York.

Congressman Charles Buckley, successor to Edward "Boss"

Flynn and a "100 per cent organization man" in the Bronx, vigorously disagreed with the tactics of delay. He announced for Senator Kennedy the day following the West Virginia primary, saying, "We'd better get on the bandwagon or it will run us over." DeSapio and Prendergast stated that they were "impressed" with Kennedy's West Virginia victory but refrained from any public endorsement. The apparently uncommitted public attitude displayed by DeSapio led former Senator Lehman to charge that their delay was calculated "so that they could 'make a deal' for the votes of convention delegates they control." Lehman advocated a Stevenson-Kennedy ticket.

A few days prior to the Albany caucus, Buckley again called for early support of Kennedy. Buckley has been described as a leader who "runs a taut ship. There are no leaks and there is swift, long-lasting discipline for anything that has the odor of mutiny." He pointed out that "this is no time for cute politics. Those who play it usually wind up behind the eight ball." He insisted, "the sentiment is all for Kennedy. It's time we stopped pussyfooting and gave the people what they want. Kennedy is the only candidate who can help us elect our local ticket." The following day Mayor Wagner announced his support of Senator Kennedy and in an effort to create a bandwagon movement stated that he was prepared to urge the New York delegation to support Kennedy.

The Stevenson forces, the only serious contender against Kennedy, never gained a foothold among the New York delegation. At the most they were able to muster only a single vote in preconvention polls of the delegates. This did not discourage a spontaneous burst of activity in behalf of the reluctant Stevenson by an assortment of supporters in New York. The Stevensonites of 1952 and 1956, many insurgent political clubs, some liberals, and others joined together in petition-signing campaigns that resulted in half a million signatures in New York alone. They urged the voters of the state to impress the delegation with the growing support for Stevenson.

Before the delegates were polled at the Albany caucus, they were informed by chairman Prendergast of the results of a statewide public opinion poll which the state committee had requested. He reported that Kennedy outdrew Stevenson upstate 57 to 18 per cent and in the suburbs 43 to 41 per cent. But Prendergast chose not to report what the pollsters had found among the Democrats of New York City, where the majority of the state's Democrats reside. Here Stevenson outdrew Kennedy 53 per cent to 32 per cent. Therefore, Stevenson was still preferred by the Democratic voters in the state by a margin of 44 to 38 per cent. When challenged, Prendergast replied that among the total voting population (that is, Republicans as well as Democrats) Kennedy was still the favorite.

At the Albany caucus Prendergast, DeSapio and former Governor Harriman urged the delegation to support Senator Kennedy. This completed the list of key party leaders who favored Kennedy. Not a single major party figure spoke against Kennedy. The results of polling the caucus gave 87½ votes to Senator Kennedy, 2½ to Senator Johnson, two to Senator Humphrey and one each to Stevenson and Senator Symington. There were 12 abstentions and 8½ absentees. The results led the *New York Post* to ponder in an editorial, "Who Speaks for New York?" pointing to the "astonishing disparity" between the delegate strength for Kennedy and the voter sentiment in favor of Stevenson.

Developing a Party Platform

The pre-convention activities seemed devoid of any public policy attitudes. Even in the factional disputes there was little evidence of explicit differences on the policy issues confronting the national polity. Of course, there was the expressed issue of "bossism" between insurgent and regular party contenders and the struggle for power and recognition of the Negro on the part of the Harlem political leaders. But there appeared to be no, or only minor, ideological differences expressed by the New York Democrats as they chose their delegates, leaders and presidential candidates. This would lead one to believe that there is little or no relation between party personnel and the public policy positions taken in New York politics or in large urban organizational politics. Such a statement may be an over-simplification of the very complex process of expressing policy attitudes.

The New York party took the initiative in declaring their position in regard to the shape of the national party platform to be developed in Los Angeles. During the preceding year they created a Public Affairs Committee of the Democratic State Committee, headed by former Governor Averell Harriman. This committee released a series of statements which reflected the policy positions of the party. They took positions on such matters as medical care for the aged, civil rights, and highway programs.

In addition, New York City was the setting for one hearing in a series of ten panels held throughout the United States to tap public sentiment concerning a proposed Democratic platform. On this occasion the party leaders headed a list of fifty witnesses from a wide variety of groups and organizations representing civil rights, education, consumer, nationality, labor, and veteran interests. Harriman sought a change in foreign policy to restore the image of the United States as "one of sympathetic understanding and friendly concern for the welfare of others." Wagner called for a strong civil rights program and suggested the enactment of federal laws similar to those of New York City and New York state, prohibiting discrimination in housing, employment and other fields. Levitt called for federal aid to education, asking for "bold departures from traditional thinking on education finance."

The Convention

The New York delegation arrived in Los Angeles with an apparent air of unity. They were overwhelmingly agreed upon the presidential nominee and the party platform, the two major decisions to be made at the convention. This unity in part was derived from their common identity as members of the regular party organization. The insurgent faction was represented by a mere handful and the Harlem faction was still smaller. Also, the factions, as well as the individual leaders, generally had all been given some recognition or reward in the pre-convention phase— the insurgents now had their Lehman, the Harlem leaders no longer had to fear a purge attempt by Tammany, Harriman had won recognition as honorary chairman, Wagner had gained public acknowledgment as mediator between the factions in his role as delegation chairman, DeSapio retained his position of national committeeman which provided him the opportunity to work toward national Democratic chairman, and Prendergast retained organizational control as caucus chairman.

The air of unity concerning the presidential nominee and the platform did not reveal the continual tension that lay close beneath the surface. A number of factors relating to this tension should be pointed out. First, the existence of three chairmen reflected the loose coalition arrangement contrived to create a unified effective voice in the convention procedings in behalf of

New York interests; it reflected the still unsettled struggle for power between DeSapio, the resilient Tammany "boss," and Wagner, the mediator of insurgency. Second, the New York delegation was not absolutely certain that Kennedy was the right candidate. They mirrored what James Reston of *New York Times* pointed out on the eve of the convention:

> The Democratic convention is off in a cloud of doubt, not about what it is going to do but why. It is going to nominate Senator Kennedy of Massachusetts because, somehow, it doesn't quite know how it can do otherwise and the balance of doubt runs that way. But it is still distressed because the delegates have made a decision before they have made up their minds.

The delegation and its leaders gave little thought and no public expression to what alternatives they would pursue should Kennedy fail to gain the nomination on an early ballot. Had Kennedy failed there is ample evidence to contend that the New York delegation might have split into three camps behind Stevenson, Johnson, and Symington. Finally, the mobilization of Stevenson strength in the state, although it had found little response among the delegates, was being prepared to bombard the delegation and the convention with a dramatic display of popular support.

Let us examine, then, the critical points and the activities of some members of the delegation during the convention period to perceive the tension underlying this seemingly calm surface.

Shaping the Party Platform

Mayor Wagner was the only New York delegate to testify before the platform committee in Los Angeles. On this occasion he spoke in behalf of the United States Conference of Mayors which formerly he had headed. He called for the establishment of a Department of Housing and Urban Affairs with cabinet status, and for increased federal financial support of urban redevelopment, transportation, and air and water pollution. The final draft of the Democratic platform adopted a considerable number of recommendations of the Conference of Mayors. The same proposals were presented to the Republican convention in Chicago with much less success, particularly the proposal for a department of urban affairs.

The Hotel Accommodations

The New York delegation was assigned to the luxurious Ambassador Hotel, some thirty minutes from the convention hall.

The state committee was in charge of arrangements. Wagner took violent exception to assignments which placed DeSapio, Prendergast, Harriman and himself in adjoining guest cottages. He immediately transferred to a suite in the main building where he would be "closer to the members of the delegation." With this gesture he also asserted his independence of DeSapio and his own attempt to lead the delegation. At the same time he took up separate personal quarters in a hotel in far-off Beverly Hills. Senator Lehman, the mainstay of the Stevenson forces, also found himself new quarters downtown at the Biltmore Hotel, the center of convention activity.

Seating and Ticket Accommodations

Miscalculations by the convention officials resulted in chaos, frustration, and anger in the first two days. It has been said by some that there was more concern, energy, and heated argument displayed over these matters than over the presidential nomination or the platform. Some members were required to sit behind the Tennessee delegation because of an obstructed view caused by a television platform. The delegation's headquarters staff unintentionally failed to seat State Comptroller Arthur Levitt and national committeewoman Edna Kelly in the front row on the convention floor, among the prominent members of the delegation. A hurried reshuffling of seats averted a major eruption in the delegation, but not before Levitt threatened to resign. A minor incident, which produced more laughter than concern, was the placement of the Kennedy organization telephone under the seat of Herbert Lehman. The delegation was allotted a very limited number of passes to the Sports Arena. This placed a hardship on many delegates who brought members of their families, because their relatives were unable to attend the convention sessions. Scarcity of tickets placed DeSapio and Prendergast in an unusually influential position, for they controlled the tickets. In fact, Mayor Wagner's staff had to apply pressure to receive tickets for the Wagner entourage. It also encouraged considerable absenteeism among the delegates. They chose instead to visit the race tracks, tour Los Angeles, or sit in their hotel rooms and discuss New York affairs.

The Caucus for Presidential Preference

On Monday the delegation caucused to express their presidential preference. This had already been done in Albany three weeks before, but the present caucus was official and would instruct the leaders how to cast the state's vote on the following Wednesday night. Three major candidates—Johnson, Symington, and Kennedy—spoke briefly to the caucus. Senator Lehman spoke for his candidate, Stevenson.

The caucus then closed its doors and a roll call was ordered by the chairman, Prendergast. The polling was brief. The wait for the tally, however, produced another example of the friction between the leaders. Since Prendergast was chairman of the caucus, it was expected that he would announce the outcome of the vote. But Wagner arose, hovered over those counting the vote, picked up the tally sheet upon its completion and announced the results. There was some elbowing between the two chairmen but nothing to resemble the squabble a moment later when the press was called in to hear the outcome. Joyce Martin, public relations officer for Prendergast and the state committee, was about to announce the results to the press when Frank Doyle, executive secretary and public relations officer for Mayor Wagner, grabbed the tally sheet and gave it to Wagner so that he could make the announcement to the press. There was a considerable amount of confusion involved in the open display of "leadership." Incidentally, the delegates voted as follows: Kennedy, 101; Johnson, 4½; Stevenson, 3½; Symington, 2; Humphrey, 1. Three delegates were absent, each with a half vote.

The Caucus on the Platform

On Tuesday the New York delegation held an open caucus on the party platform; Congressman Emanuel Celler and Julia Crews, members of the resolutions committee, reported back to the delegation on the draft of the platform. Celler touched briefly upon civil rights, while Mrs. Crews discussed foreign policy. Congressman Powell told the caucus that this was "the best platform either party has written in the history of politics." He added, "the civil rights plank is totally acceptable to my group. It is perfect." After other brief comments from such leaders as Wagner, Prendergast, Lehman and Levitt, the delegation endorsed the 1960 party platform unanimously by voice vote.

Support for the Presidential Nominees

The New York delegation participated at three levels in support of their favorite presidential nominees. They made formal speeches before the convention; they held informal discussions among themselves and members of other delegations; and they participated in floor demonstrations. Four New Yorkers made seconding speeches in behalf of candidates. Governor Harriman seconded the Kennedy nomination. He praised Kennedy's "courage," "heart," and "indispensable capacity to make up his mind and act." Both Mrs. Eleanor Roosevelt and Herbert Lehman seconded the Stevenson nomination. Mrs. Roosevelt, who had spent the evening moving from one place to another in the gallery to create attention for her favorite, Adlai Stevenson, exclaimed to the convention, "we want the best." Her son, Franklin D. Roosevelt, Jr., a strong Kennedy supporter, sat with moist eyes as he viewed his dignified mother. He joined a half-dozen other members of the delegation who stood and applauded her at the conclusion of her brief speech. Senator Lehman, disappointed with the lack of support for Stevenson among the New York delegation, declared that the people of New York were "overwhelmingly" for him. Congressman Celler, seconding Symington, told the convention that history would charge them with "vast criminal neglect" if they made the wrong choice.

Such leaders as Wagner, DeSapio, Prendergast, Mrs. Roosevelt, Lehman, Finletter were busy making a wide variety of contacts and holding informal discussions in behalf of their candidates. Relying on assurance that he "would be chairman in fact as well as name," Wagner issued a series of news releases which indicated he planned daily conferences with other party leaders including upstate groups. It should be pointed out that few rank-and-file delegates availed themselves of this opportunity to meet with their leader. Wagner sent a letter, financed by the Kennedy headquarters, praising Kennedy's qualifications to all convention delegates. In addition, he met with various leaders of other state delegations such as Governors Lawrence of Pennsylvania, Ribicoff of Connecticut, Di Salle of Ohio and Brown of California, as well as Mayor Daley and Jacob Arvey of Chicago.

DeSapio and Prendergast, characterized as "an inseparable pair who stalked about together, almost hand in hand, as if dazed and lost and afraid to be alone," also conferred informally with those listed above who met with Wagner. They were in closer contact with the members of the New York delegation than any other leaders.

The Roosevelt, Lehman, Finletter triumvirate spent most of

their time working on delegates from other states. They also persuaded some twenty New Yorkers to attend a Stevenson gathering on Tuesday night. This move was interpreted by some as a reflection of "an easily detectable undercurrent of second thinking and, in some cases, outright dissatisfaction at the course the delegation was taking."

The New Yorkers gaily joined the Kennedy demonstration, but most of them did so from their seats because there was no room to march in the aisles. Participation proved hazardous for those who did. Nonetheless, the New York standard was carried joyously among the demonstrators while the delegation made the customary noisy display.

The Stevenson demonstration was another matter. While the New York banner was raised in the Stevenson rally, the delegates reacted coolly. They had been receiving hundreds of letters and telegrams from home urging support of Stevenson. The initial reaction of coolness soon became intensified. A hostile, negative mood set in among the delegates when they saw the odd assortment of demonstrators—youngsters, women and "beatniks"—and the gallery support for Stevenson. Some delegates bantered with the demonstrators, asking them, "When did you vote last time?" and telling them to "go home," and exclaiming, "No wonder we lost the last two times." Among themselves the delegates were angry to see the gallery filled with Stevenson supporters. This, they said, accounted for their own failure to secure tickets for their families and friends. And when the large "snowball" containing the half-million signatures came to the New York area the delegates cursed at it and hastened it to the back of the Sports Arena and off the convention floor. The delegation then began to chant, "We want Kennedy," under the direction of Franklin Roosevelt, Jr.

Selecting a Vice President

The nomination of Senator Kennedy scotched the aspirations of fellow Catholic Mayor Wagner to the vice presidency. But Wagner had been realistic about his chances all along. He knew a Kennedy victory was likely and that DeSapio's statement upon his departure for the Los Angeles convention concerning Wagner's availability for a possible nomination as vice president, even if Kennedy won, was unrealistic. Wagner instead began to campaign for Senator Henry ("Scoop") Jackson of Washington. To advance Jackson's candidacy, Wagner brought him to the New York delegation reception and introduced him to the party leaders and delegates.

DeSapio and Prendergast joined Governor Lawrence of Pennsylvania and other leaders of big states to advance the candidacy of Lyndon B. Johnson. This reflected the support Johnson claimed from the New York delegation in his bid for the presidential nomination, should Kennedy slip. Some estimated that Johnson had as many as fifty delegates.

Congressman Powell now appeared to be the New York leader for the Symington candidacy. With the Kennedy victory the Stevenson forces collapsed completely.

When Kennedy announced his preference for Johnson, the New York delegation supported his decision. They had no opportunity to register their dissent, if any, for the convention made the nomination by acclamation.

Leaders and the Led

The air of unity which prevailed when the delegation arrived in Los Angeles evaporated shortly after the pulling and hauling of the convention began. The leaders pursued different courses of action with other delegations, candidate organizations, and members of the New York delegation. Wagner continued to play the role of leader in the public eye. He focused his attention on the leaders of the other delegations and candidate organizations. He operated as though he controlled his delegation and represented the best mediating influence among the warring factions within the delegation. He maintained a prominent public role, issuing numerous news releases and making television appearances as head of the delegation. He even insisted that he release the results of the caucus to the press. But he had a minimum of contact with the rank-and-file members of his own delegation. DeSapio and Prendergast, on the other hand, were in their element both with the leaders of other large urban states and with the rank-and-file of the New York delegation. They continued to operate as though they were the unquestioned leaders of the delegation. Wagner objected to their conferences with the heads of other delegations. He told them that "they had no right to speak for the New York delegation without consulting him." They chose not to contest Wagner's public display of influence. They were silent, for example, when he ordered a close friend of DeSapio out of a delegate seat. DeSapio and Wagner agreed on Kennedy for president but disagreed on the candidate for vice president. DeSapio won out with Johnson, but Wagner at least saw his candidate, Jackson, promoted to the position of national Democratic chairman.

The leaders assumed that they were in fact the leaders and that they did have sufficient influence to deliver the 114-vote delegation. At times, however, it was evident that communications channels between the various leaders and the delegates in general were at a minimum level. A discussion with a number of delegates during the evening of the presidential nomination revealed a considerable lack of knowledge about what forces were at work within the delegation and in the convention as a whole. They appeared apathetic about the events transpiring around them, as though they were in Los Angeles simply to ratify a decision already made elsewhere—in the presidential primaries, on television or in the "bosses'" inner sanctum. They could change their decision about the candidates. The opportunity was left open to notify Mayor Wagner of a change of heart. Of course, some may have felt that to change would mean disloyalty to the leaders who, at the time of the convention, had stated clearly their preference for Kennedy. Those in the Bronx, for example, would think twice before switching, for it is said, "when a man goes out of favor with Mr. Buckley he goes equally out of fashion in Bronx politics, and he is about as likely to make a comeback as are tarred braids." Others might have been willing to risk political ostracism if there was no practical alternative. But in New York politics, at least, there were few suitable alternatives. In the last analysis they could not cast their votes for a reluctant candidate who had spurned the party organization on two previous occasions. Kennedy looked and acted like a winner who could come into New York, boost the local ticket and bring harmony to a party loosely held together for public display.

CONCLUSION

The awe of those assembled in the galleries when New York cast its 114 votes for Senator Kennedy reflected the surface influence of this largest delegation upon the outcome of the convention. But it required more than impressing the galleries, as the Stevenson forces learned, to dominate or influence the outcome. No one would assert that New York dominated the convention. New York, together with other large delegations from Pennsylvania, Illinois, and Ohio, did play its expected part in the broad determinations at the convention. There was no political boss to dominate the 1960 convention. Despite Harry Truman's allegations of rigging, the Kennedy victory was not the result of the actions of a single boss who whipped the majority into line. The importance of the presidential primaries, television and pre-convention commitments appeared to have a telling effect upon this convention. Most of the delegates were aware that they were engaged in a validating instead of a decision-making process.

By the same token there was no single boss dictating to the New York delegation. The charges of bossism launched against DeSapio were ill-conceived. DeSapio was in too precarious a position to assume the image of a boss. His recent defeats in New York City, his inability to sanction Lehman, his sharing of leadership not only with Prendergast but also with Wagner, Buckley and others, and his inability to time the New York commitment to Kennedy in order to maximize his own and the party's interests certainly were not characteristic of a boss. It was apparent that DeSapio and Prendergast had more influence in the selection of the delegates than the other leaders, but here, too, they shared power with others. In the case of the district delegates, the local county organizations and political clubs played an effective role. This was also true of the delegates-at-large. If DeSapio and Prendergast were indeed bosses, then we were witnessing a different kind of bossism than that of the leader who dictates decisions and applies sanctions and manipulations to enforce them. The contemporary New York boss went into the 1960 presidential convention very sensitive to a multitude of pressures.

The large New York delegation, then, was headed by a number of leaders, each with a different set of objectives and power bases to gain the acquiescence of the rank-and-file delegates. No leader had exclusive control of the application of sanctions or the reward system of New York politics. There were few rewards available for the state Democratic party, which is still out of power. In New York City, Wagner controls many positions; he had chosen not to embrace DeSapio too closely for fear of the consequences of public reaction in the forthcoming mayoralty election which had threats of anti-Tammany reformism and fusion of the many minority parties. Each of the leaders had a deep interest in promoting his own political career. Wagner, for example, wanted to prove that the position of mayor is not a burial ground; DeSapio viewed a national reputation with interest. In such a fluid state of affairs no leader can hope simply to maintain the status quo, for this fluidity frees the rank-and-file to make demands upon the leadership for support in the struggle between the political elites. The net result is a more responsive relationship within the party between the leader and the rank-and-file. This explains in large part the support of Kennedy not by dictatorial boss methods but as the result of a cautious "feeling out" process between leaders and the other members of the delegation to determine which candidate would yield most toward victory on the local as well as the national level.

If the leaders found themselves adjusting to a variety of pressures within the party, it was equally apparent that the Democratic party itself was adjusting to a variety of changing conditions in the political context of New York. The city-federal relationship has broadened enormously since the early New Deal days of 1935. This has occurred mainly in the area of social welfare, which traditionally has been a function of machine politics and religious charities. New York City, for example, is undergoing a major metamorphosis in its physical plant, particularly with respect to the urban redevelopment program sponsored largely by the federal government. The changing nature of the physical plant produces interesting political consequences—anticipated and unanticipated—in residential patterns, shifts in ethnic composition of certain areas, and the loss of those citizens dependent upon and accustomed to the political machine and boss. This new dependence on the federal government has made the citizen cognizant of the importance of presidential politics. The party is confronted more and more with a constituency whose focus is quite different from its own local orientation. Thus the party is gradually being forced to respond to the changing focus. The insurgents, for example, stand ready to burst into the regular party and infiltrate it not only with an interest in presidential politics but with a concentration on policy issues which will contrast vividly with the patronage concerns of the regular party of a dying era.

The decision to support the Kennedy nomination, then, de-

rived from conditions within and outside the party. The factionalism within the party, which in turn reflected the changing conditions outside the party, left the Democrats with competing
leaders willing to mediate their differences and/or to exploit the
disparate elements in order to further their personal political
careers and produce an open, responsive relationship between
the leaders and the delegates. Of course, at no time did the
leaders allude to the tenuous nature of their control over the
delegation when negotiations were underway with out-of-state
leaders and candidate organizations. And it was not long before
a perceptive Robert Kennedy "understood" the New York situation well enough to make arrangements which maximized his
brother's interest, molding together an effective campaign effort
which would minimize the tension between the factions.

19. Leadership and Party Unity: The Kentucky Democratic Delegation

MALCOLM E. JEWELL

University of Kentucky

One feature often neglected in analysis of national conventions
is the critical role that state political considerations may play
in the decisions of any delegation. In a deeply divided state party,
for example, the caucuses of its delegation to the national convention may represent only a skirmish in the prolonged battle for
control of the state party. The Kentucky delegation did not play
a major role in the 1960 Democratic convention, but an account
of its activities illustrates well the dominant role of party interests. In the case of Kentucky, Democratic leaders consistently
sought to minimize their differences over presidential candidates
in order to maintain harmony within the dominant faction of
the party, the faction represented in the delegation.

Political Background and Personalities

Factionalism is a perennial feature of the Kentucky Democratic
Party. In recent years this factionalism has become particularly
intense and has centered around the conflict between groups led
by A. B. (Happy) Chandler and Earl C. Clements. Clements,
who was elected governor in November of 1947 and served three
years, retained a strong influence in state politics after he was

elected to the Senate in 1950. His lieutenant governor, Lawrence W. Wetherby, succeeded him and was elected to a full term in 1951. In 1955 Clements was instrumental in picking a relatively unknown state judge, Bert T. Combs, to run in the gubernatorial primary against Chandler, who had served in the past as governor and senator. Chandler won the primary and the general election in 1955. Chandler's action or inaction is generally believed to have been responsible the next year for the defeat of both Clements and Wetherby by Republican candidates for the two United States Senate seats. In 1959, Combs ran for governor again. Initially he faced two opponents in the primary—Harry Lee Waterfield, who was strongly endorsed by Chandler, and Wilson Wyatt, formerly mayor of Louisville and later federal housing administrator. Clements negotiated an alliance between Combs and Wyatt, both of whom were strongly anti-Chandler; Wyatt ran for lieutenant governor. Combs and Wyatt, with the political assistance of Clements, won the primary and the election. Combs then chose Clements as his highway commissioner, and the Combs-Clements forces consolidated their control over the party at a state convention in June of 1960.

The story of the Kentucky delegation is largely the story of political relations among three men: Clements, Combs, and Wyatt. Clements was a firm political ally of Lyndon Johnson. He had served as deputy Democratic leader in the Senate under Johnson from 1953 through 1956 and had remained in Washington as executive director of the Senate Democratic Campaign Committee and one of Johnson's key aides until returning to Kentucky early in 1960. Combs had no strong personal attachment to any presidential candidate but personally preferred Johnson and remained loyal to him also because of a massive political debt to Clements. Wyatt had a strong personal loyalty to Adlai Stevenson, whom he had served as personal campaign manager in 1952 and adviser in 1956. His activity on Stevenson's behalf was limited, however, by the latter's reluctance in 1960 to seek the nomination.

Former Governor Chandler was also a member of the delegation, *ex officio*, as outgoing national committeeman. Chandler announced his support first of Stevenson and later of Kennedy, choices dictated by process of elimination. Although Johnson best suited Chandler's conservative philosophy, Chandler would not support him because of antipathy to Clements. He may have been deterred from supporting Stuart Symington by differences with former President Truman. Chandler controlled his own vote in the delegation and no other.

Among the other leaders in the Kentucky delegation were former Governor Wetherby, whose alliance with Clements precluded any independent influence, and John Crimmins, head of the powerful Democratic organization in Jefferson County (Louisville). Crimmins was the most prominent Kennedy supporter in the delegation and had some influence over other delegates from Jefferson County.

Preliminaries to the National Convention

When Combs and Wyatt joined forces in January of 1959, they issued a joint platform including this plank:

Abolition of the unit rule for Kentucky's delegations to the Democratic national conventions, enabling each delegate to support the candidate of his choice and removing the possibility of the coercion of the delegation by any official.

This was an important part of the agreement because it provided assurance that Wyatt could support Stevenson, or anyone else he chose, whatever stand other state Democratic leaders took. Moreover, Wyatt objected to the unit rule in principle and had been criticizing it in his campaign. Under the rule in 1956 the entire delegation had been bound to support the hopeless presidential candidacy of Governor Chandler. In 1952, operating under the unit rule, the delegation had given Governor Wetherby complete discretion in casting the vote. Wetherby had voted consistently for Vice President Alben Barkley even after Barkley's withdrawal. The agreement in 1959 on abolishing the unit rule set the stage for the atmosphere of harmony that prevailed during the preparations for the 1960 national convention.

Former Senator Clements and Governor Combs assumed primary responsibility for preparing the slate of delegates to the national convention. It is impossible to tell the exact influence of either man or whether there were any important disagreements on the choice of delegates. Both were supporting Lyndon Johnson for President. The fact that several important party leaders were placed on the delegation despite the probability that they would not support Johnson suggests that Combs, at least, felt it necessary to satisfy major forces in the party even at the risk of losing a few votes to other candidates. Presumably local party leaders were regularly consulted in the choice of national delegates representing the various districts. In particular the Jefferson County organization must have had a strong voice in choosing delegates from its congressional district, several of whom backed candidates other than Johnson. In some cases Clements and Combs picked as delegates persons who were known to support Lyndon Johnson while in other cases a specific commitment to Johnson may have been demanded as the price for a place on the delegation. In one case an attempt was made to get a commitment from a prominent party leader who wanted to be on the delegation; when he refused to support Johnson, he was put on the delegation anyway at the last minute. Attempts to apply such pressure to potential delegates known to favor other presidential candidates appear to have been rare, however.

Primary responsibility for preparing the list of delegates and assuring maximum support from them for Johnson was in Clements's hands. It was widely believed that he had sought the post of highway commissioner partly to strengthen his influence over the choice of delegates. In view of the widespread support for Johnson among party leaders in the state and the harmony between Clements and Combs, it is doubtful whether Clements's considerable powers as a master politician were seriously taxed in the process of producing a pro-Johnson delegation. The list of delegates prepared by the administration represented a cross-section of state and county leaders in the Combs-Clements-Wyatt wing of the party. Aside from the outgoing national committeeman and committeewomen, who were *ex officio* delegates, it did not include any members of the Chandler wing of the party. The slate of delegates was approved without opposition in the congressional district conventions and the state convention, both meeting in Louisville on June 25.

In keeping with the Combs-Wyatt agreement, the state convention avoided adopting the unit rule. One issue that may have caused some disagreement among the leaders, however, was convention endorsement of a presidential candidate. In the absence of the unit rule such an action would have had little practical effect, and in view of most national delegates' support for Johnson it was unnecessary; nevertheless, some steps were taken toward an endorsement. Governor Combs publicly urged that both the county "mass meetings" (choosing a slate of delegates to the district and state conventions) and the congressional district conventions avoid endorsing any presidential candidate or instructing national delegates to support any candidate. Nevertheless, the press estimated that a substantial majority of the delegates to the state and congressional district conventions had been instructed by county meetings to support Johnson. Moreover, in four of the eight congressional district conventions rather informal action was taken to "advise" support for Johnson or to endorse him. Former Senator Clements apparently paid more attention to preparations for county meetings than did other leaders of the administration and may have been partially responsible for the instructions adopted in many of them. He took an open part in the proposal of one district convention to "advise" support for Johnson. In keeping with Combs's desire, however, the state convention endorsed no candidate. None of the speakers at the state convention, and these included Combs and Clements, mentioned any of the presidential candidates.

Although Wilson Wyatt is particularly influential in Jefferson County, he made no effort to gain endorsement of Stevenson by mass meetings or the district convention in that county. Stevenson supporters made some weak and unsuccessful efforts to gain some changes in the slates of state and district delegates selected in Jefferson County mass meetings.

Forces loyal to former Governor Chandler sought in only a few counties (including Chandler's home county) to challenge the election by mass meetings of delegations loyal to the Combs administration. Four years earlier, Chandler—then governor—had gained control of the party after a series of bitter hassles in the county meetings and district and state conventions. This time he recognized the futility of a convention fight against the administration.

The Delegation at the National Convention

By the time the Kentucky delegation reached Los Angeles, virtually all of its members had decided how to cast their votes on the first ballot. The state leadership at the convention did nothing to change minds of the delegates.

Governor Combs set the tone for the delegation's procedures at the first breakfast on Monday, the opening day of the convention. He reiterated briefly his own support for Lyndon Johnson and said that no poll of the delegation was necessary until Wednesday because he knew how the delegates stood and was not interested in trying to put pressure on them. In subsequent meetings he reiterated his support for Lyndon Johnson and privately pointed out that, in the event of Johnson's defeat, Kentucky would gain nothing by abandoning him because of Johnson's continued influence in the Senate. On the day of the balloting, Combs announced that delegates should tell his administrative assistant how they desired to be recorded. By avoiding any public poll and promising to keep the delegates' choices private, Combs further heightened the impression that the delegates would not be pressured. Former Senator Clements, who apparently acquiesced in this strategy, made no speeches to the delegation. No presidential candidates were brought to speak to the delegation before the nominations, though many delegates shook hands with Johnson when he visited the hotel to speak to another delegation.

Combs and particularly Clements may have been more active in private contacts with the delegates than in public statements. If so, their efforts were probably directed almost entirely to assuring that no Johnson votes were lost in the rising Kennedy tide at Los Angeles. Determined efforts to convert the supporters of other candidates appear to have been at a minimum. It is noteworthy that John Crimmins—a leading Kennedy supporter —publicly thanked the Governor at the breakfast meeting after the nomination for the fair way in which the delegation's business had been conducted and for the respect shown to minority viewpoints.

The best example of smooth relations among the state leaders occurred when Stevenson's name was placed in nomination at the convention. The Stevenson leaders at the convention were having great difficulty finding a state to yield to Senator Eugene McCarthy of Minnesota for the nominating speech. (Minnesota's governor was nominating Kennedy). Combs readily agreed to Wyatt's suggestion that Kentucky serve this function and that Wyatt make a seconding speech for Stevenson. Wyatt in return undertook to make sure that these actions did not result in any first ballot increase in Stevenson votes at Johnson's expense in Kentucky. He urged several potential Stevenson supporters not to switch from Johnson on the first ballot and persuaded two delegates to vote for Johnson rather than Stevenson on the first ballot. The entire incident was handled without friction.

The Kennedy supporters in the Kentucky delegation apparently made no serious effort to have their candidate speak to the group before the nominations nor did they seem to engage in any intensive campaigning among their colleagues. The high-pressure Kennedy organization seems to have left the Kentucky delegation alone. This must have reflected primarily a recognition of political realities in the state. It seems likely, in addition, that Kennedy leaders in the state discouraged outside efforts that would have embarrassed their relationship with the Combs administration.

The Strategy of Accommodation

The primary reason why the Kentucky leaders (always excluding outcast former Governor Chandler) were so successful in avoiding friction over their differences on presidential candidates was that this strategy seemed essential to the unity of their faction of the Democratic Party. The Combs-Clements-Wyatt coalition, at the time of the convention, was united in support for the Combs administration and in the desire to prevent a political comeback by Chandler. The coalition was an uneasy one because of past political differences, and not long after the convention it fell apart when Clements reluctantly resigned as Highway Commissioner under pressure from the Governor. At the time of the convention, however, Clements expected to maintain his post, and the coalition was still serving the mutual interests of its members. They had every reason to avoid dissension brought about by differences over presidential strategy.

One important additional reason why Wyatt could work in harmony with Combs and Clements at the convention was the temporary identity of interests between the Stevenson and Johnson forces: both were trying to stop Kennedy. A symptom of the alliance was reported by one delegate who said that during the Stevenson demonstration at the convention Clements was exuberantly joining in the chant: "We want Stevenson!" This identity of interest dictated Wyatt's strategy. He knew that Stevenson could not win on the first or second ballot, not until a deadlock had clearly developed. He hoped, in that event, to lead a majority of the delegation to support Stevenson. Wyatt was not willing to jeopardize his chances for success on a later ballot by an intensive campaign to take votes away from Johnson on the first ballot.

The Kennedy supporters in the Kentucky delegation did not share in this tactical unity. They were the local vanguard of a candidate who was making every effort to win on the first ballot. But they were immune from the pressures of others. Most of them were either important individuals or represented forces valuable to the Combs administration; in either case the risks of applying pressure on them were greater than any possible advantages from Combs's point of view.

In some states, rival political factions have utilized their campaigns for presidential candidates as tools in the struggle for control of a state party. In Kentucky, the administration is able to dominate the Democratic Party and the proceedings for choosing delegates to that party's national conventions so effectively that the opposition has little to gain by trying to capitalize on presidential candidacies. Within the dominant faction, however, there may be divergent elements committed to various national candidates, as there were in 1960 in Kentucky. The Combs administration probably had the power to compel united support for Lyndon Johnson, perhaps through the unit rule. It used its authority to insure a large vote for Johnson, but it used enough restraint to avoid types of pressure that would have jeopardized support for the administration among important elements of the party.

20. A Split Delegation and a Neutral Governor: The Wisconsin Delegation*

LUCIUS J. BARKER

University of Wisconsin (Milwaukee)

The Wisconsin delegation to the 1960 Democratic National Convention was selected in a bitterly fought presidential primary. The delegation was composed of 62 persons, each of whom could cast one-half vote of the state's 31 votes. Sixty of these delegates were chosen in the April 5 primary election. Of these 60 delegates, 40 were pledged to Senator Kennedy and 20 to Senator Humphrey. The delegates were legally bound to support the candidate to whom they were pledged, at least on

*The author is grateful for the cooperation of the members of the Wisconsin delegation.

the first ballot.* The national committeeman and committee-woman, *ex officio* delegates with a half vote each, pledged themselves to Humphrey and Kennedy respectively. As such the Wisconsin delegation was a split delegation. And the split was more than legal. Involved were state and party politics, and ideological and personal differences—all of which were sharpened by the fierce Humphrey-Kennedy battle.

Throughout it all, however, the governor of the state, Gaylord Nelson, remained neutral. His party had just come into power for the first time in 24 years. Its majority status was tenuous, with the Republicans controlling one house of the state legislature (the senate), and holding one of the five** constitutional offices, that of secretary of state. In the governor's opinion, the party could ill afford the bitter strains of internal squabbles. Indeed, since state elections are held every two years, there would be little time to resolve such difficulties before the party faced another election. Thus, in a contest which loomed close and bitter as the Kennedy-Humphrey one, the governor chose to be neutral.

But even the governor's neutrality did not keep him out of trouble. His attempts to mediate disputes during the primary irritated both sides. Moreover, there persisted the impression that as between Humphrey and Kennedy, the governor privately preferred Humphrey. As a result the Kennedy people were suspicious of the governor's neutrality, while the Humphrey forces readily "understood" it. Soon after the primary, the State Central Committee made the governor an alternate delegate.***

---

*After the first ballot, the delegates may be released from the legal obligation in either of three ways: viz; (1) if the candidate himself releases them; (2) if the candidate receives less than 10 per cent of the total convention vote; and (3) if two-thirds of the delegates vote to release themselves. Prior to the convention, the attorney general was asked to render opinions clarifying two of these provisions. In one instance he ruled that Senator Humphrey's withdrawal after the West Virginia primary freed his delegates of any legal commitment imposed upon them by state law. He also ruled that since the Wisconsin delegation was legally split between two candidates, the "two-thirds release" rule applied to the Humphrey-Kennedy groups acting separately and not as a joint delegation.

**The other constitutional office, that of State Superintendent of Public Instruction, is non-partisan.

***Other public and party officials were also selected as alternate delegates. The list included the party's only United States Senator, three of the party's five congressmen, the state party chairman, the Mayor of the city of Milwaukee, and the chairman of the Milwaukee County Democratic Party.

Pre-Convention Activity

Though they lost the primary, the Humphrey forces did not give up the fight. They took the battle to the Senate Central Committee where alternate delegates were selected on May 7. In this committee the Humphrey people, or the "real Democrats" as they proudly called themselves, were clearly in command. The meeting was marked with bitterness and sarcasm on both sides. For one thing, the Humphrey people used the meeting as a forum to denounce the Kennedy organization and its campaign tactics. They charged that the Kennedy delegates were "Johnny-come-lately" Democrats, the casual type, and in any event, Democrats who were not or had not been actively involved in party work.* In addition, they claimed that Republicans crossed en masse to vote for Kennedy, and that delegates so selected did not represent the sentiment of real Democrats. It is true that most organization Democrats supported Senator Humphrey, and it was they who were most resentful of "Kennedy independents and Republicans" infiltrating their ranks. Thus to the Humphrey forces, the selection of the alternate delegates was the only chance left to see that true and dedicated Democrats were represented at the party's national convention.

Of course, the Kennedy representatives on the state committee denied these charges. They said that the people had spoken in the primary, and that their voices should be obeyed. They argued accordingly that fair play dictated that alternate delegates be selected in proportion to the delegate strength of the respective candidates, since in any event alternates would have to act for duly elected delegates. But the die was cast and the Humphrey people pushed through an alternate slate of 30 which included only three or four Kennedy sympathizers. The rest were Humphrey supporters or public officials who for the most part were

---

*Two factors might help explain the charges that the Kennedy delegates were not "real" Democrats: (1) the fact that volunteer support for the Kennedy organization came from casual Democrats, independents, and Republicans; and (2) the fact that Kennedy won areas which are normally Republican. However, it does not follow from these factors that the Kennedy delegates were any less "regular" Democrats than the Humphrey delegates. In fact, in my larger study being conducted on the Wisconsin presidential primary, preliminary conclusions indicate little difference between the Humphrey-Kennedy delegates in regard to party activism; e.g., number of years in party, number of party positions held, participation in party activities.

neutral during the primary, and were made alternates out of deference to their positions.

In addition, the Humphrey-controlled committee adopted a "loyalty" resolution which stated that an alternate, when acting for a duly elected delegate, had a moral obligation to vote as instructed by that delegate. But this did not soothe the Kennedy people. They were openly bitter and resentful of the action. And it was now their turn to act.

The next day, May 8, the Kennedy people took the fight to the first joint meeting of the Wisconsin delegation. Though the meeting was originally called for organizational and other housekeeping purposes, the furor over the selection of alternate delegates indicated that more than perfunctory business would be transacted, or at least, that such business would not be transacted in a perfunctory manner. This was even more predictable since not only were some delegates members of the State Central Committee, but many other delegates had attended the committee meeting as observers. And most of them were Kennedy delegates who did not like what they saw.

It was under such circumstances that the first joint meeting of the Wisconsin delegation was held. Of the 40 delegates attending, only about five were Humphrey delegates; the rest were Kennedy delegates. The meeting was called to order by Herman Jessen, Democratic national committeeman and a Humphrey delegate. Immediately thereafter, Ivan Nestingen, mayor of the city of Madison and chairman of the Kennedy delegation, asked for a recess so his delegates could caucus. This request was agreed to by the Humphrey delegates.

After about a 30-minute recess, the joint caucus reconvened. Immediately, the strategy of the Kennedy group was unfolded. Their first move was to push through a slate of officials for delegation leaders, all of whom were Kennedy delegates.* They handled skillfully a suggestion that Governor Gaylord Nelson be accorded some recognition by making the governor honorary chairman of the delegation. They then named two delegates to each of the four major convention committees. Of the eight persons named, only one was a Humphrey delegate. All of these actions, of course, were not unexpected.

---

*Ivan Nestingen was elected chairman. Other officers included: State Senator Robert Dean, Vice Chairman; Dora M. Krueger, Secretary; Jack Milward, Treasurer; and T. L. Russo, Sergeant at Arms.

But at this time the bitterness over the alternate delegate fracas broke into the open. To the apparent surprise of the Humphrey delegates, the Kennedy forces presented a resolution condemning the manner in which the Humphrey-dominated State Central Committee had selected the alternate delegates. The resolution called the committee's action "illegal and undemocratic" and asked that the entire matter be "referred to the national committee for its interpretation and ruling.** In the debate that followed, Frank Nikolay, chairman of the Humphrey group and a member of the state legislature, stoutly defended the action of the committee. He chided the Kennedy delegates for acting like a "bunch of cry babies" who could not stand to lose in a fair and honest fight. But his voice was unheard. He was rebutted time and again by Kennedy delegates, some of whom apparently relished the opportunity to denounce the Humphrey people in a forum in which they were certain of victory. The Humphrey delegates soon recognized the futility of the debate and the resolution was accordingly shouted through on a voice vote.

Such was the first meeting of the split delegation. Soon after this meeting, however, events in West Virginia threw a new light on the Wisconsin situation. Senator Kennedy's victory in that state's primary, coupled with Humphrey's defeat and subsequent withdrawal from the presidential race, had a telling impact on the behavior of the Wisconsin delegation. For one thing, the Kennedy people were now ready to forget their past feuds with the Humphrey delegates. They dropped the idea of protesting the manner in which alternate delegates had been chosen, and did not forward the resolution to the national committee. They openly welcomed and solicited the support of the Humphrey delegates. In addition, the state attorney general, himself a Kennedy delegate, issued a formal opinion stating that Humphrey's withdrawal freed his delegates of any legal commitment imposed upon them by state law.

But the Humphrey delegates were cautious. They repeatedly refused to abandon Humphrey. Even definite overtures by Senator Kennedy himself could not lure them. Neither for that mat-

---

**Minutes of the Wisconsin delegation to the 1960 Democratic National Convention. Meeting held Sunday, May 8, 1960, at the Schroeder Hotel, Milwaukee.

ter were they ready to support other candidates* Indeed, as late as June 26, they reaffirmed their moral and legal commitment to Senator Humphrey and agreed that no decision would be reached until they personally discussed the matter with Humphrey.

Thus, the Wisconsin delegation which went to Los Angeles was still divided. But the fact that the Humphrey delegates had no avowed candidate, coupled with the now friendly attitude of the Kennedy people, minimized the friction and factionalism within the delegation.

Caucuses and Early Activity at the Convention

By convention time, the bitterness which characterized the earlier meeting of the delegation had considerably lessened. In general, the joint meetings of the Humphrey-Kennedy delegates were routine affairs. The distribution of guest tickets provided the most controversial issue in the four meetings which the delegation held. Beyond this, the meetings were little more than friendly gatherings. But beneath the surface the split remained. Separate caucuses of the Kennedy and Humphrey delegates, more than anything else, emphasized the split.

Both groups held their initial caucuses immediately after the first joint meeting of the delegation on Monday, July 11. The Humphrey caucus, and the group's only formal one, created a great deal of interest. For the most part, the Humphrey delegats were a confused group.** This much they knew—Humphrey had that certain type of liberalism they liked; Kennedy did not. But under the circumstances, they pondered how best they could fight for their liberalism, how best they could express their feelings. They considered whether they should stick with Humphrey or switch to a reluctant Stevenson where many of their sympathies were anyway. And in either case, they questioned whether or not the effort was futile. They considered "accepting" Kennedy, but were troubled lest they sacrifice principles for political expediency. In every case, they pondered the probable impact of their action on the liberal cause, on the future

---

*A special caucus of Humphrey delegates was held on June 26 at which spokesmen for Kennedy, Johnson, Symington, Stevenson, and Bowles urged the delegates to join their respective camps.

**A few Humphrey delegates, however, reiterated their intention to switch to Kennedy if Humphrey released them. They stated that local conditions primarily influenced their decision.

of liberalism within the party. Thus were the delegates torn in their attitudes as they entered their first caucus in the convention city.

The caucus itself did little to clear up anything. The only decision made was to withhold a decision until Senator Humphrey had explained his intentions. This the senator did at a noon luncheon the same day.

The luncheon, ostensibly held for some fifty delegates Humphrey had amassed in his pre-convention activity, was a gala social affair attended by more than 400 persons. In fact, Humphrey himself quipped that if he had known he had so many delegates he probably would have still been an active candidate. But the meeting proved a disappointment to most of the Humphrey delegates, including those from Wisconsin. True, Humphrey stirred their enthusiasm as only he could, but he did little more. They wanted an indication of Humphrey's presidential choice, but this they did not get. Instead, he left that decision up to the "consciences" of the individual delegates.

Thus, the Wisconsin Humphrey delegates were still without direction. A few reiterated their intention to vote for Kennedy, but most declined to jump on the bandwagon. Though no other formal meetings of the Wisconsin Humphrey delegation were held, informal attempts were made to keep as many of them together as possible.*

The Wisconsin Kennedy delegates were also active. Their initial caucus was devoted mostly to routine matters, none of which excited any interest. For the most part, the caucus appeared designed to preserve the spirit and interest of the delegates. Ivan Nestingen, who had been elected earlier as chairman of the full delegation, was also chairman of the Kennedy group. He, as did most of the Kennedy people, exuded confidence. There was little discussion concerning the Humphrey delegates. So confident were the Kennedy delegates of victory that they appared little concerned with what the Humphrey delegates would do. They were convinced that the bandwagon was rolling.

However, this confident attitude was short lived. Late Tuesday (July 12) top Kennedy strategists evidenced mounting con-

---

*At a secret caucus held in the hotel room of Representative Lester Johnson, a leader of the Humphrey group, plans were reportedly made to hold the delegates together for an expected Stevenson boom. See *Milwaukee Journal*, July 13, 1960, p. 1, col. 5-8.

cern that their bandwagon would not develop enough momentum for a first ballot victory. Consequently, in their second caucus (held July 13), the Wisconsin Kennedy delegates hurriedly mapped plans to corral the uncommitted Humphrey delegates. This changed attitude toward the Humphrey delegates was so apparent that one or two Kennedy delegates privately expressed the apprehension that Kennedy was losing strength. Nevertheless, the Kennedy group went about the task systematically. Under the astute leadership of Chairman Nestingen, "persuading teams" of two or three Kennedy delegates were assigned to each of the uncommitted Humphrey delegates. Individual rather than team contact was stressed. These individuals were carefully selected on the basis of their friendship with the particular Humphrey delegate involved. Where rank and file delegates were not familiar with a Humphrey delegate, well-known public officials such as Senator Proxmire or Congressman Reuss and Congressman Zablocki were assigned the task. Pep talks were even in store for those Humphrey delegates who had indicated they would switch to Kennedy. In addition, the Kennedy people sought and received Governor Nelson's endorsement of Kennedy in this all-out drive to win the Humphrey delegates. Up to this time, Nelson's position was unclear and unknown.

In their persuasion efforts, the Kennedy people decided to use three main talking points: (1) that Kennedy would win in Wisconsin and thus help the local ticket; (2) that it would look good for the state to be united behind a winner; and (3) that Kennedy could beat Nixon. They carefully avoided any comparison of the abilities or caliber of candidates for fear they would arouse Stevenson sympathies.

The drive was thus on in full force. It lasted until the clerk called the roll for balloting. During this period every Humphrey delegate was contacted. For the most part, however, they proved a stubborn lot. They were aware of the all-out drive, and some of them resented it. They appeared quite irritated by the persistent prodding. And if anything, the drive only rekindled their resentment at Kennedy and what they called his "organization tactics." But the pressure on the Humphrey delegates became greater as the balloting drew nearer. In fact, last-minute efforts by one or two Kennedy people especially angered some Humphrey delegates. For example, one Humphrey delegate said that a Kennedy supporter told him in a very sarcastic and vengeful manner that "he'd be sorry" if he did not vote for Kennedy. Another delegate said he was "threatened by some one in the state who had very little power," and accordingly he (the Humphrey delegate) was not bothered by it.

Most of these tactics proved unsuccessful. Only five of the 21 Humphrey delegates switched to Kennedy on the first ballot, several less than the number who had indicated such intentions.*
Thus, on the first ballot, 46 delegates cast 23 votes for Kennedy while 16 delegates cast 8 votes for Humphrey.

In retrospect, it appears that the voters of the Humphrey delegates represented as much "Stop Kennedy-Pro-Stevenson" sentiment as they did pro-Humphrey sentiment, though it was the latter which held the delegates together. Had the Humphrey delegates switched to Stevenson, as many of them wanted to do, Kennedy would probably have picked up another one and a half votes.

The Fight Over the Johnson Nomination

The selection of Senator Johnson as vice presidential nominee severely tested the degree to which the Humphrey-Kennedy factionalism remained in the delegation. But more than this, it seemingly penetrated the ideological convictions of the entire delegation. As a matter of fact, there was so much apprehension among the delegates that an emergency caucus was called only one hour before the roll call. The caucus was held in a room just off the main convention floor.

In the caucus itself, Senator Proxmire led the fight to win approval of Johnson. Proxmire reasoned that the executive qualities of Johnson's senatorial leadership, which he had criticized in the past, were the very ones which would make the Texan a great vice president. He accordingly praised Johnson's great executive ability. Furthermore, Proxmire thought that supporting Johnson for the vice presidency would enhance rather than retard the enactment of liberal legislation. He felt that Wisconsin's interests would be served better if Johnson were in the vice presidency rather than in the crucial post of majority leader. Other state and party officials followed Proxmire's lead; and, as

---

*On Sunday prior to the convention opening, as many as eight Humphrey delegates were reported to switch to Kennedy. See *Milwaukee Sentinel*, July 11, 1960, Pt. 1, p. 1, col. 5-8.

one journalist aptly put it, "one by one . . . purged themselves of anti-Johnson sentiment."

But some of the delegates were very outspoken and bitter in their denunciation of Johnson's selection. Certainly it was not unexpected that the Humphrey delegates would denounce Johnson since to them even Kennedy's commitment to liberal principles was questionable. And though one or two Kennedy delegates joined in the criticism, vestiges of the old Humphrey-Kennedy split were evident. Herman Jessen, retiring national committeeman and a Humphrey delegate, referred to those who supported Johnson as a "bunch of reactionaries." Another Humphrey delegate, State Senator Carl Lauri, who had voted for Kennedy on the first ballot, was particularly bitter. Lauri said that Kennedy told him that "under no circumstances did he want a Kennedy-Johnson ticket." He thus accused Kennedy of breaking a promise. And even though most of the Humphrey delegates went along with the Johnson selection, they did so begrudgingly. The sentiment of this group was well expressed by Frank Nikolay when he said that "since the mistake of sacrificing principles for political expediency was made the night before" (referring to Kennedy's nomination), political etiquette required him to go along with the choice of the presidential candidate.

However, the criticisms of Johnson were not confined to the Humphrey delegates. Indeed, apparently the most depressed and disappointed person at the caucus was a Kennedy delegate, James Arena. Coming from a labor area (Racine), Arena said he did not believe in talking out of both sides of his mouth. He was especially incensed with delegation leaders who were now pleading with the delegates to support Johnson. "Last night Johnson was no good," said Arena, "and today we are supposed to think he's Almighty God."

As the caucus dragged on, it was evident that the overwhelming majority of the delegates had resigned themselves to going along with the wishes of the presidential candidate. Before doing so, however, State Assemblyman Norman Sussman, a Kennedy delegate, demanded to know the position of the governor who, after all, said Sussman, is "our leader." However, Sussman was immediately assured by Pat Lucey, pro-Kennedy state party chairman, that the governor had been consulted prior to Johnson's selection and had given his approval.

Although the governor's attitude was reassuring to many of the delegates, it did not resolve the mixed feelings with which they approved of Johnson. There was even an argument as to whether those who opposed Johnson would have the chance to record their opposition. But those who opposed the Texas senator demanded that they be so recorded. "I wouldn't dare go back to my district," said one Humphrey delegate, "without recording my opposition." To bring the caucus to an end, Chairman Nestingen ruled that it was the right of any delegate to have his vote recorded. Six delegates took advantage of this ruling and the chairman accordingly announced that he would record the vote as 28 to 3 in favor of Johnson.

In the end, Johnson was nominated by acclamation on a voice vote. And though the Wisconsin delegates who opposed him were not so recorded by the convention, they were nevertheless recorded in the home state press."* This was the important thing.

In retrospect, the Humphrey-Kennedy split definitely had an impact on the behavior of the delegates in the Johnson situation, though by no means was it the only factor. The Kennedy delegates felt obliged to support Johnson. To have done otherwise would not only have shown a lack of confidence in the man they had supported all along, but it also would have impugned their political adeptness in selecting a nominee they could trust and support. So whether supporting Johnson was right or not, most Kennedy delegates agreed that it was proper.

To the Humphrey delegates the situation was less difficult, though no less emotional. They felt no special allegiance to Kennedy, and had no interest in Johnson. They were thus free to take any position they desired. To them the positions they took were readily justifiable. Hence, those who opposed Johnson did so for the same reasons they opposed Kennedy—on the basis of ideological commitments. Those who did not oppose the Johnson nomination reasoned that any successful presidential candidate should have the right to choose his running mate. In both instances, the Humphrey delegates remained uncommitted to the principles of the Kennedy-Johnson combination.

All in all, the caucus proved an excellent safety valve for the feelings of the delegates.

---

*In addition, the *Madison Capital Times* devoted almost a full page spread, complete with pictures of the "liberals who dared to keep the faith." July 18, 1960.

The Governor and the Delegation

One of the most intriguing aspects of the Wisconsin situation was the behavior of its neutral governor, Gaylord Nelson, vis-a-vis its split delegation. And quite obviously, the governor's neutral position in the primary greatly affected his subsequent role and influence in the delegation. It likewise affected the delegation's behavior toward him. For example, in organizing the delegation, there was some feeling, particularly among the Humphrey delegates, that Nelson would be the ideal chairman for a split delegation. They reasoned that his neutrality in the primary, as well as the prestige of his office, put him in a good position to promote harmony in the delegation. But the Kennedy delegates, who had fought hard to win the primary, thought that one of their number should be chairman. They accordingly elected Ivan Nestingen chairman of the delegation, and made Governor Nelson honorary chairman.

However, Nelson's selection as honorary chairman was not a perfunctory thing. In a separate caucus the Kennedy delegates agreed to support their own slate of officials for the delegation. Then when the Humphrey and Kennedy groups met jointly, Nestingen read the Kennedy slate which made no mention of the governor. Immediately, Frank Nikolay, chairman of the Humphrey group, ventured that since the governor was a member of the delegation he should be accorded some role. Nikolay's suggestion obviously created uneasiness among the Kennedy delegates. For a moment they appeared uncertain how to deal with it. But in the hurried and cautious discussion which followed, someone put forth the idea that the governor be made honorary chairman. This provided the Kennedy people a very palatable way out of an otherwise ticklish situation. By making Nelson honorary chairman, the Kennedy delegates not only showed the expected sense of affection and respect for the governor, but they also preserved the chairmanship for a loyal Kennedy supporter.

At the convention itself, the governor was not involved in, and indeed was somewhat withdrawn from the operation of the delegation. It was only after Lieutenant Governor Philleo Nash "threatened to blast the convention in language that would make former President Truman's criticism [charging a rigged convention] sound like tea table talk" that floor privileges were extended to himself and the governor. Alternate delegates were seated in the balcony, far away from the delegation, and it was there that the governor and the lieutenant governor sat during Monday's opening session of the convention. Calling this to the attention of the delegation, Nash decried the fact that the "governor of our state should have to sneak in the convention." Nash did not blame anyone for the situation, but it was quite apparent that the Kennedy leadership of the delegation was the target. And though most of the delegates appeared rather chagrined by the incident, the matter was passed over without comment.

The governor attended about two meetings of the delegation. In neither case did he assume, nor was he accorded, a leading role. It is true that in one of these meetings the governor charged the delegation to work for strong planks on agriculture, labor, and civil rights. However, this was a little more than a pep talk since there was not the slightest bit of disagreement on these matters. And accordingly, the delegation unanimously passed a resolution supporting the governor's attitude.

Only at one meeting was concern expressed over the governor's role. And this was in a Kennedy delegate caucus in which last-minute and somewhat desperate plans were being mapped to garner the Humphrey delegates. The caucus, held on Wednesday July 13, was a highly emotional affair in which the governor's neutral position was attacked time and again. The Kennedy people seemed agreed that the governor could do much to influence the Humphrey delegates. They lamented the fact that he had not made his position clear by "coming out for Kennedy." As one delegate put it: "The governor should declare himself, he can't be neutral in politics. He has to come out and not straddle the fence. He can put the screws to them [the Humphrey delegates]."

The Kennedy delegates also felt that Nelson did not fully appreciate that his own reelection depended greatly on Kennedy being the presidential candidate. Delegate after delegate testified that the governor's own reelection would be jeopardized, and even doubtful (in their particular areas) if Kennedy was not the head of the ticket. As one delegate angrily shouted: "I think we ought to let the governor know that he will not be a shoo-in if Kennedy is not nominated." At this point Nestingen

attempted to terminate the discussion by appointing a representative from each of the state's congressional districts to call
on the governor and ask him to use his influence on the Humphrey delegates. However, there were some delegates who demanded action.* They insisted that the governor be summarily
invited to state his position before the caucus, and they had
their way.

While the governor was being paged, the caucus was fever-
ishly deciding the best way to present the issue to him. Senator
Proxmire, for example, warned the delegates against emotional
outbursts, since after all, he said, the position of the governor
must be respected. Another delegate warned: "Don't push him
[the governor] because if you do he'll get stubborn and we'll
get nowhere." After a few more admonitions, the caucus pushed
through a resolution asking the governor to come out for Kennedy, and urge the Humphrey delegates to do likewise. The
strategy was to read the resolution to the governor and ask for
his reaction.

By the time the governor entered the room, the atmsophere,
though still tense, was considerably calmer. He was given a
standing ovation and was escorted to the front of the room.
The presiding officer then read the resolution to the governor
and asked for his reaction.

The governor began his reply by recalling his neutral role in
the primary and up until the convention. Then in an announcement which obviously surprised but pleased the delegates, the
governor said he was now supporting Kennedy since he feared
a developing "stop Kennedy" movement might prove unfortu-
nate. Nelson indicated that he had already been talking to the
Humphrey delegates trying to persuade them to vote for Senator Kennedy. But the governor declined to make a public
statement endorsing Kennedy since, in his opinion, public
statements do not change any votes. Furthermore, he reiterated
that he would not be disappointed with either Humphrey, Kennedy or Stevenson. On this note the caucus adjourned.**

---

*It was about here that Nestingen left the meeting to keep a previous
appointment. State Senator Robert Dean, vice chairman, took over the
chair.

**After the caucus, several Kennedy delegates persuaded Nelson to per-
mit the issuing of a statement by the Kennedy headquarters announcing
his support.

In retrospect, the caucus placed the governor in a most difficult situation. He was the only major state official who had not embraced Kennedy. The pressure on him was great.* However, he calmly and in seemingly good spirits stated his position, and stuck to it.

Later, the emergency caucus on the Johnson vice presidential nomination also focused attention on Governor Nelson's role in the delegation. The governor did not attend the caucus, but the delegates nevertheless wanted to know his attitude. And undoubtedly his reported approval of Johnson had a soothing impact on an otherwise troubled delegation.** Indeed, Johnson's support among the Wisconsin delegates was so unenthusiastic that the governor's opposition could have proved an irritating obstacle to the Kennedy leaders of the delegation.

Why the governor's opinion on the Johnson nomination was important may not only shed more light on his role and influence in the delegation, but it may also clarify the role and influence of other delegation leaders. For one thing, the governor had remained neutral during the primary fight. It was only hours before the nomination, when it was obvious that Kennedy would be nominated, that Nelson reluctantly sided with Kennedy and urged Humphrey delegates to do likewise. On the other hand, most state and party officials had long been in the Kennedy camp. One such official was state party chairman Patrick Lucey. As state party chairman, Lucey had declared himself officially neutral in the primary contest between Kennedy and Humphrey. But as a private individual, Lucey worked hard for Kennedy and was one of his most trusted supporters. As a result, Lucey was charged with using his party position as well as the state organization to support Kennedy.*** Neverthe-

---

*The *Madison Capital Times* reported that some of the delegation leaders, mainly Proxmire, delegation chairman Nestingen, and state party chairman Lucey "brought persistent pressure through the caucus for Governor Nelson to abandon his neutral position. . . ." July 15, 1960, p. 4, col. 7.

**In a subsequent news conference, the governor denied that he was consulted or that he had approved Johnson's selection. Said he: "I would not have selected Johnson myself and I would have counseled against the selection if I had been asked." *Milwaukee Journal,* July 18, 1960, p. 2, col. 1.

***From the time of his election in 1957, Lucey has been under constant criticism for his partiality in primary contests. In the 1958 Democratic primary, for example, Lucey was bitterly attacked for supporting one can-less, he continued to support Kennedy in the primary and convention. Lucey's role in the Johnson caucus illustrates well his political acumen.

He sensed that the Johnson nomination had cut beneath and across the Kennedy-Humphrey factionalism and ran counter to deep ideological convictions of many Wisconsin delegates. And though Senator Proxmire's support of Johnson was important, it had one serious weakness insofar as its impact on the delegation was concerned. Proxmire's support of Johnson, no matter how hard he tried to explain it, appeared hyprocritical since his previous attacks on Johnson, perhaps more than any other factor, were responsible for the anti-Johnson sentiment in Wisconsin.

Most of the other delegation officials were so firmly committed to Kennedy that their support of Johnson could be interpreted as the practical expedient thing to do. Only Governor Nelson, who had been aloof from both Humphrey and Kennedy camps and from the delegation itself, could be represented as viewing Johnson's nomination from a detached point of view. Lucey no doubt detected this and was in a position to do something about it. Thus, when the question was raised concerning Nelson's attitude, Lucey immediately stated that Kennedy had cleared Johnson with the governor. Lucey said he had "just seen" the governor and that the governor was in accord. And whether by coincidence or design, Lucey's statement erased much of the uncertainty and indecision within the delegation.

Conclusion

Such was the role of the governor in a split delegation. In the primary Nelson found it difficult to choose between Humphrey and Kennedy. Humphrey, for example, typified everything for which Wisconsin Democrats stood. He was the farmer's friend, the civil rights advocate, and the laboring man's candidate, and he articulated those positions well. He had great appeal to organization Democrats, including Governor Nelson, who made no secret of his admiration and affection for Humphrey.

---

didate over another as the party's nominee for attorney general. But to his critics Lucey replied: "I have never been neutral about anything, and I don't intend to be now . . . I'm aware that it is a tradition in the party that the state chairman should remain neutral. It's also a tradition that we usually lose elections." (*Milwaukee Sentinel,* May 19, 1958.)

On the other hand, Kennedy posed a problem to Wisconsin Democrats. While he could not seriously challenge Humphrey's leadership in those fields most crucial to Wisconsin politics; viz. agriculture, civil rights, and labor, Kennedy's personal appeal was nevertheless tremendous. His stand on issues was neither that of a Humphrey nor a Nixon. He appealed to liberals and conservatives, Republicans and Democrats. As such Kennedy's winning potential in Wisconsin's open type primary was greatly enhanced, and Governor Nelson knew it.

As leader of a Democratic Party newly come to power, Nelson perhaps did not wish to risk splitting the state party for the sake of either Humphrey's or Kennedy's presidential campaign; he wanted to be in a position to restrain the candidates themselves if need be; and perhaps also he wanted to keep the Wisconsin delegation in a more maneuverable position pending further clarification of the nominating picture.* In any event, Nelson sought to accomplish his objectives by seeking agreement on a favorite son delegation. But this strategy failed, and under the circumstances the governor chose neutrality.

After the primary the governor remained neutral despite mounting pressure to declare for Kennedy, and at the convention he disappointed his followers by failing to take a leading part in the deliberations of the delegation. Perhaps he did so because had he broken his neutrality he might have been forced, as a practical matter, to take a pro-Kennedy position, and this he seemed reluctant to do. There persisted the impression, for example, that the governor and those close to him were so ideologically attached to Stevenson that they found it difficult to support Kennedy. Still further, Nelson might have believed that Kennedy would have been of no help to his own (Nelson's) candidacy in 1960.** On the other hand, Nelson's neutrality was consistent with his past behavior on matters of intra-party conflict, and as such may be viewed as part of his overall temperament.

Generally, Nelson's neutrality seems to have impaired his standing as a leader. For example, at the convention many dele-

---

*It was generally believed, for example, that Nelson preferred Stevenson above all other probable candidates, and wished to be in a position to support the Illinois governor had the opportunity been available.

**Nelson won reelection while his party generally, including Kennedy, suffered heavy defeats in the state.

gates expected him to act like a leader and were disappointed that he did not do so. In addition, Nelson's neutrality has apparently minimized his influence in the subsequent distribution of federal patronage. Federal patronage in Wisconsin has been channelled through a seven-man screening committee,* and it is generally believed (and not without reason)** that state party chairman Patrick Lucey, rather than the governor, has most influence in these matters.*** This becomes important when it is recognized that relations between Nelson and Lucey have been far from ideal. Moreover, control of federal patronage in Wisconsin, perhaps more than many states, can be crucial to the party in power since so little patronage exists at the state level.

Over and above these considerations, however, Nelson's behavior raises the more fundamental problem as to whether or not his neutrality, assuming it served his own political interest, was also in the broader interest of his party. Here is a matter on which there is bound to be varying opinions. As a general proposition, it does not seem appropriate from the viewpoint of the expectations, requirements, and responsibilities of party leadership in a democracy for a governor to remain neutral in presidential politics. However, as regards Wisconsin, there is no doubt that state law discourages a governor's more active participation and leadership by requiring him (and other officials as well) to run as a delegate-candidate in the primary and thereby risk defeat. But whether due to state law, or to a governor's own choosing, or to both of these and other reasons, neutrality circumvents the leadership direction one normally expects from the governor's office.

---

*This committee includes the national committeeman and committeewoman, three officials of the state party organization, including Lucey, and two members at large. Four members of this committee, including Lucey, the national committeeman and committeewoman, have been pro-Kennedy from the start, while the three others had supported Humphrey in the primary. There is, of course, some consultation with the party's congressional delegation.

**Appointments thus far have generally been strong pro-Kennedy people and favored by Lucey. Perhaps more important, however, is that Lucey enjoys the image (as portrayed in the press and otherwise) of being closer to the White House than the governor. Lucey's influence undoubtedly lies in the access he established during the presidential primary with the Kennedy organization.

***The party's only United States Senator, William Proxmire, was also pro-Kennedy and is a close associate of Lucey.

21. Rationality and Decision-Making: The Illinois Democratic Delegation

JAMES A. ROBINSON

Northwestern University

This paper is not a comprehensive critique of the convention but instead reports data on one delegation relevant to one criterion likely to be on any list of standards for evaluating the convention system. This criterion is rationality. Rationality is a word with many usages,* but in spite of its ambiguity, most people will surely say that the process for making a decision or nominating a president ought to be rational. For our purposes, we may define a rational nominating procedure as one which selects candidates with qualifications similar to those required by the office.** Nothing about the presidency requires that the chief executive have a full head of hair, so we could say that any nominating process which discriminated against baldness per se would be non-rational.

In addition to casting 69 votes, the Illinois delegation exercised its formal decision-making power on three other occasions, spending no more than a minute on each. It elected Mayor Richard J. Daley of Chicago and state party chairman James A. Ronan, also of Chicago, as chairman and secretary, respectively, of the delegation. It confirmed preliminary appointments to the platform, resolutions, credentials, and rules committees of the convention. It reelected the state's national committeeman and committeewoman for four-year terms. These decisions were all taken in the delegation's one caucus held in a large room on the

---

*The philosopher Alfred Schutz lists eight or nine usages in his paper, "The Problem of Rationality in the Social World," *Economica*, 10 (1943), 130-149. More recently the sociologist Harold Garfinkel has called attention to as many as fourteen possible meanings of the term, "The Rational Properties of Scientific and Common Sense Activities," *Behavioral Science*, 5 (1960), 72-83.

**This use of the term corresponds to two of Garfinkel's definitions. It focuses on *rules of procedure and grounds of choice. Rules of procedure* are two kinds: "Cartesian'" and "tribal." Cartesian rules apply when a decision is reached without regard for social affiliation of persons involved; tribal rules designate decisions in which "the person counts his decision right or wrong in accordance with whom it is referentially important that he be in agreement." Grounds of choice designates the bases upon which a decision is made among alternatives as well as the bases for legitimizing the decision (p. 74).

third floor of the Hayward Hotel in Los Angeles shortly after three o'clock on Sunday afternoon, July 10, the day before the convention opened. The delegation did not caucus again, nor had it caucused prior to its arrival.

Who Were the Delegates?

The delegation was chosen by a combination of two methods. Each of the 25 congressional districts elected two delegates and two alternates in the April primary. Each of these delegates had one vote. The remaining votes were alloted to 38 delegates-at-large chosen at the party state convention in late May. At the same time, 18 alternates-at-large were selected by the convention.

In the primaries, a few delegates ran committed to particular candidates. One who did was Paul Powell, Speaker of the Illinois House of Representatives, who committed himself to Senator Stuart Symington. In the 13th district, which embraces part of Cook County and runs along the lake shore to the Wisconsin border, a candidate pledged to Chester Bowles ran a poor third. In most parts of the state, however, delegates ran uncommitted to any particular candidate, and many of these apparently ran with the blessing of the state or local party organization leadership.

Half of the elected delegates were chosen in contested primaries with low rates of voter turnout, and many held party positions, public office, or were candidates for office at the time of their selection as delegates. Of the 12 contested districts, only two fell within Cook County where party organization is observably more disciplined than the rest of the state. But even in the contested districts, voting was lighter for delegates than for other offices. Data are available for nine of these and the difference between total vote for delegate and the total vote for all offices ranged from 16 per cent to 33 per cent.

Virtually all of the delegates had a record of prior activity in local, state, or national politics. Several well-known people were chosen by the state convention as delegates-at-large without any request on their part or without any advance notice by the party leaders. These were at-large delegates, each of whom had one-half vote and included such figures as former Governor Adlai E.

Stevenson and Senator Paul H. Douglas.* More than half of the delegates held party or government positions. Data are not available on the occupations of all delegates, but 51 of the 88 occupied or aspired to positions over which party leaders possessed discretion on nomination or appointment. In these circumstances, it is not surprising that the leadership exerted a high degree of control. The only possibility of a split lay in the cleavage between the leaders in Cook County and those downstate, including Paul Powell, John Stelle, former governor, and Scott Lucas, former United States Senator.

Delegate Participation

Several indicators reveal the low degree of individual delegate participation in Illinois. The first sign was the response among delegates to the nationwide CBS telecast prior to the convention on what the convention floor and the proceedings on the floor would be like. The network in Chicago invited all Illinois delegates and alternates to a special showing. Thirty-two responded that they planned to attend; only seven did. A second indicator is the number of absentees among the delegation during sessions of the convention. Although no exact count could be made, the many vacant seats during the proceedings of the convention made the delegation conspicuous. A third indicator of a low level of involvement among individual delegates is the observed reactions to such convention activities as demonstrations following the nomination of candidates. When Senator Kennedy was nominated, Mayor Daley marched through the convention hall carrying the Illinois standard and wearing a Kennedy hat, and there was considerable cheering among people sitting in the Illinois delegation. With this exception, and one other, Illinois delegates neither participated in nor reacted visibly to the demonstrations.

The further exception took place during the demonstration for Adlai Stevenson. About half of the Illinois delegates were on their feet during the prolonged demonstration for their governor, but they were not standing or cheering for Stevenson. In fact, those who participated waved Kennedy signs and many cheered "we want Kennedy" rather than "we want Stevenson."

One other reaction to convention activities on the part of indi-

---

*Governor Stevenson did not attend the caucus on Sunday afternoon, and his alternate, Mr. James O'Keefe, voted for Senator Kennedy. Senator Douglas did not go to Los Angeles.

viduals sitting with the delegation can be reported: several joined in the clapping of hands during the speech by Judge Tom Brady in which he nominated Governor Ross Barnett of Mississippi as a favorite son candidate. This clapping was meant to stop Judge Brady, who was making the last of the nominating speeches after several wearying hours of speeches and demonstrations. From my observation these people were not delegates, but were guests or friends who had been admitted to Illinois' space. In fact, during the nominating speeches, a woman was observed writing a letter home, which letter passed on such facts as that one member of the family would always remember that Senator Kennedy had stepped on his foot in a crowd, and that the weather was absolutely lovely. These observations support the statement that (for most members of the delegation) participation in the convention was very limited, amounting to no more than casting a vote or half-vote in accordance with instructions received from Mayor Daley at the Sunday caucus.

The Presidential Decision

Many have remarked that Senator Kennedy's campaign for the presidency began the afternoon during the 1956 convention when he narrowly lost the vice presidential nomination. If this be so, it is relevant to recall that Illinois gave an overwhelming majority of its 64 votes that day to Senator Kennedy. Inasmuch as 40 of the 69 votes in the 1960 convention had been members of the 1956 delegation, a substantial portion of the Illinois delegates had previously voted for Kennedy.

During the first half of 1960, the newspaper speculation was that Mayor Daley again hoped to be for Senator Kennedy, but the Mayor did not commit himself publicly prior to the convention. Throughout the spring, speculation also held that regardless of the Mayor's preference, there would be considerable downstate support for Senator Symington. In February, even before the delegation was chosen, political reporters thought they could find 20 votes for the Missouri neighbor.

During the spring and early summer, party leaders had various opportunities to hear something of individual delegates' preferences. These opportunities included the state convention at Springfield, visits around the state during the primary campaign, and other political conversations. Delegation leaders say that they did not ask delegates their preferences or put pressure on them for a particular candidate, but that as they talked with them, they learned of the growing favor for Senator Kennedy. Kennedy visited the state more often than any other candidate and drew exceptionally large crowds downstate even in bad winter weather. Symington and Hubert Humphrey made occasional stops in the state, but Lyndon Johnson came only once and then for a non-political speech. Kennedy's crowds indicated to delegates and local precinct committeemen that he might run well in their areas. This, added to Symington's failure to make noticeable gains in other states, helped Kennedy at Symington's expense.

On June 16, the Kennedy staff issued a state-by-state survey of their strength and claimed 57 votes in Illinois. The same week former Governor Stelle was said to be discouraged about Symington's prospects. Outwardly, Speaker Powell remained confident, nevertheless, and said he expected 18 to 20 votes for Symington.

In the Stevenson camp, it was believed that Kennedy would receive a minimum of 49 votes. Symington would have 13, Stevenson 4, and they believed 3 were still undecided the day before the caucus.

Meanwhile, Chicago papers predicted 50 to 56½ would go to Kennedy. This was on the strength of what Mayor Daley was expected to do, because many delegates declined to answer reporters' polls, stating that they would follow the Mayor's judgment. Just before the caucus the delegation leaders themselves expected about 55 votes for Kennedy, 6 or 7 for Symington, 2 for Stevenson, and perhaps 2 for Johnson. This, then was the situation when the Illinois delegation caucused.

Caucus

The Sunday afternoon caucus was closed to the press and to representatives of candidates. Mayor Daley spoke for about fifteen minutes reviewing Senator Kennedy's qualifications for the nomination with overriding emphasis on the Senator's vote getting prowess, his excellent organization, and his capacity to help Democratic candidates up and down the ticket.

The Mayor noted that some delegates had been elected pledged to other candidates and their promises should be respected by all. However, he hoped that every delegate who honestly could, would support Kennedy, and that the Senator would obtain the overwhelming endorsement from Illinois.

Following the Mayor's speech, 21 delegates and alternates arose to speak in behalf of candidates. Former Senator Lucas, who had been Majority Leader of the Senate, pointed out that he should probably be for Senator Johnson, who had succeeded him as Majority Leader. He knew the great burden of that office; he knew the responsibilities it required; and he had great admiration for the man who now held it. But he did not believe that Johnson could be elected. He thought the perfect candidate was Senator Symington who, he emphasized, had "no political scars." Another speech for Senator Symington was made by Speaker Powell who explained that he had promised President Truman that he would support Senator Symington. He did not intend to go back on his promise as long as Symington was a candidate.

A crude content analysis conducted on the spot reveals that the reasons offered for supporting candidates were primarily related to strictly political qualifications, such as capacity to mobilize support for one's program, rather than for administrative, intellectual, or technical qualifications of the office. All but two of the speakers supported Senator Kennedy, and several listed more than one reason for favoring him; but in all but one of the speeches it was possible by the length of time devoted to each theme or by judging the intensity of speech on each theme to isolate the major reason offered by the speaker for supporting Kennedy. It was possible to classify these themes into a few categories. Listed below are the major categories of themes used by the speakers and the number of times each appeared as the major theme:

1. Winner, great organization strength will help the ticket most—10
2. Youth—5
3. Issues (labor)—2
4. Veteran—1
5. Loyalty for former commitments—2
6. Announcements of position—3
   Total—23.

The theme recurring most often was Kennedy's strength as a candidate and the help he would bring to the state and local tickets. References to his youth were almost all defensive and apologetic. The apology, however, was sometimes turned to an advantage, as in the case of a prominent elder party official who said that the older generation had not done very well with the world and that perhaps it was time to turn to the younger generation.

With the exception of the two references to the labor issue, there were few reasons which related directly to issues or to the responsibilities of the presidency. That is not to say that sometime during the speeches references were not made to other issues, the most frequent ones being to civil rights and to the great needs of the country and the current international situation; but these were never the major themes of individual speeches. What concerned delegates the most was who would win in November, and more particularly, who would most help the state and county tickets in Illinois. On this question Senator Kennedy clearly had the advantage. As the Mayor emphasized, the Senator had won seven primaries, and this figure was repeated by other speakers.

When the roll was called, 59½ votes were given to Kennedy, 6½ for Symington, 2 for Stevenson, and one delegate passed. All those who voted for Symington were from downstate, but not all downstate delegates supported Symington. Governor Stelle split from Speaker Powell and Senator Lucas, and voted for Kennedy, an action which the *Chicago Tribune* interpreted as an assist to Mr. Arvey's desire to be reelected national committeeman. Others from downstate joined Kennedy because as George Saal, the sheriff of Tazewell County, told a reporter: "Shucks, I want to be with a winner."

Post Caucus

In the two days between the caucus and the balloting, Mayor Daley was said to be urging other delegates to help raise the 59½ votes for Senator Kennedy to a higher figure. For example, the *Chicago Tribune* reported that the Mayor sent word to Harold Pogue, a trustee of the University of Illinois, which is an elective position, urging him to support Kennedy rather than Governor Stevenson. Indeed, at one point it appeared that 62 votes would be cast for Kennedy, but one of the delegates-at-large who possessed a half vote finally decided to stay with Symington. When it came time to cast Illinois' votes during the balloting on Wednesday night, Mayor Daley had picked up two votes (one shift from Symington and one from the uncommitted delegate) and was able to announce 61½ votes for Kennedy, 5½ for Symington, and 2 for Stevenson.

External Influences

After the caucus, the Kennedy floor managers had checked daily to see that there would be no depreciation in their ranks. When the delegation met on the floor, one could see members of the Kennedy family and the Kennedy campaign organization very much in evidence around the Illinois delegation, many brought there because one of the six Kennedy telephones on the convention floor was installed at a corner of the delegation. Also visiting the delegation from time to time was R. Sargent Shriver, Jr., a brother-in-law of Senator Kennedy, and President of the Chicago Board of Education. Mr. Shriver's wife, Eunice, a sister of Senator Kennedy and other sisters also appeared, presumably, as a Kennedy campaign worker said, to distract them. Representative Charles Brown, Symington's campaign manager, came to talk to Speaker Powell, Colonel Arvey, and other delegates.

But Stevenson forces made the most evident attempt to influence the delegation. In Los Angeles the delegation had received thousands of telegrams from Stevenson supporters in and out of Illinois. The state chairman received a telephone call at 11 p.m. on the Saturday night before the convention from an individual in Long Island, New York, who had once resided in Illinois. It was two o'clock in the morning when the call was placed from New York, and the message was that it would be morally wrong for the Illinois delegation to support, and the convention to nominate, any candidate other than Stevenson. Throughout the week, the secretary of the party received telegrams, opened them and passed them to their addressees. All bore essentially the same message—vote for Stevenson. One alternate, on receiving such a telegram, crumpled it in disgust and threw it to the floor. Not long before the balloting took place on Wednesday night, Stevenson supporters rushed on the floor with a copy of a United Press International dispatch quoting a statement by a Western Union official that the company had received more than 25,000 telegrams endorsing candidates since the first floor demonstration for Stevenson. UPI said the deluge of telegrams was so heavy that it had impeded the outgoing press traffic which was then more than a million words a day. Although the Western Union spokesman declined to divulge the count for each candidate, it revealed that the telegrams were running heavily in favor of Stevenson.

These telegrams did little to influence the attitudes or the behavior of the Illinois delegation in Stevenson's favor. The delegation was not only firmly for Kennedy but was firmly opposed to Stevenson and seemed to become confirmed in this stance as the telegrams flowed in. Many were not amused, but annoyed, and some remarked on the naivete of anyone who believed that he could influence the decision of the delegation by something as anonymous and indirect as a telegram.

A second effort by the Stevenson campaign organization to influence the decision of the delegation in particular and the convention in general was the visit by Stevenson to the convention floor on Tuesday night. Stevenson called the state chairman of the Illinois party at noon and advised him that he would be coming that evening. The party chairman, Mr. Ronan, and Stevenson's alternate, Mr. O'Keefe, met him off the floor and escorted him through the press and admirers to the delegation. This was interpreted within and among the members of the Illinois delegation as a withdrawal from candidacy for the presidency. They noted that it was customary for candidates to remain off the floor and away from the proceedings. This, of course, was not at all the intent of Stevenson or his campaign managers. He was urged to make such a visit for the purpose of giving renewed impetus to his campaign and encourage his sometimes disappointed supporters.

Another attempt to involve members of the Illinois delegation occurred just prior to the demonstration for Stevenson on Wednesday night. Miss Mercedes McCambridge, the television and movie star, was among those trying to organize a demonstration. Periodically she cajoled, shamed, and argued with the delegation to support Stevenson, or at least to carry a banner in his behalf during the demonstration. Her efforts met no success, and during the demonstration which followed, about half the delegation remained seated, and those who stood waved Kennedy banners and to the chants of "we want Adlai" joined in with "we want Kennedy."

The final effort to influence the Illinois delegation came at about ten minutes to seven on the night of the balloting, while the roll was being called by states for nomination of candidates. Senator Mike Monroney, the campaign manager for Stevenson, came to the Illinois standard and asked Mayor Daley to come to the telephone. There, Stevenson, at the urging of Mrs. Franklin D. Roosevelt, was on the line and asking Daley about his support in the Illinois delegation. Stevenson inquired whether he really had as little support as the two votes would indicate, and whether there was some misunderstanding of his own position. The Mayor indicated that not only was Stevenson not regarded as a candidate, but he did not have much support in the delegation. The call was one of Mr. Stevenson's few direct efforts to influence the outcome of the convention's decision and was no more successful than other efforts on his behalf.

Several Illinois residents favorable to Stevenson hovered about the delegation, seeking out friends among delegates, trying to find out what was the support for one candidate or another. Others from Illinois were active in the Stevenson organization at one place or another during the convention.

All external efforts to influence the Illinois delegation had no discernible effect. The decision reached Sunday remained firm, except for the slight increase in Kennedy support which Mayor Daley's efforts had secured.

The Illinois leader also attempted to assist Kennedy in other ways. He tried, for example, to induce Stevenson to second Kennedy's nomination, arguing that because Kennedy had nominated Stevenson in 1956, it would be appropriate for Stevenson to second the Senator's nomination in 1960. This effort, however, came to naught.

Few other states were as solid for Kennedy as was Illinois, and it was doubtless appropriate that Mayor Daley should be among those called to the rostrum to be on the reception committee when Kennedy came out to deliver a short speech following his nomination. But before the presidential choice was final, the Mayor was already at work with leaders of other delegations to try to get a favorable candidate for the vice presidency.

Illinois Participation in the Vice Presidential Decision

The leadership of the delegation favored Senator Symington for vice president, and as early as Tuesday Mayor Daley was involved in conferences concerning the second place on the ticket. Newspaper reports linked him with Carmine DeSapio of New York, Governor David Lawrence of Pennsylvania, and Governor

Michael V. DiSalle of Ohio, in urging the nomination of Senator Symington.

Daley and other Illinois leaders backed Symington for the same reason they supported Kennedy: they believed that he would help the party's state and local candidates. In a television interview after the nomination of Senator Johnson, Senator Lucas reaffirmed his support for Symington, again noting that of all the candidates he had "no political scars." Powell, who had indicated that he thought Mayor Daley had done all he could to get the nomination for Symington, thought that Johnson would cost the ticket as many as 75,000 or 100,000 votes in Illinois.

But the nomination of Johnson was certainly acceptable to the delegation, who reasoned that while he might not run strongly in the northern parts of the state, he would surely be an asset to the party in the more conservative and rural downstate Illinois. Congressman William Dawson, one of the leaders in Negro politics in the state, vice president of the Democratic National Committee, and long an influential member of the House, was asked by Mayor Daley to second Johnson's nomination. On Friday, after Johnson's nomination on Thursday night, Representative Dawson gathered together a number of Negro leaders at the Biltmore Hotel to hear Johnson speak on civil rights. There is no question, then, that Lyndon Johnson was an acceptable vice presidential candidate to the Illinois leadership.

The leadership reached the vice presidential decision without a caucus. When the time for balloting arrived on Thursday night, fewer Illinois delegates were on the floor than at any previous time in the convention. Friends and guests of the delegates who previously had been in the galleries took the places on the floor. To a man they rose to applaud Dawson as he went to the rostrum to second the nomination of Johnson.

Conclusion

It would be easy to interpret the lack of participation, listlessness, and sheep-like behavior of the Illinois delegates as a failure of representative democracy. That sort of criticism should not be drawn from this description. The unity of the Illinois delegation was, of course, a function of the strength and capacity of its professional party organization. The success of a president in carrying out his and the party's program depends upon his capacity to marshal the kind of political support which Kennedy was able to obtain from Daley and the Illinois delegation.

A second characteristic of this delegation is similar to one which could be observed in other delegations. This is that the major reason which brought Illinois to Senator Kennedy's side was that Kennedy was expected to deliver the largest number of votes in November. This was not the only or the sufficient condition for winning Daley and his colleagues to Kennedy's candidacy. There were other reasons that they were disposed to support Kennedy, but it seems clear that what made it possible for Illinois to support Kennedy in such strength was that he more than any other candidate had proved his electoral magnetism.

It is easy to regard the behavior of the Illinois delegation as an example of non-rational decision-making. The model, which many of our textbooks and commentators still retain, holds that the individual voter and the individual delegate evaluate (or should) presidential nominees in terms of their positions on the issues and their administrative qualifications. To be sure, other delegations, notably Michigan and the District of Columbia, gave great weight to candidates' stands on issues. Illinois was not uninterested in these questions, too, as witness the leadership's tentative search for a vice presidential nominee who would appeal to a wide variety of interests in the state, interests reflected in political issues. Yet among the Illinois delegates and their leadership, concern for the administrative capacities and the stands on issues of the candidates seemed clearly secondary to their belief that Kennedy promised to be a winning candidate in Illinois.

Surely, however, the ability to win and to help local candidates are related to the requirements of the presidency. If the president must call upon the state party leaders for support in adopting his programs, he may surely be expected to help the local party organizations.

Moreover, to the political professionals, the machine which Kennedy organized was a remarkable demonstration of leadership. While one might prefer that more weight be given to factors other than the capacity to win in November, one could hardly deny that this factor is directly related to the needs of the office. Indeed, it is one sign of skill as a leader. If a rational nominating process is defined as one which focuses on factors related to the qualifications for the office, this delegation acted rationally when it gave great weight to the electoral strength of the candidates for president and vice president.

Part V:

State Delegations: Organization and Candidate Communications

22. *Organization and Administration of a Large Delegation: California Democrats*

EUGENE LEE

University of California

The literature of organization and administration has seldom included discussion of the organization of state delegations to a national convention. Yet, as Paul David and his colleagues suggest, "Any clear understanding of the convention must involve some systematic consideration of the position and make-up of the state delegation as an organized group." This is the subject matter of this paper.

That the organization of the state delegation has not been made a subject of intensive investigation is not surprising. For one thing, the delegation is an elusive subject to capture. Its life span is short, its existence hectic, its records fragmentary. Its formal characteristics, moreover, are frequently but a facade masking the realities of the delegates' true behavior. And on those occasions when the delegation has been made a subject of study, the emphasis has—as in the 1952 studies—been placed on the politics and decision-making activities of the group, not on the more mundane aspects of its machinery and adminstrative processes.

This is not an account of the decisions reached by the California delegation, the pressures which featured the decision-making process, or of political strategy. Rather, this is an attempt to describe the organizational and adminìstrative framework within which these more dramatic and colorful events took place.

The Legal Framework

The California Elections Code, (1960) contains but brief reference to the manner in which a delegation is to be organized. The initial provision calls for the organization of a small executive committee to assume responsibility for the selection of delegates and alternates and to undertake to secure signatures on petitions sufficient to qualify the delegation to appear on the primary ballot. (Signatures equal to ½ of 1% of the party's last gubernatorial vote must be obtained.) Importantly, the *Code* requires that the committee secure the endorsement of the candidate to whom the delegation is to be pledged. In reality, of course, the candidate almost always selects the committee.

The California presidential primary ballot contains only the names of the candidates to whom delegations are pledged (only one delegation per candidate), not the names of the delegates themselves. Although the delegates must be distributed geographically throughout the state, the voter casts his ballot for the slate as a whole. (In all of the other thirteen presidential primary states, except South Dakota, at least some delegates are separately elected by districts). The election is on a statewide winner-take-all basis. There is no provision for a delegation pledged to more than one candidate.

The successful elected delegation is subject to few legal requirements. The first is that delegates must meet together before leaving the state for the convention and select a chairman. The second is that individual delegate must, "to the best of his judgment and ability," support the candidate to whom the delegation has pledged itself. What this actually means is not very clear. The generally accepted interpretation is that the delegation is required to support the pledged candidate on the first ballot and/or until the candidate releases the delegation.

The Executive Committee and the Selection of the Delegation

The organization and membership of the executive committee of the 1960 Democratic delegation from California, as well as many subsequent developments, were dictated by a major political decision agreed to by almost every important party leader in the state. This was to present to the voters a single and unified Democratic delegation pledged to a favorite son, Governor Edmund Brown. The intent of this decision was to deter bona fide candidates from entering the primary, thus to avoid forcing the party leadership to take sides in opposition to one another and publicly to engage in fratricidal strife. An ancillary objective was to enhance the power of the state and its Democratic leaders by taking to Los Angeles a large bloc of uncommitted delegates which could be used to advantage in convention maneuvering.

Because of this key decision, the formation of an executive committee representing the various elements of the party was almost *pro forma*. With the approval of the governor, these officials took the lead in the organization of the delegation: the national committeeman and committeewoman, the speaker of the assembly, the president *pro tem* of the senate, the dean of the congressional delegation and a second congressman designated by the U. S. senator from California, the women's chairman of the state central committee and, acting as chairman of the executive committee, the chairman of the state central committee.

The principal task of this committee, both in terms of the convention and the party's place in the state, was the selection of the delegation. This involved the choice, from among perhaps a thousand or more party leaders, of 160 delegates and 80 alternates, a responsibility sufficient to tax even the wisest politician of the Golden State. In accordance with recent Democratic practice, congressional district caucuses of local party leaders were invited to submit nominations to the committee for consideration. In addition, important party and state officials provided the committee with their suggestions as to those who should serve on the delegation.

The final selection of the delegation by the committee took place at a two-day session late in February. The locale was certainly one of the most unusual in American political history, the wedding chapel of the Carmel Highlands Inn, a handsome resort on the California coast. The chapel, chosen because of its relative remoteness from passers-by, including the press, soon was labeled the "smoke-filled sanctuary." While it is questionable that the committee sought divine guidance, the delegation which did emerge from their deliberations was broadly representative of the party leadership throughout the state. It is clear, too, that it was sufficiently representative of the supporters of the several presidential candidates to induce these candidates, particularly Senator Kennedy, to remain out of the California primary.

The executive committee list of delegates and alternates was presented to the governor for his approval and, with only one or two exceptions, was accepted. With the selection accomplished, attention was next turned to the task of qualifying the delegation to appear on the primary ballot. Petitions containing the names of at least 15,000 Democrats were required to be filed. Official party staff, for the most part, took the lead in the organization and administration of this activity, while the actual work of signature solicitation was divided throughout the state among the delegates, party officials and club members. The "official" nature of the delegation was evident in this activity, but a challenge to the formal leadership soon arose in the declaration by George McClain, long-time California old-age pension promoter, that he would enter a delegation pledged to his candidacy in the June primary.

Both this late-developing opposition and the desire to produce a greater vote than that for the G. O. P. slate pledged to Vice President Nixon led to the development of a modest campaign throughout the state to encourage registered Democrats to go to the polls and support the governor and the official leadership. The governor himself took to the hustings—using a sidewalk poll of public preference for Democratic presidential aspirants as his vehicle—to beat the drums of the delegation. Each of the major candidates entered the state to express his affection for the governor at $100-a-plate dinners and to urge the election of the delegation. Pamphlets, and television spots were utilized. The total cost of this primary campaign was $60,000, the funds being provided partially from the above dinners and partially from a portion of the $100 fee required of each delegate and alternate.

The results of the June primary were never in doubt, although their interpretation remains anything but clear. The Brown delegation received 1,354,000 votes to McClain's 646,000. At least 180,000 Democrats, it is estimated, went to the polls but failed to vote for either slate. In any event, formal ratification by the majority of the Democratic voters of the slate had taken place, and the delegation could proceed to its next order of business. The Executive Committee, in effect, went out of existence.

The Formal Organization

As set forth in the statutes, the delegation was required to meet prior to the convention, its only legally prescribed duty being to select a chairman. Such a meeting was duly called and attended in Sacramento by all but 26 of the 162 delegates. Ten of the absent group were congressmen, and many of these as well as other missing delegates were represented by alternates.

The meeting, held on a Saturday three weeks prior to the convention, had as its order of business the election of officers, the discussion of convention procedures and arrangements, and the election of the national committeeman and committeewoman. Of these items, only the national committeeman decision proved controversial (and deeply so). For all other offices, the delegation ratified unanimously the choice of a small group of five or six party leaders who had assumed responsibility for the formal structure of the delegation. Clair Engle, the ranking elected official other than the governor, was the obvious choice for chairman of the delegation, and the governor had early indicated that this should be. Although in Washington, Engle played an active role, along with representatives of the governor's office and key party officials, in the final determination of the other officers to be presented to the delegation. The six officers—two vice chairmen, a secretary, a parliamentarian, a treasurer and a sergeant at arms —were equally divided north and south, a pattern of organization which had featured and continued to dominate all of the activities of the delegation. The choice of almost all of the officers was obvious in view of their official party status, and—as with the selection of the executive committee initally—elicited little surprise and no adverse reaction.

The choice of the national committeeman, on the other hand, was a hotly contested race, representing a factional struggle within southern California as well as a dispute over state party leadership. Here it is important to note only that the above-mentioned formal leadership of the delegation was openly divided. The governor favored one candidate; the chairman of the delegation, Senator Engle, favored his opponent, and other divisions could be cited. In short, the attempt to build a delegation which cut across factions, and which included contesting elements within the party, extended—as indeed it had to—to the officers of the delegation as well.

The obvious implication of this is that formally designated leaders of the delegation each played two roles. As officials of the delegation they were expected to, and did, perform as neutrals in the various contests that ensued during the life of the delegation. As delegates, on the other hand, each was a partisan—at times highly so—in the support of a candidate or faction. Significantly, too, none of the officers was expected—as an *officer*—necessarily to support the governor in his actions or decisions. They had been selected, not as governor's men, but in view of their official status in one or the other of the several arms of the party.

Other important actions were taken by the Sacramento caucus which concentrated authority and responsibility in the hands of the chairman. Senator Engle was authorized to appoint a steering committee for the delegation, to appoint a committee of alternates to advise on their role at the convention and appoint the representatives of the delegation to the various committees of the convention, the most important being the Platform Committee.

The Officers of the Delegation.

Some of the responsibilities of the chairman have been suggested, but this most important duty was to preside over the caucuses of the delegation. The powers of the chair included those of fixing the caucus agenda, recognizing delegates during caucus debates, rendering a decision on voice votes at caucuses, making parliamentary decisions with the advice of the parliamentarian, and authority to call the delegation into caucus at his pleasure. (The last named power was never utilized.) To the chairman belonged, also, the dramatic responsibility of announcing the vote of the delegation during the roll call of the states. In these various prerogatives resided much opportunity for discretion and for parliamentary manuever. The composition of the delegation and the events surrounding it dictated, however, that the chairman act impartially and as a neutral. In short, the power and authority of the chair were removed from the area of political strategy within the delegation, although the chairman—as a delegate—was actively engaged in furthering the cause of his favored candidate. The *vice chairmen*, the two ranking party officials north and south, had no formal duties other than to occupy the chairman's seat on the convention floor during his absence.

The other officers had duties suggested by their titles. The *secretary*, president of the statewide club movement, was responsible for the polling of the delegation, the procedures for which are discussed below, and for keeping the minutes of the caucuses. A not inconsiderable responsibility was that of designating the seat which each delegate was required to occupy on the convention floor. The *treasurer*, who holds the like title in the state central committee, was responsible for the collection and custody of the $100 fee required of every delegate and alternate and for the disposition of the resulting sum ($24,000) in accordance with the decisions of, first, the executive and, subsequently, the steering committee. (The budget is discussed below.) In addition, the treasurer accepted responsibility for assisting the delegates and the official delegation hotel in the conduct of the financial arrangements governing room deposits and the like. The *parliamentarian*, a veteran congressman with a long record of convention attendance, advised the chairman of the delegation on convention rules and practice, and made rulings on points of order. At times, he was in a highly strategic and important position resulting from his ability to influence the order and conduct of the delegation's business. The *sergeant-at-arms*, an active party worker from Southern California, was responsible for custody of the floor microphone and telephone assigned to the chairman and for maintaining the security of the two caucus meetings which were held behind closed doors. The staff which assisted the officers in the performance of their duties is discussed below.

Although not strictly officers of the delegation, special mention should be made of the role of the *national committeeman and committeewoman*. To differing degrees, both acted as liaison between the delegation and national committee and convention officials in the solution of problems arising both before and during convention. These concerned such matters as the designation of the delegation hotel, which caused a minor controversy, and the distribution of tickets, a major and continuing controversy. The role of the committeeman was seriously affected, to say the least, by the fact that he was one of the centers of the major factional dispute which divided the delegation, other than the selection of the presidential candidate, and that he had been defeated in his bid for reelection. In addition, his duties as the host committeeman involved him in activities and provided him with prerogatives, namely the distribution of tickets, that strongly influenced his activities.

In retrospect, both the method and timing of the selection of the national committeeman and committeewoman would seem ripe for further analysis. The relationship between a state delegation and a national committeeman selected by a completely separate delegation four years previously does not appear to be completely satisfactory. A closer tie-in with state party machinery and a mid-term election are possibilities for examination.

The Steering Committee.

In accordance with the authorization of the delegation, the chairman proceeded to the appointment of a steering committee to consult with him regularly concerning the conduct of the delegation. The membership of the twenty-man committee differed slightly and was somewhat larger than the original executive committee discussed above but, again, was broadly representative of the different groups and factions within the party. The committee was frequently joined by the governor.

If the California delegation had been pledged to a bona fide candidate, it might have been expected that the steering committee would have been the chief instrument in developing political strategy for the delegation. In view of the division among the 162 delegates and the committee itself, however, it assumed responsibilities only of an administrative and housekeeping nature: the expenses and budget of the delegation, the participation of the alternates, the distribution of guest tickets, the seating of the delegation on the floor, parliamentary procedure, whether the caucuses should be open or closed to the press, and procedures for voting, to cite several examples.

Because it included leaders from all factions, the committee served as an indispensable center for the discussion and ratification of decisions concerning the activities of the delegation. All groups were equally aware of timing of caucuses, of seating arrangements, and so on. But not once in its three meetings did the committee discuss questions of candidates, delegate strength, convention strategy or he like.

Caucuses and Roll Calls.

Although the public view of the convention suggests that its business is conducted on the convention floor, almost all of the deliberations of the California delegation were undertaken in caucuses far removed from the Sports Arena. It is almost literally true to suggest that the delegation could just as well never have left the hotel. That this was the case is fortunate, for no environment known to the writer could have been less conducive to deliberation or decision than the convention floor. A close analogy would be that of attempting to conduct a college class in Times Square on New Year's Eve.

The delegation held four caucuses, one of which has already been discussed, the organization meeting in Sacramento. The primary business of the second session, held in Los Angeles on the day preceding the convention, was to hear the statement of the governor declaring his support for Senator Kennedy and to come to a decision as to when the delegation should be polled as to its preference for the presidential nominee. The alternative strategies and tactics of the various candidate factions are outside the scope of this paper. Suffice it to say that the Sunday meeting produced a stalemate. At the third and most critical meeting of the delegation on Tuesday afternoon, the delegation was formally released by the governor and was addressed by Senators Kennedy and Symington and by Oscar Chapman, representing Senator Johnson. Representatives of the delegation who had been attending meetings of the various convention committees—rules, credentials, permanent organization, and platform—presented reports which were duly accepted. The battle of strategies over the timing of the presidential polling continued and resulted in a closely contested decision to poll the delegate or authorized alternate substituting for an absent delegate to determine his preference for one of the candidates.

This was the official roll call which the chairman announced the following evening during the roll of states, with the exception that delegates were permitted to change their earlier votes or the votes of alternates. Under rules set forth by the steering committee, these changes could be accomplished only by utilizing a written form prepared by the secretary and available on the floor of the convention. Some twenty changes were recorded. Of the 162 delegates, 161 were present at either the caucus or the convention; only one alternate replaced a delegate in the vote for the presidential nominee.

The final caucus of the delegation was held on the last day of the convention and constituted a "kiss and make up" meeting of the factions which had been jousting with each other during the week. No business was transacted other than the adoption of several resolutions of appreciation.

Two comments suggest themselves in a review of the caucus and floor activities of the delegation. The first concerns the role of the mass communications media in covering delegation meetings. The decision of the chairman and most of the leadership to hold the initial meeting in Los Angeles behind closed doors resulted in an outcry of indignation from the dozens of media representatives covering the delegation. As a consequence, the ensuing session, at which the delegation heard from the candidates and was subsequently polled, had to be moved to a much larger room, adequate to house the press, and more importantly, the extensive equipment of the television reporters. No such space existed in the delegation hotel; thus it was that the California Democratic Delegation held its most important meeting and cast its vote in a Hollywood television studio under a battery of lights and faced by more than one-hundred reporters, cameramen, and commentators. The delegation had come a long way from the "smoke-filled sanctuary" of some four months previous.

Secondly, if the delegation had been required to conduct its business and make a decision on the convention floor, two procedures had been planned. Upon the call of the chairman or petition of twenty per cent of the delegation, a caucus could have been held off the floor. As no room in the Arena was large enough to hold the California delegation, arrangements were made to hold meetings in a neighboring public building some two blocks away. (Such a caucus would have been called if there had been a contest for the vice-presidential nomination.) An hour would be a safe estimate as to the time such a caucus and the movement incident thereto would have required.

Arrangements were also made to poll the delegation on the floor. Inasmuch as oral communication was impossible, this could be accomplished only by a written ballot. Sign-up sheets for each row, indicating the name of each delegate opposite his assigned seat, were prepared with space provided for the delegate to indicate his presence and, if the occasion arose, his preference on the candidate or issue in question. Designated row captains were assigned responsibility for totaling the ballot for their row, and provision was made to bring the fifteen row sheets to the secretary for final totaling on an adding machine which had been squeezed under his seat.

As suggested, it is fortunate that this procedure was never required. The inability to communicate with the delegation due to the noise of convention suggests one initial problem, and the difficulty of negotiating the crowded aisles another. A third obstacle to the conduct of deliberations on the floor was that access to the seats of the delegation was available to anyone persistent and lucky enought to gain entrance to the floor of the arena, and the section was frequently inhabited by reporters, friends from out of town, weary strangers needing a rest, and movie starlets. A related problem was that alternates were seated in the farthest reaches of the arena, some five minutes fast walk away. With the use of walkie-talkie and a page to carry a floor pass, an alternate might be seated within a ten minute period. When the presence of several alternates was called for simultaneously, the problem was compounded geometrically.

These seemingly technical matters are stressed here because they affect materially the ability of the delegation, particularly a large delegation—and the convention—to make a responsible decision. If, in fact, floor decisions seem likely, convention machinery should be revised to make this possibility practical.

Evident throughout the convention were what David describes as the "consequences of massive size." In terms of responsibility and practicality, California Democratic leaders—more than most—should be sympathetic to proposals to reconsider the questions of fractional votes and the role of the alternate.

The Alternates.

At the pre-convention caucus in Sacramento, the chairman of the delegation was authorized to establish a committee from among the 80 alternates to make recommendations as to their role at the convention. Inasmuch as they were selected in much the same manner as delegates, included in their midst many party leaders and had paid the same $100 fee required of all delegates, the alternates were jealous in their demands to participate to the full in the life of the delegation. At the same time, the question of their participation was a matter of importance to the morale of the party organization in the state, and officials and staff of the delegation did their utmost to satisfy the alternates' desires to the maximum degree practical.

The alternates' committee proposed that in off-floor caucuses the alternates be permitted to vote on all matters except the choice of the presidential and vice presidential nominees, unless the delegates voted to exclude the alternates from the debate and vote on any particular question. This proposal was modified by the delegation steering committee to the effect that the alternates could attend all caucuses, sitting in a separate section from the delegates, and could have a voice but no vote in all proceedings. Alternates officially substituting for a delegate could vote, of course.

The principal desire of the alternates was to be seated on the floor of the convention during at least part of a session. As noted above, the mechanics necessary to accomplish this were extremely cumbersome and occupied much of the time of the delegation staff on the arena floor. The problem was aggravated—and the desire for floor seats accentuated—by the fact that national convention officials had chosen to place alternates in the worst seats in the Arena. Nevertheless, every alternate was, by deliberate design, given the opportunity during one or more of the sessions to join the delegates on the convention floor.

The Informal Organization.

The preceding discussion has stressed the fact that the formal leadership of the delegation did not—*as officials*—participate in the political deliberations which occupied much of the time of the delegates. Behind the formal pattern, which has been outlined above, existed a separate organizational structure, which had an equal role in shaping the activities of the delegation and certainly a greater role in shaping its decisions.

This structure was organized basically around the several candidate factions which, combined, constituted the delegation. Each faction had its leaders and meetings and made its decisions. Two of the factions, the Kennedy and Stevenson advocates, were quite formally organized; the Johnson and Symington forces, on the other hand, were much less formal in their activities and met less frequently, both consequences of the much smaller size of these two groups.

Both the Stevenson and Kennedy delegates met daily, discussed alternative strategies, the best approach to wavering delegates, and the latest information from the candidate's headquarters. From these meetings, intelligence was transmitted back to the headquarters as to the direction in which California was moving. Of the four groups, the Kennedy faction was unquestionably the best organized. However, it is far from evident that the vaunted efficiency of the national Kennedy machine penetrated the jungle of the California delegation, and one should not overestimate the effectiveness of the operation merely by a glance at its surface appearance.

The most prominent member of the delegation was, of course, the governor. His role as head of a large, uncommitted bloc of delegates, as well as the fact that the convention was being held in his state, made him the center of attention. In addition, he held in his hands the important power to decide when and if to release the delegation, a power based on tradition, not law. As a leader of the Kennedy cause, the governor was heavily occupied with the deliberations and decisions which would best advance the senator's cause within the delegation. These involved contacts ranging from personal meetings with the senator to individual sessions with on-the-fence delegates who might be subject to gubernatorial persuasion.

The governor brought with him to Los Angeles a staff of about a dozen persons, half of whom were secretarial personnel. The full time of several was occupied with such matters as the preparation and dissemination of news releases and the arrangement of television appearances. The governor's executive secretary, a delegate, served as a principal political advisor and represented the governor at strategy meetings, while others assumed responsibilties for appointments, schedules, the handling of mail and phone calls, and similar matters involving state as well as convention business.

In addition to these more obvious aspects of the informal structure of the delegation, there were a host of other patterns of inter-relationships which were essential to its organization. Each of the three legislative groups—congressional, state senate, and assembly—possessed channels and opportunities for communication which cut across candidate preferences. Delegates from the same congressional district were generally seated together on the convention floor and tended to associate with each other at the delegation hotel. Officers and active members of the Democratic club movement had a history of personal acquaintance and shared activities, and a similar comment could be made about those active in the official state party machinery. Labor and minority groups constituted two other identifiable elements among the delegates which served as vehicles for the dissemination of information and decisions. Other groups could be cited.

And, of course, there were constant opportunities for contact and communication at the bar, in the dining room, in delegates' rooms, at the delegation headquarters, and in the lobby. Hosted cocktail parties in the hotel for the entire delegation were held on three occasions and were well attended. Brunches were held each morning at the hotel in a separate room for the delegation. Charter buses transported many of the delegates to the convention each day.

These informal associations are common to any organization, of course, and are always of extreme importance to an understanding of its behavior. Given the short and hectic existence of a convention delegation, however, they unquestionably play a more crucial role than in a more permanent and stable organization. Time and the pace of the convention simply do not permit the creation of new channels of communication and personal leadership unique to the delegation itself, and in their absence pre-existing ties loom large.

Such internal contacts as those described above were maximized in Los Angeles because of the fact that the delegation was housed in a hotel far removed from other delegations and from the convention headquarters at the Biltmore. As a consequence, the California delegates talked and met largely with each other. Theodore White suggests that this dispersal of the delegations was one of the key characteristics of the Los Angeles convention:

> A national convention, always a universe in itself, is usually bound together in a compact huddle of down-town hotels in some compact, clotted city so that geographical nearness throws delegates together until they can simmer into a common boil. But this convention was a diffuse one with only two focal points, the Biltmore Hotel and the Sports Arena. . . . The universe of this convention was atomized and dispersed—as was the greater universe of reality outside and beyond it.*

The Staff and Budget of the Delegation

A delegation does not run itself, at least not a large one. Behind the activities of the California organization were a score or more of workers who devoted long hours to the administration of the delegation's affairs. Some of these were paid personnel, some were loaned by other party organizations and officials, some were volunteers.

The key man in the group was the executive secretary of the northern California Democratic State Central Committee, who served the delegation in the same capacity. For almost all of the delegates, politics is an avocation or a pursuit ancillary to some other occupation; for the party secretary it is a full-time job. His

---

*"The Changing of the Guard," *Saturday Review*, August 6, 1960

connections with the delegation commenced long before it was ever organized, and his responsibilities ranged from strategic political advice to the governor as to the desirability of a favorite son-delegation through the conduct of the primary campaign, to the smallest detail of convention arrangements.

Politics aside, housing and communications typified the matters which occupied the staff prior to and during the convention. The housing of 162 delegates and 80 alternates and their families, plus 40 press and media representatives, and a dozen or more staff personnel, arrangements with the hotel assigned by national convention officials—and with the surrounding motels, necessitated by the fact that the hotel was too small, the assignment of rooms to delegates, the establishment of delegation headquarters and a press room, the preparation of a caucus room with public address equipment, all suggest the myriad of problems which surround the conduct of an important meeting in a convention environment.

A related problem concerned communications within the delegation. A daily mimeographed newsletter was prepared and distributed to each delegate's hotel room advising him on such matters as pending meetings of the delegation, of social events, of steering committee decisions regarding the manner in which a delegate could change his caucus vote for the presidential nominee. Incoming mail and wires to the delegation ran into the thousands, and volunteers worked full-time at the simple task of sorting and distributing these materials. Anticipating the deluge of phone calls, which did ensue, the telephone company installed a message center in the lobby of the motel, which was manned by company personnel around the clock. To it were referred all calls to delegates not in their hotel rooms and messages were recorded and available to delegates when they called at the center.

To those two examples may be added problems of ticket distribution, of transportation, of the taking and preparation of minutes of the delegation, of communication with convention officials and the headquarters of the several candidates, of press and public inquiries, to suggest some of the activities which were essential to the conduct of the delegation, but which required personnel other than the delegates themselves.

Not all of these items are of equal importance, of course. But evident in the above recital is the fact that the California delega-

tion was greatly aided by the fact that this was an "official" delegation supported by the party machinery and leadership. This
assistance was evident in every chapter of the delegation's history, at its inception, during the primary campaign, at the convention itself, and in the "mop-up" following the week's activities. The obstacles which would be imposed on a "rebel" delegation, without staff and experience in convention affairs, might
not be insurmountable. They would greatly weaken such a delegation's effectiveness, however.

If a delegation cannot run itself, neither can it run without
funds. As noted above, each of the delegates and alternates was
required to provide $100 for the delegation treasury as a condi-
tion of his selection. This sum of approximately $24,000 was used
to cover hotel charges for the headquarters, press and caucus
rooms; telephone installation and service; the rental of duplicating equipment and paper; and payments to a small number of
staff carried on the delegation budget. Approximately one-third
of the total amount was used to meet a portion of the expenses
of the primary campaign, almost all of which went for television
spots. The funds were administered by the delegation treasurer
under the supervision of a special three-man budget committee
appointed by the chairman. No special comment need be made
concerning the finances of the delegation except to note that it
was generally agreed that, in the future, alternates should not be
required to make the same level of payment as the delegates.

In Retrospect: The Statutes Revisited

This was the first favorite-son Democratic delegation to be
elected in California since the inauguration of the presidential
primary in 1912. At all other conventions, from 1912 through
1956, the delegation was either pledged to a bona fide candidate
or, in one occasion in 1920, was elected on a "no preference"
basis under the law prevailing at that time. This, then, was a
unique delegation, but from a study of it emerge generalizations
which provide insight not only into the organization and administration of a large delegation but into the convention as well.

Although the statutes governing the presidential nominating
process in California are brief, several provisions were of critical
importance for the Democratic Party in 1960. The first of these
was the requirement that the delegation be elected as a statewide slate on an all-or-none basis. Although delegates must be

representative of all sections of the state, there are no separate district elections; only South Dakota has a similar provision. The implications of this upon questions of organization are at least two-fold.

First, the system strengthens the hands of the statewide leadership responsible for the selection of the slate of delegates, whether this leadership be that of the official party organization or of some faction. The process would be different, indeed, if the selection were forced to consider the prospect of contested races at the district level. On the other hand, the requirement that the delegates be almost entirely apportioned among the several congressional districts seriously hampers the freedom of the leadership on selecting the delegation. The party leadership is not distributed, in fact, in accordance with district lines, and the limited number of at-large seats available forces any selection committee to eliminate eminently qualified persons from the delegation. Appointment as an alternate is regarded for what it is, second best. This problem of geographical distribution has been mitigated in the large multi-district counties by a provision that delegates within the county may be assigned without regard to district lines. (Thus the 16th District in Los Angeles was represented by 13 delegates, more than four times as many as the 18th Congressional District, which had but three.) Nevertheless, the problem of the geographical distribution of seats and its implications for the character of the delegation and the party leadership remain clear.

Secondly, the party leadership was the prisoner of the calendar set forth in the *Elections Code*. If one of the important factors in political success is timing, the politicians of California are required to operate under rules which seriously limit their freedom of action. This was particularly evident in 1960. The Democratic leaders of California were forced to make decisions of strategy well in advance of most of the state conventions and primaries and without the benefit of much of the political intelligence that became available later in the spring.

There is little question, too, that the calendar shaped the composition of the delegation and its subsequent behavior. The governor was in the middle of a session of the legislature at the time the delegation was being selected. Legislative support was essential, and the chief executive felt he could not afford to lose any substantial number of votes from disgruntled senators and assemblymen, angry at being excluded from the convention. As a partial result, 56 of the 73 Democratic state legislators were on the delegation, and 41 of these were delegates. This was an extremely high proportion of the 162 delegates, both with respect to California delegations from both parties in earlier years and the practice of other states. As it turned out, the legislators—of all the delegates—seemed most vulnerable to local pressures and newspaper positions and least sensitive to the pleas of the governor to support the party leadership and maintain the semblance of statewide unity.

For the reasons noted above, it would seem desirable for leaders of both parties to reevaluate the presidential primary calendar. While it requires a substantial amount of time in a large state to name a delegation and to organize a campaign, it would seem possible that the statutory schedule could be shortened by up to a month without seriously hindering the election process.

Of even greater importance in 1960, however, was the fact that, unlike almost all of the other large presidential primary states, the California party leadership could not legally organize on a "no preference" basis, but had to adopt the fiction of a favorite son. (New York, Illinois, Pennsylvania, Massachusetts, and New Jersey are examples of states which require or permit a "no preference" delegation; in 1960 only California, Ohio, and Wisconsin of the larger states prohibited this pattern of organization.) As noted, California Democrats elected a "no preference" delegation in 1920 under the law then existing, but never before in modern times had they made use of the favorite-son device.* It must be stressed that at the time of the election of the delegation in June, the governor was no longer even a nominal candidate for the presidency and had removed himself from consideration as a vice presidential hopeful. Thus, whatever had been the case in 1959 or early 1960, the California delegation was in no wise pledged to Brown in any meaningful sense of the term, either morally, emotionally or practically. Only the exotic requirements of California law required that delegates go through the formality of agreeing to support the governor at the convention to the "best of their judgment and ability."

---

*The definition of a favorite son used here, i.e., a local figure who is not in fact a bona fide candidate, eliminates the McAdoo slate of 1924. McAdoo was a local figure, but he was a strong candidate.

The requirement forced the favorite son into a position of public leadership far beyond the realities of the situation. The full implications of this, political and otherwise, are beyond the scope of this paper. From the standpoint of organization and administration, however, the statutory provision created a situation where the formally declared goal of the delegates was completely at variance with their intention. Paradoxically, the only delegates in Los Angeles who wished to follow the legal fiction through to a first ballot vote for Governor Brown were those who, in fact, opposed the governor and his declared preference for Senator Kennedy and wished to use a first-ballot vote for Brown as a holding action in support of one of the other candidates.

The total impact of the delegation is difficult to assess, but the artificiality of the instrument appeared to damage rather than assist the delegation in its mission, the nomination of a candidate. While the favorite son requirement may have aided the party leadership in maintaining control over the selection of the delegation and its subsequent organization, such control could probably have been achieved just as well with a "no preference" slate. Similarly, it is true that the ability of the governor to decide when to "release" the delegation provided him a significant instrument of control. In the 1960 context, however, the price paid for this power was much too high, for it involved putting the governor into a spot where the public was led to expect that which he could not possibly deliver, namely the delegation. Strong parties cannot be built upon legal bases which leave the leadership so vulnerable to attack. This lesson was taken to heart by the 1961 California legislature, which approved a bill making it permissible to organize future delegations on a "no preference" basis.

It is clear from the above discussion that this favorite-son delegation was one of a peculiar species of organization. Its formal and legal mission was never taken seriously. Its goals and aims were never clarified, and its leaders possessed few instruments—either favors or sanctions—to promote the development of a consensus. Its official leadership was selected because of their role in distinct and separate organizations and held widely divergent attitudes regarding the direction in which the delegation should move. The delegates themselves were members of different and, at times, competing factions and were subject to a great variety of external pressures and loyalties. Given these attributes, *which were inherent in the situation,* it is surprising not that the delegation acted in the manner which it did but, rather, that anyone anticipated it would act differently.

In the future, it will undoubtedly take a commitment to a bona fide candidate to produce a California Democratic delegation capable of acting in a coherent and unified fashion.* Such a delegation will almost certainly be one which has emerged the victor in a contested primary, for a delegation committed to but one of the major candidates will attract other delegate slates into the field. Similarly a favorite-son delegation subject to "control" from any one person or group would inevitably be so narrowly drawn as to encourage competing factions (and candidates) to enter the race, and the prospects of a favorite son in such a competition would not be bright. The final alternative, a broad-based delegation such as that of 1960, designed to *forestall* the entrance of competing candiates, would be subejct to the cross-pressure and divisions of any multi-factional group.

In short, California Democratic leaders cannot anticipate, as apparently many of them did in 1960, that they can have it both ways. A broadly-based delegation, elected without opposition *and* subject to "control" or pleas for unity simply involves too many contradictions. It is not likely that this lesson will be lost on potential Democratic candidates of future years, for as Paul David has commented, "California, especially, may be too much of a prize to be allowed to lock up its convention strength very often behind a favorite son without a challenge, unless he has genuine national strength." And, one would add, especially when it is clear that no favorite son—be he governor, senator or leader representing a party faction—is likely to have the power in the foreseeable future to "deliver" a delegation.

---

*The extent to which these comments might also apply to the Republican Party is not at all clear. The G. O. P. has frequently throughout its history in California employed the favorite son device and has generally maintained a greater sense of unity and discipline than was evident in the Democratic delegation of 1960. Whether this is indicative of a fundamental difference between the two parties or whether the Republican record is merely one of more favorable circumstances remains speculative.

23. *Presidential and Vice Presidential Candidate Communications As They Reach a Delegation:*

Kansas Republicans

HARLEY J. STUCKY
Bethany College

I prepared a questionnaire to ascertain as systematically as possible under the circumstances the origin, type, quantity, and the effect of the communications about the candidates and platform reaching the members of the Kansas delegation. One of the questions was: what was your chief source of information on the candidates? The delegates suggested that their chief source of information was the news media, the press was more significant in helping them get a picture of the candidates than the other news media. One delegate said most of his information on Thruston Morton and Barry Goldwater came from the press while his information on Henry Cabot Lodge came from newscasts and TV programs. Another individual reported that he was helped in his thinking by a series of informal conversations which he had with a group of his friends. It is significant to note that the general framework of the delegates' thinking had been molded by the maze of newsworthy activity carried on in the years prior to the convention and not by the welter of activity carried on by the promoters for the sake of nomination.

In contrast with this rather subtle intrusion of the delegates mind, I want to note one personal call. On Sunday afternoon, July 24, I was sitting in the office of the Kansas delegation when Mr. X. rapped at the door. When the receptionist opened it he asked, "is this the headquarters of the Kansas delegation? Do you have any Fred Seaton buttons?" Her response was to the effect that there were a few around but not many. Whereupon he proceeded to deliver an assortment; and, as he fumbled through his wares, he asked, "is the chairman of the delegation in?" The receptionist replied that he was out. Mr. X continued the conversation with his query, "what do you think about Dick's deal with Rockefeller? Dick made a mistake. Maybe he was ignorant, but it's the most disturbing thing I've seen. We're receiving a lot of telephone calls suggesting that Dick's slipping. Hope you're not for him!" At this point the confused receptionist queried, "who?" Mr. X replied, "Rockefeller—sure would be a shame if Dick made a deal with Rocky. Have you got any Seaton literature?" The one-sided conversation continued as the receptionist tried to encourage him to leave without being discourteous. When he left, the receptionist closed the office door with a sense of relief and as she made her way back to the desk she declared, "God! He's a pest. He's been in the office—before!" Needless to say, little was communicated for Fred Seaton on the occasion. In fact, the irritation and annoyance which emerged in the course of Mr. X's visit suggested that the inning ended with no hits, no runs, and a series of errors. In most instances, however, those who called upon the delegates to share their concerns on the platform or to leave their promotional literature were appreciated.

Much of the promotional material for Vice President Richard Nixon reached the delegates by late spring or early summer. The promotional materials for other candidates arrived later. The Kansas delegates declared that they received a number of literature packets, perhaps five or six, and that they received from 25 to 30 printed letters and circulars. One delegate estimated that he had received about 35 printed letters and circulars. These items were received from various groups and organizations which were actively engaged in the business of promoting a particular candidate.

In addition, the delegates received a number of personal letters and postcards from individuals. These items were mailed spontaneously and demonstrated that the individuals were sufficiently concerned to express their views to the chairman, or other members of the delegation. One delegate reported that he received personal letters and postcards "by the bushel" but when I questioned him further as to precise number he estimated it to be "about 35." Another person estimated he received about 150 pieces of mail of which the majority were telegrams. This person noted that he looked at them and then tossed them into the wastepaper basket. This practice was not uncommon among the delegates.

In response to the question as to whether there were any telephone calls from the constituency back home, one delegate stated that he had received nine such calls before he left for the convention but none since his arrival in Chicago. The experience of other delegates was quite similar.

During the national convention, the chief method of reaching the delegates was by telegraph. In analyzing the mail reaching the state chairman, Sam Mellinger, there were 73 telegrams out of 96 pieces of mail from July 25 through July 27. Of these 73 telegrams, six dealt with the platform; one suggested that Lodge be saved and used as Secretary of State rather than Vice President; one urged the nomination of Rockefeller, while still another repudiated him and urged that Goldwater be nominated; one called for Goldwater and Nixon; and all the rest were for and in behalf and support of Senator Barry Goldwater. In all, there were 54 telegrams from Kansas that urged his nomination for President or Vice President with only six advocating the latter position. In addition to these, there were eight out-of-state telegrams from such places as Arizona, Texas, Louisiana, and Indiana urging the nomination of Goldwater. In some instances these telegrams were duplicated and sent to all the members of the delegation.

The chairman of the delegation also received a series of printed postcards, identical in format, with Goldwater's picture with 385 words of the fine print and the challenging assertion, "nominate anybody you please, I'm voting for Goldwater." Two of these postcards came from Arizona, two from Texas, one from New Hampshire and five from California.

The state chairman also received a number of personal letters from out-of-state people—two from California, three from New Orleans, Louisiana—all for Goldwater. There was also one from New York, one from Massachusetts and one from Minnesota urging the nomination of Rockefeller. One letter addressed to the Republican delegates from Texas declared, "as a conservative Texas Democrat, it seems to me that the intemperate performance at the Los Angeles Democratic Convention has unwittingly handed the Republican Party an unbelievably great opportunity to serve America in the November election IF . . . If the platform is sound on fiscal policy . . . If questions relating to civil rights are left to the free choice of the people themselves . . . If the nominee for Vice President is a conservative—Senator Goldwater would be ideal. . . ." Another telegram from Houston, Texas, read, "Two displaced Jayhawkers will cast votes for Barry Goldwater regardless of convention nominee for President."

The following telegram probably received the personal attention and presence of the Kansas delegation: "The Nebraska Delegates and Friends of Secretary of the Interior Fred A. Seaton invite you to a reception . . . Secretary Seaton would add tremendous strength to the Nixon ticket . . ."

When did these communications reach the delegates? The Kansas delegates noted that a number of people expressed their views shortly after the April State Republican Convention where they were selected, and that they received from a dozen to two or three dozen communications in the two or three weeks immediately prior to the convention.

Each delegate received a package of promotional materials from the active candidates—Nixon, Goldwater, Seaton (for Vice President), and from the National Draft Rockefeller Committee. Except for Nixon's materials, these kits reached the delegates at Chicago.

Among the extremist literature was a pamphlet entitled "If Kennedy Wins—The Forces Behind the Kennedy-Stevenson-F. D. R., Jr. Axis and Its Drive on the White House." The pamphlet suggested that Kennedy's voting record is in accord with the ADA (Americans for Democratic Action) and other organizations which it labeled Communist fronts. It attacked his Roman Catholicism by suggesting that he has been presenting a false picture saying in essence: "Look, folks, I'm a Protestant at heart; the Catholic label does not mean a thing." It cited his father as helping to wreck the 18th Amendment. Another piece of extremist literature mixed religion, politics and economics into one packet under titles "Christ on Socialism," "Socialism Ex-Cathedra," and "Liberty League News." These were flyers urging that we return to "free enterprise": that Goldwater ought to be the candidate because he "is an American." It equated the Farmers Union Cooperative movement with socialism. Another flyer was on a book entitled "Disarm" picturing a skull against a black background. The words "disarmament will be a major issue in the 1960 U. S. presidential election" were encircled.

Now that we have analyzed the promotional literature we can return to our story of these communications in relation to the Kansas delegates. Most of the delegates I contacted suggested that they received few communications, letters, telephone calls, telegraphs, etc., for Nixon from the folks in Kansas. In analyzing their mail, they suggested that from five to 25 per cent of it was for Rockefeller; about 65 to 80 per cent was for Goldwater; and the rest of communications were scattered among other potential candidates. One delegate reported that he received "quite a few" for Thruston Morton as Vice President; "one" for Henry Cabot Lodge; "two or three, or maybe a few more" for Fred Seaton; and "three or four" for James Mitchell. Another delegate received a letter for "Governor Gerald Ford" of Michigan.

Did the supporters or promoters of a particular candidate call you? The chairman of the delegation reported that he had a call from the Rockefeller headquarters in which they suggested that they thought that Nelson Rockefeller would be available and would probably be willing to address the Kansas delegation if he were invited and asked to do so. The chairman declared that he replied that if Rockefeller wanted to address the delegation that he should request such an opportunity. The delegates asserted that they had received no such requests.

Did you attend any dinner or other social function in behalf of a particular candidate? Here there was some variation in answers of the various members of the delegation. Some declared that they had attended a number. A former Governor of Kansas who was a delegate asserted that he had lunch with a number of his former friends. He asserted that during his term in office he had acquired a wide circle of friends and acquaintances and that some of the proposed candidates or their promoters were in this circle. Others declared they attended no dinners or teas in behalf of the candidates. The state chairman noted only one such occasion and that was the reception for Fred Seaton.

Did you have an informal dinner or other social function with representatives or others promoting a particular candidate? Here again the range was from those who said "no" to those who said they had a number of such experiences at the convention. Did you hold or were you engaged in an informal conversation supporting particular candidates? Here again the range was from those who had none to those who had three or four such experiences or more. One person noted that he had these informal conversations "by the dozens" and added that they were usually over a cup of coffee or a coke.

All in all there were probably not as many of these contacts or messages as there might have been in a high conflict situation with numerous candidates of nearly equal strength and appeal. In such an imaginary situation one might have anticipated a more impressive array of brochures, circular letters, and many more communications from the constituency. The 1960 convention undoubtedly produced the form and style of other campaigns, but maybe the punches were not as vigorous or as enthusiastic. I think this was in the mind of the chairman of the Kansas delegation when he declared in reflecting upon the communications and campaign literature which he had received: "Nobody's really campaigning."

What effect did these communications have upon the delegates? During the convention some members of the Kansas delegation were a little annoyed by the telegrams and other materials which came urging the nomination of Barry Goldwater. This being the case they often found their way into the wastebasket. One delegation suggested that he didn't like form letters and reacted negatively to them.

The Kansas delegation denied any influence by these brochures or other promotional literature or by any communications upon their thinking. They suggested that they had thought of all the potential candidates prior to the convention and that they had obtained a general background of the potential candidates from the news media. Certainly it can be said that the Kansas delegation did not waver from its unofficial endorsement of Richard Nixon. Through the months preceding the convention it was simply assumed that the Kansas delegates would cast their votes for Nixon and there was no defection from this proposition. When the delegates had their caucus on July 27, 1960, at 11:00 a.m. the chairman declared: "We didn't come to caucus. We came to help nominate the next President of the United States." A motion was made that the chairman be instructed by each of the delegates to cast the vote of each delegate making a total of 22 for Richard Nixon. The motion passed unanimously.

INDEX